Advance Praise for *The Navigation Case*

"To the military historian, contemporaneous documents are the gold
standard of research. With the discovery of his father's long-lost
personal papers chronicling his adventures during the air war against the
Japanese Empire in the Pacific Theater, John Happ has hit the mother
lode. The immediacy with which Happ chronicles the courageous
if outgunned American airmen propels the powerful narrative of
The Navigation Case with the intensity of a bombing run over enemy
territory. This sometimes reckless and often tragic tale of survival and
heroism belongs on the bookshelf of any student of World War II."

—BOB DRURY, bestselling author of
Lucky 666: The Impossible Mission

the NAVIGATION CASE

Training, Flying and Fighting the

1942 to 1945

New Guinea War

JOHN E. HAPP

A KNOX PRESS BOOK
An Imprint of Permuted Press
ISBN: 978-1-64293-961-3
ISBN (eBook): 978-1-64293-962-0

The Navigation Case:
Training, Flying and Fighting the 1942 to 1945 New Guinea War
© 2021 by John E. Happ
All Rights Reserved

Permuted Press, LLC
New York • Nashville
permutedpress.com

Published in the United States of America
1 2 3 4 5 6 7 8 9 10

In memory of

Duncan Stuart Robertson

US Army, CIC

"Battle of the Occupation"

Long before I was your pallbearer
I was fortunate enough to be your protégé.

TABLE OF CONTENTS

CHAPTER I

Discovery

During my school days we were exposed to very little about World War II in the Pacific. Where I lived, Americans were largely of European ancestry. Our parents and grandparents were all Irish, Italian, German, Polish, or Greek. "The War" in my memory largely meant the European Theatre; the Nazis and the evil associated with them consumed almost all of the attention in history classes. Furthermore, I grew up in a town next to Skokie, Illinois where in the 1960s and '70s you could still meet men and women in local shops with numbers branded onto the insides of their forearms, concentration camp survivors. The shorthand, or the sound bite for the Pacific War, was always something like, "we had to get the Japs because they bombed Pearl Harbor." It was simple and easy to understand, with helpful racist overtones to motivate a bellicose hatred of an enemy we barely knew.

English have been known to quibble with Americans who claim to be from a "dysfunctional family"—to them the term is redundant. Over the many years, some in my family did not communicate very well with each other. My parents worked three jobs outside of the home to keep things together. Then my grandmother moved in with us. Ultimately we found ways to coexist, tolerate, and sometimes even enjoy each other.

During the Vietnam War our house was full of anxiety about my older brother's high lottery number. I still retain an image of that exact *Chicago Tribune* reporting the results of the lottery draft sitting on our dining room table. My family was relieved to no end to see his birth date drawn late. It was a high lottery number, diminishing the chances that he would be called to enlist. Yet the chance remained that they could call up those with that number. A grammar school friend of my brother, a friend from church, a guy who used to be a part of pickup basketball games and flag football teams as a kid, escaped it all by fleeing to Canada. It was eye-popping and gut-wrenching in those days, the fact that a seventeen-year-old kid, a "boy next door" had to flee the country to avoid the draft and the horrors of that highly unpopular war.

After sheltering six children, my crusty grandma, and my parents over the span of some forty years, our family house was uneasily cleaned out. Furniture, beds, china, glassware, and keepsakes were distributed among us, or resolutely dumped, and it was put on the market. A lingering curiosity was stirred when a mysterious brown leather briefcase, found stored in our long-ignored attic, came into my possession. It was quite battered, very dried out and worn raw at the corners. One of the buckles was hanging by its last fibers, the other long torn away. The handle was intact and the brass closure still functioned and shined. It was stamped on the face of it in gold lettering "Navigation: Dead Reckoning" and marked TYPE A 4, with specification numbers, order numbers. The name NATIONAL BRIEFCASE MFG CO INC was still quite clear. I had never seen this bag before in my life.

The volume of papers in the Navigation Case was staggering. As I leafed through the yellowed documents, scanning over neatly preserved letters, photos, military aircraft accident reports, citations, and awards, my eyes grew wide and paused on pages bearing the name MacArthur. The military jargon was often tough for me to understand. Growing up at the tail end of the baby boom, mine was the first high school class not to have to register with the Selective Service after Vietnam. Recruiters came to our high school. It went nowhere. I was scared. My little underdeveloped brain kept those TV news images of combat in foreign jungles rolling around in my head. Stuck were the images of young guys, helmeted in green fatigues, rifle ready, tiptoeing among moss-draped trees and tangled brush, not knowing who or what was ahead of them. Fear I understood.

There was a lot of material to sort through, organize, and understand. My father appears to have written letters all throughout his service: pages and pages of correspondence carefully returned to their stamped and post-marked envelopes. It tells of natural wonders, technical innovations, and heartbreaking loneliness. While heroic on the surface, at every turn the letters are permeated with unsettling circumstances throughout his military life. Where words failed, he brought home photographs: men in uniform, various crude looking airplanes and several National Geographic-style images of innocent natives in their birthday suits outside of grass huts.

Then, from among the papers, a news article tumbled to the floor. It described an event in New Guinea filled with "horror and tragedy," characterizing this particular mission as the single biggest weather-related loss of men and aircraft in US Air Force history. I had vague memories that when asked about his service, my father would briefly reply that he was "a pilot in New Guinea." I thought he implied he'd been involved in a transportation service, moving men and equipment

I do not recall my father ever speaking about his time in the war. He took flying lessons on his own not far from where he grew up in Park Ridge, Illinois. I was told he took his younger brothers up on practice flights on his own well before the US got into the war. He was proud to wear an air force ring and he still maintained his pilot's license as we kids were growing up in the '60s. For the most part we all have stories about "going up" with him in small planes from a local airfield. He kept a pistol locked in his dresser drawer. It came out only late at night on December 31 when we would make ice for a skating pond in our back yard. At midnight he would fire it into the air to ring in the New Year. For years I honestly imagined he took it off some dead German soldier. That's how little I knew about my father's actual role in the war. And no one I knew had ever heard of New Guinea. For me, those vague names were tied up in my own failed history class memory with the Dardanelles, the Ardennes, and the Bridge on the River Kwai. You have to be a real historian or geography buff to know what land was fought over in many instances.

As I picked that news story off the floor, vivid images of Vietnam crept back into my head. The fact that the episode involved my father both worried me and piqued my interest further. I wondered what my father and his transport plane were doing in New Guinea; and if we were supposed to be fighting the Japanese, why there? The Coral Sea battle, Midway, Guadalcanal, and Leyte Gulf are all generally familiar to historians today. But when I inherited this Navigation Case, the word Guadalcanal, while somewhat familiar, carried no historic or geographic meaning in my mind whatsoever. I could tell you the name of the nun who twisted my ear off in sixth grade though: Sister Ethelina.

This article went on to state that the episode was turned into a book by an Australian foreign service officer named Michael Claringbould. I wrote the author requesting a copy, and soon, a humble paperback book called *Black Sunday*[1] appeared in my mailbox. The author had attended my father's air force reunions, looking in part for the men's stories. But his primary interest was to gather information about the possible locations of downed airplanes, lost in the jungles of New Guinea. He hoped to find and restore them for Australian museums. The resulting book was largely an inventory of aircraft types, focused on performance specifications and serial numbers. In my ignorance I could not get a good feel for what happened. My quest for answers continued when I later identified several letters, found in the Navigation Case from Claringbould. They showed my father had been working through some basic questions about his time in New Guinea. Eventually, in turn, Mr. Claringbould sent me copies of my father's correspondence, which revealed my father's contributions to the story and miscellaneous aerial photography for the book. These letters launched an enduring preoccupation to learn more. Imagine my surprise when I came to find that my father piloted something called an A-20, which was by no means a transport plane. It was a heavily armed combat aircraft. His squad came to be known as the Roarin' 20's.

While the context of this horrific story was still a mystery to me, on a given Sunday in April of 1944, General Douglas MacArthur ordered a strike on a Japanese base putting the lives of six hundred American airmen in the greatest of danger. His aim was to overrun a bustling logistics center, far up the northwestern coast of New Guinea at a port town then called Hollandia. From various bases in eastern New Guinea, some three hundred combat airplanes prepared for takeoff. But the men were held on the runway, engines idling, as the mission was being reevaluated. Months of experience in theater taught the men that nasty weather was as much of a deadly threat to pilots as enemy guns. That Sunday morning commanders were especially concerned about unusually heavy torrential storms over the imposing mountains. Air travel through those passages was severely impeded. Finally, command decided that the timing of a complex mission such as this one was too far along to be canceled. After hours of sitting in their rattling cockpits, the men were finally sent into battle.

The mission was deemed an extraordinary success, a veritable milestone in the war. But the story lies in the fact that "the whole damn 5th Air Force and the 3rd Attack Group," all of some three hundred aircraft, got trapped behind an ungodly storm. As the men were bombing the enemy encampment, an equatorial typhoon built up behind them leaving them cut off from their bases. Their route home took them over churning seas, heading toward uncharted, cloud-shrouded and unexplored mountains, to their base in a jungle basin still some four hours distant. The storm scattered the planes like autumn leaves. Men fearing for their lives, tried to find a way out of the pounding rain and tempestuous winds. The sea was churning up a fury of white caps. Tumbling while navigating, the wind rocked pilots off balance every which way. The closest Allied bases were overwhelmed with crews trying to land their craft. Unable to wait their turn, being so low on fuel, fighter planes pathetically crashed into each other on crowded runways. Still other pilots pressed further east hoping the clouds would break so they could find a point on the ground to orient themselves toward their home. By the time the few lucky pilots found refuge, gas tanks exhausted, they were quick to learn of the demise of their mates. The survivors revealed years later that twisted black clouds released pelting buckshot-like rain upon their cockpits. But it was the storm, not the Japanese, that delivered what was at the time, the largest noncombat loss of men and equipment in the history of the nascent US Army Air Corps. Yet this deeply tragic episode in a long war was seemingly recorded only by the men of that bomb group, and only decades later referred to as "Black Sunday."

Except for Claringbould's lonely book, not one word of this is found outside of their own group histories and private journals. As I dug deeper into the correspondence and records, I found reports from other pilots and crewmen which corroborate or contribute significantly more to the overall treachery of the New Guinea air war. Monumental complex operations devised by General MacArthur and carried out by these pilots are apparently revealed nowhere else. Together these several tragic and triumphant episodes, written out firsthand in this long campaign, evolve into an amazing story.

I had no idea of the man with whom I grew up as my father. All who knew him considered him a gentle and warmhearted person. But I had no idea he was a combat pilot. I had no idea he dropped bombs in the service of his country. And with the imprint of Vietnam in my head, I feared thinking, "On whom?" The practicing Catholic I knew as my father would have been troubled by those thoughts as well. Until I translated the military jargon in those orders and unraveled the mysteries of the maps and photos, I could not buckle the Navigation Case and put it away.

The research and the writing took years. I was distracted by the responsibilities of marriage, parenting, and work—all of which kept me from answering my questions sooner. The endeavor, consequently, has been fit in over many weekends and evenings of reading, making notes and connecting dots. Now, with my own children building independent lives for themselves I am able to summarize, in colloquial terms, what happened; why young Americans were sent to New Guinea to fight and too often die.

The material in the Navigation Case tells of Len's life from becoming a private pilot during college days to his life-threatening missions in the Battle of New Guinea—the greatest campaign victory in the history of the US Air

Force. His correspondence details the rigors of cadet training camps. Many during that period washed out, and a staggering number were killed. But having survived all the pioneering aviation training and the fury of overseas battle, Len was later "redistributed," assigned to another unit. This next tour placed him in battle against a most insidious and pernicious enemy. And yet he was stateside, operating from a base in Indianapolis, Indiana.

CHAPTER 2

Stout Field, January 1945

In December of 1944 the Nazis launched a westward offensive through the snow-caked Ardennes Forest of Luxembourg and Belgium in a drive toward the port of Antwerp and the English Channel. In spite of the virtually impenetrable winter conditions, they amassed 200,000 troops and 1,000 tanks for the push. It was a complete surprise to the American troops, some four divisions of 20,000 men each, totaling 80,000, poised roughly north to south along the Belgium-Germany border. This unanticipated lunge slogged arduously forward. It pushed the Americans back and bent their defensive line; it created a so-called "bulge" in their defensive formation. The Allies scrambled reinforcements into position and the enemy offensive was repulsed by the end of January 1945. The Germans never broke through. As the Battle of New Guinea over in the Pacific Theatre became the greatest campaign in air force history, this "Battle of the Bulge" was considered the greatest stand in the history of the US Army. But the cost was astonishing: it is estimated that a total of 42,000 American men were killed and another 47,500 were wounded. At about the time Len was "redistributed" to Stout for a second tour of duty, American commanders in Europe were assessing the devastation from this "Battle of the Bulge." Len's new assignment was as a MAET pilot (Medical Air Evacuation Transport) for a unit at Stout Field in Indianapolis. The numbers of injured were overwhelming field hospitals; many extreme cases needed to be evacuated out.

By contract the soldier's commitment to serve was indefinite: "the duration of the war plus six months." In their enthusiasm to sign up, many servicemen had not grasped that. The men gave it their all on the battlefield, and so did the men performing noncombat work, both overseas and stateside. In his correspondence Len would remark repeatedly that he felt as though he got all the breaks—but a second tour of duty in the cockpit was really bucking the odds. While Len was at Hunter Field in October of 1943, air force planners were already seeing a "loss rate" of 25 percent of their pilots in combat actions.[2] They used that number to train and send over replacement crews for those lost in action. Disasters due to inexperience, bad weather or faulty new equipment noted anecdotally throughout Len's service seem to bear out a similar number. On occasion, up to 20 percent of those young pilots did not even survive training exercises or the benign transport missions they undertook back to Allied supply bases.

The truth was, with the generals pushing the war "further, faster!" something had to give way. Bedazzled by the slick new planes, with their new speeds, higher altitudes and sophisticated radio communications, air force field commanders often neglected to notice how the new technologies impacted pilots' bodies and brain functions. Doctors, who until then had little experience in aeronautics (a term not yet in common use), were therefore granted little respect from the brass running the war. Mysteriously and for the first time, medics came to the conclusion that pilots simply wore out faster performing their duties compared to enlisted men. Senior officers, too, witnessed the mental health of their pilots deteriorate over the course of about a year, no matter how it was defined: fatigue, mood, courage, or enthusiasm. Most commanders took special note because their pilots were flying expensive and, certainly in the beginning of the war, almost irreplaceable machines. In their unemotional calculations, any tragedy meant a multiple loss in men and equipment. After approximately fifty combat missions, a senior officer could see what doctors saw—his pilot was a changed man. In New Guinea, Len had flown sixty-four.

UP IN THE AIR, AGAIN

Len's very first transport mission to and from Bergstrom Field in Austin, Texas, was a routine repositioning of men and aircraft. It was a 2,400-mile round trip that took twelve to fourteen hours, by far longer than any New Guinea mission.

Immediately after that flight Len felt uncharacteristically frustrated and tired and went to see the base medical officer. A letter home to his finacée Julia tells of his mood at the time:

> On this last trip to Texas [January 3, 1945], I was miserable. I've never felt quite that discontented about anything...I'm completely fed up on the life I see around me...leading a lonely life.... When I returned today, I saw our flight surgeon and he grounded me for this month to work something out.

Len's doctor determined that he was in questionable shape and that by continuing to fly he could be getting progressively worse, risking his own life, those he was transporting and that of his eighteen-thousand-pound C-47 aircraft. You could not see it, but Len could feel it. It was a condition defined by a dizzy mix of fatigue, frustration, and discontentedness. His lovesick correspondence to Julia revealed clues to this degradation. Based on his observation and experience, and recognizing that Len had only recently come back from a hot combat zone, the medic grounded Len for a month and ordered him to rest, eat well, and get some exercise.

COWARDICE AND INSUBORDINATION

During the first few days of Len's supposed rehabilitation, as the commanding officers were preparing their duty rosters for upcoming flight missions, it must have surfaced that Captain Happ was not available, medically "grounded." Yet, he was seen around base hitting the punching bag at the gym, shooting pool at the club, in and out of the movie theater, and no doubt at the club bar. His grounding must have looked, on paper, to be based on dubious medical reasons. According to a report called, *The Medical Service of the AAF*[3] (Army Air Force), "In the 'old army' and the 'old navy' there were no psychiatrists messing around with the men, acting as confidants and intermediaries, and inventing excuses for downright cowardice and insubordination." The way those commanders saw it, the air force had invested eight to ten months of expensive training in each flyer,[4]

> [therefore] the flight surgeons lost the privilege of grounding a man for anything except symptomatic medical conditions or well-established neuropsychiatric disorders: psychoneuroses and psychoses... When the [military] administration took a hand in diagnosis, the sensitive care of the flyer relationship was compromised, and this led inevitably to degradation in diagnosis.[5]

In other words, if a commanding officer thought a soldier was faking, he could override the medical staff and get the pilot back in the air. In this way, someone must have said, "Bull roar!" to Len's grounding orders; he was at the base as a transport pilot, an officer after all. Ironically, as surely as Len had written Julia on January 9 "not to worry" about his one-month grounding, within that same week, on January 16, a colonel by the name of Johnson issued another order called a "Revocation of Grounding." The revocation was authorized by the Office of the Base Flight Surgeon—probably involuntarily.

And thus the medic was overruled by a commanding officer within the week. Len's grounding was voided and he was immediately reinstated to resume the medical evacuation missions that very same day. His mission, to San Antonio's Randolph Field, took him on a six-and-a-half-hour flight of 1,200 miles. The next day it was on to Washington, DC, then immediately farther north to Boston, Massachusetts. It had been hard flying: a total of some 2,050 miles that day, over eleven hours in the air, the majority of it cruising around 10,000 feet. Furthermore, he had been flying in darkness, on instruments, in the dead of winter, after a year flying along the sun-soaked and humidity-laden equator. Those were already more consecutive miles and air hours over two days than he ever flew in New Guinea. As usual, he wrote to his girl Julia in Chicago, this time from the Hotel Bradford where he had settled in for the night of January 17, 1945:

Well, here I am in Boston. We landed here in the dark, so I didn't get much of a chance to see the town. They've had considerable snow here, and the runways are banked high with snow.

We had very fine flying weather all day. I got my first actual look at the White House. Don't get around much, do I? Of course I also recognized the Washington Monument, etc.

I really wanted to R.O.N. [remain over night] at Bolling Field, Washington, D. C. but we stopped there just long enough to drop off a litter case. We are dead-heading [traveling with an empty ship] from here to upper Maine, Presque Isle, I think it's called. Here we pick up more patients. Our itinerary calls for a stop in Chicago where we will have a patient for Vaughn General Hospital. We should be able to stop overnight in Chicago if orders permit…we're taking off at 8 A.M. if weather permits.

His mission continued the next day, January 18, almost just as he had written. Len flew from Boston to Presque Isle, Maine, then to Ayre, Massachusetts, and on to Bedford, Massachusetts, before finally settling at Mitchel Field on Long Island, New York—not Chicago after all. His hopes of seeing Julia were dashed. It had been a giddy schedule with many unpressurized ascents and descents to and from 10,000 feet in altitude, covering some 975 miles in more than six hours of flight that day. He was lonesome for Julia. As he wrote, he noted that the blues song *Don't Ever Change* was playing in the background of the lounge.

In Presque Isle it's very cold, people dress like eskimos. We landed here at 7 P.M. tonite from Bedford, Mass. By the time we had our patients off and paper work complete, it was 8 o'clock. By 8:45 we were signed in at the B.O.Q. [Bachelor Officer's Quarters] and washed up for supper.

As he became more familiar with his new duties he described the essence of flying MAET:

> Here was the order of the day: at Presque Isle in northern Maine we picked up 18 litter cases, injured from overseas. We left Presque Isle this afternoon and stopped at Ayre, Mass. to drop off 1 case. At Bedford, Mass. we dropped off 1 case. We are now on our way to Atlantic City to drop off some patients. We stopped at New York where there is a hospital large enough to take care of our patients over nite. On our hospital ship we have a flight nurse and a med technician besides a radio man and engineer. The itinerary from here will be to Atlantic City, Indianapolis (to check the airplane), Louisville, Memphis, El Paso and the west coast. These 16 cases we have left will be dropped one by one from here to upper California. What a business!
>
> Most of the patients are in a bad way—paralyzed from hips down, etc. If a guy thinks he has troubles, he should just look at these men being loaded and unloaded on litters.
>
> I didn't get any farther than the Club here tonite. At a field like this, it is not necessary to go in to town for hotel accommodations. Besides, we [Len and his copilot] are both awfully tired tonite.

Alternating between bases around Austin and San Antonio, Texas, Len's next several weeks whirled breathlessly by. His flights took him over many famous landmarks, both historic and natural wonders, en route to regional hospitals with his banged-up passengers. He flew from sea to shining sea, spanning the four corners of the continental USA. His correspondence painted a romantic picture of early 1945 America, reminiscent of a gap-year adventure. And yet, there were still misunderstood issues and unsolved mysteries impacting pilots within the pioneering development of aviation.

After an uncharacteristic period of silence, Len's correspondence picked up on January 23 at the Hotel Moran in Springfield, Missouri. He wrote that during that period he had flown from Mitchel Field on Long Island to Memphis, Tennessee (1,100 miles). Then he flew a back-and-forth mission east from Memphis to Augusta, Georgia (535 miles), then finally back west to Springfield, Missouri (825 miles). At the very least, those daily flight times amounted to more than thirteen hours, and much of them at altitudes of 10,000 feet. Len called it a "heavy day," which it was: some 2,460 miles in the air. His body was physically subjected to the effects of alternating degrees of air pressure as he ascended and descended in his unpressurized cabin. What Len was experiencing was much like what we know today to be metal fatigue, that disastrous phenomenon which weakened the frames of aircraft. It worked like the bending back and forth of a paper clip before it brakes, catastrophically. Unfortunately, engineers would not begin to identify and understand metal fatigue until the mid-1950s. Furthermore, while the first prototype airplane with a pressurized cabin was tested in September of 1942, the second experimental plane called the Boeing XB-29 Superfortress, crashed due to engine trouble in February of 1943 killing eleven crew members, among whom were Boeing designers and engineers. Twenty-two employees of a nearby meatpacking plant into which the plane fell were also killed. Further development was temporarily halted and neither Len and nor anyone in the entire 5th Air Force ever had planes with pressurized cabins where Len had served in New Guinea. Len's letter was without emotion, until he dramatically asked Julia to pray to God on his behalf.

> Landed here tonite at 7:10 P.M. It was 8:30 before we sat down to supper. This was an exceptionally heavy day. We flew from Memphis to Augusta [Maine] and from Augusta to here. The total mileage was over 1200 and we flew for about 8 hours…for the 700 miles from Augusta to Springfield we had CAVU weather [Ceiling and Visibility Unlimited].

> It is now about 12:15 A. M. or 15 minutes into tomorrow. We had a busy day. I just walked out on a brewing party. To the fellow I'm with, this means a spree to relax and have fun. He is the eager

type and I left him to his fun. To me this life, or the way of relaxing, is and always will be a bore. Because you are as close to God as anyone...please ask God that I find my way out of all this, and to a happy life with you.

The next day he got up and out: from Springfield, Missouri, to San Antonio, Texas, then on to El Paso. The pace of his flying these consecutive long distance MAET missions was already more demanding, the flights more frequent, than those Len flew in in New Guinea just a few months back. At Biggs Field in El Paso on January 24, he expressed his pride in his manual navigation skills while also managing a hectic schedule.

Today we flew from Springfield, MO to Randolph, in San Antonio, Texas then on to El Paso here [1,000 miles taking 6.5 hours]. What we went to Randolph for was some more patients, and a change in original itinerary.

Surely brushing up on my navigation on these trips. Came here from San Antonio straight as an arrow today. [The one-way trip is 550 miles, almost four hours]. Today we also got a new Med Technician, and a Capt. Flight Surgeon instead of a Flight Nurse. We are now carrying patients who are worse off than the first ones we had. Some like to fly, and others dislike it.

On the trip from Springfield to San Antonio it was beautiful today. It was overcast around Randolph, but we broke out into the clear Texas plains just a few miles out. At Randolph I picked up my mail, first in almost 10 days. Honey, your letters are a wonderful thing. It will be three or four days before we get back there. Got letters today from Hop [Hopperstad of his former unit] and from Tim [Dillon, a college buddy]. On gypsy runs like this, it will be difficult to keep in contact with these friends. Things are rough all over, huh? I feel great tonite of course I'm tired....

Len was then ordered to fly from El Paso, Texas, to Ogden, Utah, and finally Walla Walla, Washington, all on January 25. He wrote from the Marcus Whitman Hotel after that 900-mile segment taking over five and a half hours. His adventure took him above the wide, painted gaps of the Grand Canyon and wove him through the gusty white peaks of the Rocky

Mountains. The mission then continued on to Walla Walla for another 550 miles. That day's flying totaled over 1,450 miles and nine and a half hours in the air.

> Left El Paso this A.M., arriving here this afternoon after stopping at Ogden, Utah. We delivered 6 patients today, 3 in Ogden and 3 here.

By any definition, any normal person would be fatigued by all of this travel. But then who would not be thrilled by these experiences? Julia could only marvel, letting herself drift into vicarious adventure upon reading of all these romantically far off destinations. It was unusual, in 1945, for anyone to crisscross the resplendent American continent by air, an awe inspiring opportunity by anyone's barometer. As Len described:

> We flew all day under clear skies and quite a treat. It is hardly for me to describe the beauties of this western territory. The canyons and gorges are a site to behold, especially at this time of year with the table lands covered with snow to match the red rock of the canyons...The country around Salt Lake City is especially beautiful. We [pilot and co-pilot] both wanted to jump right into the hills around Mt. Pleasant. But what would the patients say! It was surprisingly warm here tonite. We couldn't get a room at the air base, so here we are in town. The other pilot and I are both willing to hit the sack early tonite. Day break isn't until 9 A.M. around here. Tomorrow we go to Sacramento, Cal. At Modesto we leave our last patient and then [head] back to Randolph for some more customers. We should stay at Randolph for at least a day or so tho. This going for days without hearing from you, honey, is not good...but it doesn't get me down. When we get all our patients delivered, will have a little more time to ourselves.

However, like a spinning odometer the miles were rolling higher and higher through January and well into February: Indianapolis to San Antonio, 1,100 miles; San Antonio to Washington, DC, and Boston, 2,050 miles; Boston to Presque Isle, Maine, to Ayre, Massachusetts, to Bedford, Massachusetts, to Mitchell Field, Long Island, 975 miles with eight ascents and descents; Mitchell Field to Memphis, 1,100 miles, back east to Augusta, Georgia, 534 miles, back west to Springfield, Missouri, 822 miles (all on the same day); then down to San Antonio and El Paso, 1,000 more miles; to Walla Walla, Washington, 1,450; to Sacramento, California, to Modesto, California, on to Bakersfield, California, up and down, 1,200 miles. On and on the steel engines of the C-47 Skytrain chugged, propeller blades spinning invisibly round and round on sky-bound tracks, spewing clouds of smoke, racing forward into a dark tunnel, further, faster.

THE FINAL FLIGHT

When Len was assigned to Stout, Chicago and Julia had seemed so easily accessible and close. But fate did not bring them together. This reassignment and his MAET schedule afforded not one free getaway (leave of absence) as they hoped. On the night of March 13 Julia beseeched him longingly on the phone to find a way home. In response later that night he wrote a deeply melancholy note lamenting yet another failed reunion with her. They were perhaps the most painful lines written throughout Len's whole ordeal since enlistment: "Darling, I do want to get to Chicago to see you. It just seems that I can't get away [from] here long enough."

It had been barely two months since the doctor's orders grounding Len were revoked. Self-pity did not come easily to Len. He preferred to recognize the suffering and sacrifices the patients he flew had made, while enduring those of his own. Between these latest missions records show that Len had just recently read and certified his compliance with Form 24-A and its subsequent updates, twenty pages of instructions and regulations directed to "all AAF pilots, flight surgeons, aviation medical engineers and flight engineers" in order to keep him current. He was scheduled to go up again but then, there was nothing, emptiness. No more phone calls, no letters, no orders, or entries in this MAET travel diary. There were no more verses of despair or longing. Nothing.

Julia had never gone more than a few days without hearing from her aviator since he was back in the States. But following a broken date, St. Patrick's Day weekend, as described in his somber letter, an unsettling anxiety pervaded her entire family home. Up to this point, Len's letters had arrived like clockwork, describing missions and painting grand scenes of America's natural beauty. Now time was slowed, ominously marked by a hollow mailbox and a silent telephone.

It may be hard to grasp in today's world of Zoom meetings and Google Maps, but in Julia's day one waited for a phone line to become available in order to "place" a call. One spoke into a mouthpiece connected to a handset for hearing the caller, which you "hung up" on a hook when you were finished with a call. Like most American homes, Julia's had one telephone wired into the house. It sat alone on a slim, polished walnut table before the kitchen entrance and next to the dark brown wooden staircase leading up to the bedrooms. A single ceiling lamp illuminated the gloomy hallway.

Julia was an active woman. She had a full-time teaching job and a full social life to distract her from dwelling on her decorated pilot's absences as he darted back and forth throughout the country. She was proud of him and envious of the travel, but his schedule was awful and she could not sit and wait. It would make her go crazy. So she stayed involved socially, went out, kept up her fundraising for war bonds, and stayed current on civil defense activities. When he'd been overseas, she'd gotten used to the volatility of the mail delivery. But now, two days without a letter became three days, and three days became four.

The green of St. Patrick's Day had come and gone. Shamrocks had long wilted. Now Julia was chilled with doubt and longing. Again and again her mailbox was empty; no word from him as the bleak endless days turned into fretful empty weeks. Evenings were made tense by Julia defensively guarding the phone, rashly arguing with her sisters so they did not tie up the line.

She made a habit of carrying individual letters from Len as she traveled around the city to school or to her activities. She opened them now and again on the bus or at her desk at lunchtime. Len's flights up and down and across the country had naturally fed her vivid imagination. Rereading his letters she could imagine flying over the White House, or over the snow-capped peaks of "our western territory" as Len had written. Tucked into each letter were the words: "You make the sun shine for me…. Hugs and kisses, Len," or, "Life will be beautiful with you. Your loving, Len."

After repeated and countless prayers, it would not be uncommon for a separated lover to become hesitant and worried. She was overtaken by the horrifying thought that he had crashed somewhere into oblivion. Then longing, frustration, and worry imploded into suspicious fear and haunting jealously. Maybe a jolt of inadequacy overcame her as she imagined Len had given up and changed his mind about their future together. Maybe the distance finally became too much for him; she had felt it as well, but did not want to admit it. It had been a long, hard wartime affair.

As her bus rumbled along Kedzie Avenue, she gazed out the window, then back into the letter in her hand and again she searched his correspondence for clues to explain why she had been abandoned.

BILLINGS GENERAL HOSPITAL

Len twisted his body upright, arranging the sheets. The nurse reset his pillow behind him. Moving breakfast dishes aside, coffee to the corner of the tray, he leaned, pen in hand, into his next sheet of paper dated March 31, 1945, proclaiming:

> I can imagine what you are going thru—wondering just what is going on at this end. Darling, let's just call it a major operation, one that will be a means of accomplishing what has been my chief thought—my being worthy of you.

After establishing a regular habit of calling and writing home since the early days of his cadet training, it had been weeks since Len had communicated with Julia or his family. He was apologizing: "…they are finding me all right in every way. It is all my own doing and thinking which brought me here to this hospital. I expect to be out of here in a day or so—back to a new life." The gloom was lifting. Yet the truth tumbled out slowly, cryptically.

Unbeknownst to Julia, Len was coming through a groggy sleep barely 200 miles to the south. Len had mysteriously landed in the hospital where he was being cocooned in privacy to drive out "demons" (his words) that messed up his "own doing and thinking."

Struggling to regain himself, drifting into memories of how he came to be at Billings in the first place, he prayed that this "illness" would pass and he would be reunited with his Julia. He wrote mirthfully, lightheartedly, another week later:

> Thought I'd be out of here... but no orders yet. Getting out of a large hospital like this reminds me of stories about people getting lost in the Pentagon Bldg. Never thought I'd have to have flying 'amputated', but I guess that's the story.
>
> It was wonderful talking with you again last nite.... When I completely recover, I'll be able to tell you more about what came over me. I feel much better tonight and hope to continue.

To Len, being in the hospital must have been a nightmare and an embarrassment. Besides alluding to his own "thinking" which put him there, Len used another troubling term either literally or figuratively: "a major operation." All we know for sure was that Len was in bed, in hospital alone, reliving in his mind the last many years and how he got into this mess...

CHAPTER 3

Dreams Interrupted

It is hard to imagine today how distant the conflicts in Europe or the Pacific must have seemed to this generation of young college graduates. To them, the war in Europe was a faraway nightmare. Japan and the Pacific were further away still. When war erupted, that most unique of American attitudes reemerged: isolationism. As with World War I, people sought comfort in the attitude that the outside world, Europeans, should fight out their problems among themselves. We did not want to get involved in their battles. We certainly had no appetite to send our young men over to fight in Europe yet again.

In 1936 Italy marched on Ethiopia to annex it and colonize it for access to precious minerals.

In 1937 Japan continued expanding into China from bases in the Chinese province of Manchuria.

In 1938 Germany goose-stepped into Austria for territorial expansion, justifying it as "protection" of German speaking peoples in Austria.

In April of 1939 Italy annexed Albania for control of the Adriatic Sea. In September Germany stormed into Poland under the guise of *Lebensraum*, living space for agricultural expansion.

If any one of these headline events were occurring today, as part of the nonstop cable news cycle, the world would quake. It was continuous upheaval. Yet when World War II began, the United States declared itself to be neutral. General and former President Dwight Eisenhower wrote in his memoirs of this time in history:

> The American people still believed that distance provided adequate insulation between us and any conflict in Europe or Asia. Comparatively few understood the direct relationship between American prosperity and physical safety on the one hand and on the other the existence of a free world beyond our shores.[6]

By the summer of 1940, Nazi Germany had overrun Europe from Norway to France, including the Netherlands and Belgium. From there, they commenced aerial bombing attacks across the English Channel on Great Britain. It was with these events occurring in Europe that President Roosevelt began to rouse the country, calling for the formation of a national civil defense. He tried to move Americans from their complacency and began precautionary preparations for homeland war readiness. State governors resisted federal control extending into their backyards under the name of civil defense. So each state set up their own system. By year's end, some six thousand municipalities were actively participating in community preparedness programs; all forty-eight states had readiness and support organizations in place. Still, for the first several months and well into 1941, the American public felt itself to be distant from the war, and sensed little credible threat from abroad in spite of Roosevelt's appeals for home defense.

For his own part, just seven months since graduating from Loyola, while settling into his bookkeeping job at the paper company, Len continued to feel the easy rhythm of the school year. September for him still meant the start of the college football season. He remembered the dread of late-night studying in preparation for October midterm exams. And by December, schools were on holiday break. The city was decorated for Christmas and electric with activity. Life for the young was rollicking blissfully forward at full speed. It was Saturday night and Len was elbow to elbow with friends at the Pump Room before going to his office Christmas party. While many adults fretfully considered America's involvement in the war in Europe to be inevitable, no one seemed to have been looking out over the Pacific. Then the unexpected happened.

That morning after his first office Christmas party, Len woke up a bit groggy, running late for ten thirty mass. No one knew that Japanese dive-bombers were just then streaking their way to Hawaii. There was no way Len could have known that those events on Sunday morning, December 7, 1941, were about to change his life. President Roosevelt's precautionary preparations for war on American soil would not help the poor men and women in our Pacific paradise. The impossible had happened. Japan shocked Pearl Harbor, catastrophically, without warning, setting it ablaze. The attack galvanized the country's attention. The operation killed more than 2,300 servicemen and laid to waste countless naval vessels and aircraft. War was declared while anger, combined with fear of further bombings, triggered overwhelming public interest in local sheltering and defense schemes. Frantically, people now questioned: are San Francisco and Los Angeles next?

The civil defense organizations and their priorities varied by locale. Around the city of Seattle, Washington, small Zeppelin-like barrage balloons were put up, which lifted cables into the air meant to disable an attacking airplane. Sandboxes were placed on street corners, made available to extinguish possible fires. Neighborhoods designated existing buildings as air raid shelters while construction of new facilities for military training bases immediately took precedence.

In Illinois, community organizations formed and prepared for the "Defense of our Northern Frontier"—an attack on Chicago via the vast, undefended, open spaces over Hudson Bay and the Great Lakes. The Illinois War Council thought their state was the most attractive and accessible target for attack. It was an important and irresistible industrial center. They calculated that within a radius of 500 miles of Chicago was found approximately 40 percent of both the nation's entire war production, as well as its population.[7] Adding to the frenzied sense of urgency, millions of men rushed to sign up to serve in the military. Those who did not join the military signed up as defense volunteers, over 20,000 in Chicago area offices alone. A month later, at the end of January 1942, almost 8,500 civil defense councils were established across the country, with over 330,000 auxiliary police, 670,000 air raid wardens, and 260,000 medical professionals. Estimates counted close to 5,000,000 volunteers.

As Eisenhower wrote, Americans believed that distance provided adequate protection from the troubled world so far away. Hawaii was indeed a far-off paradise. Then suddenly, two overwhelming waves of Japanese violence and the destruction of Pearl Harbor. It lasted two throbbing hours that Sunday morning, exploding the fantasy of American isolationism. A frenzy of revenge was ignited; a deafening rally cry to civil defense blasted out. The debris of destruction left that generation of Americans with nothing but the determination to fight back. And in doing so they brought about what became the most far-reaching series of social, technological, and political changes the world has ever seen.

PROCEED WITHOUT DELAY

In the aftermath of Pearl Harbor, Len diligently made sure to have his office work in order. Then just before Christmas he humbly requested a leave of absence from Bermingham and Prosser. Immediately after Chicago's ice-cold New Year celebrations, on Monday, January 5, 1942, a sudden and unexpected journey began. He enlisted in the nascent US Army Air Corps at the Aviation Cadet Examining Board downtown, registering at "23 1/6 years of age" signing on "for the duration of the war plus six months." A Wednesday, January 7, photo in the local *Herald American* newspaper showed Len among several other young men as "the first group of recruits" being accepted for enlistment at the Aviation Examining Board in Chicago. The article stated the recruits would "proceed without delay" to Kelly Field, Texas, a Gulf Coast pilot training center near San Antonio. It was exactly one month after that groggy Sunday morning and the bombing of Pearl Harbor.

The surprise nature of the attack on Pearl Harbor revealed that the country had little in the way of trained personnel or weapons with which to wage war. The military had been depleted by years of depression combined with the national inclination toward isolationism. Len enlisted as one of the very few people in America with a civilian pilot's license. He got it through a Roosevelt New Deal program called the CPTP—the Civilian Pilot Training Program. Having learned to cruise the skies in a 750-pound Piper Cub, flying at seventy-five miles per hour, Len was soon to be trained in combat airplanes. He was to learn new aerial maneuvers under new conditions. And emerging technologies, once the stuff of science fiction, were about to become reality.

BEYOND PEARL HARBOR

The race was on: Japan's war plan called for that country to establish itself as thoroughly as they could throughout Asia before the United States could stop them. And immediately Japan made a stunning head start. From north to south, Japanese air, sea, and ground forces swept across the Pacific. Their aim was to evict the Euro-colonial powers from Asia and to colonize for themselves what they called the Greater East Asia Co-Prosperity Sphere; that area, rich in raw materials, that every explorer and conquistador had been seeking to exploit since the Age of Discovery, or what the Asians might call the "Age of Exploitation."

The Philippines were swooped down upon in the same way as Pearl Harbor on December 8, 1941, from bases in Japan and Formosa. Malaya, a British and Dutch colony since about 1824, was also attacked that same day from Japanese bases in French Indochina. British Hong Kong was attacked, and within weeks, as quickly as December 25, the British formally surrendered the colony that it had held for a century.

So, down the various stepping-stone islands and sea ports went Japan, sweeping up docile, undefended colonial lands. Almost mechanically on plan, they then set their sights on taking control over the Dutch East Indies, the so-called Spice Islands, modern day Indonesia. It was at the heart of their so-called "Southern Resource Area." Rich in rubber, oil, timber, and many other traditional agricultural products, for Japan this was the "promised land."

Over the centuries, little had changed for the ever-poor and education-starved indigenous peoples since the arrival of the Europeans. With modern technology, including arms and money, it had been easy for the European powers to control these local populations. In fact, referring to French Indochina in 1925 for example, "a bureaucracy of 5,000 Frenchmen ruled over [a] country totaling 30,000,000."[8] So when the Japanese attacked, the colonial Europeans were utterly outmanned and completely overrun.

PRESIDENT ROOSEVELT EXPLAINS THE WAR

As America's official participation in the war started, President Roosevelt regularly took to the radio in order to explain the conflict and its progress. On one occasion, February 23, 1942, he began his *Fireside Chat* by asking the American people to take out a map of the world and follow along with him as he described in detail the scope of combat. He then outlined the objectives of American (Allied) military strategies to defeat Germany, Italy, and Japan.

The president also spoke about the mobilization of American resources and the resolve of its people to win the war. And confirming American ideals that dated back to the country's founding, Roosevelt stated,

> The present great struggle has taught us increasingly that freedom of person and security of property anywhere in the world depend upon the security of the rights and obligations of liberty and justice everywhere in the world.[9]

We would be fighting to make those Asian lands free of foreign intervention, Japanese and European.

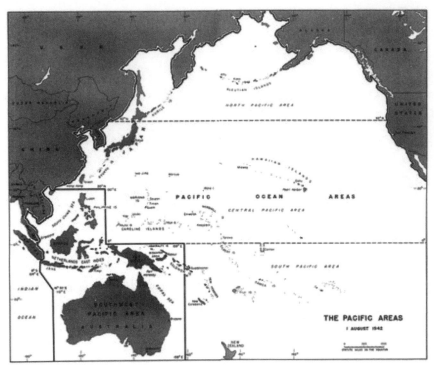

The vast Pacific, as it looked politically, on August 1, 1942. Almost every dot on the sea, large and small, was claimed as a colony by a European power. In those days it took approximately three weeks to cross the Pacific by boat, three days by airplane.[10]

THE THREAT TO AUSTRALIA

At the time Japan was blitzkrieging across the southern Pacific, Australia was meant to be isolated and marginalized in the extreme southern ocean. Incredible success was achieved by the Japanese toward encircling their Asian Co-Prosperity Sphere. Then on January 23, 1942, Japan seized the port of Rabaul on the island of New Britain. Located just below the equator it was one of many islands surrounding the Australian-held colony of New Guinea. It was known as one of the finest natural harbors in the South Pacific, with plateaus of flat land surrounding the port, which were ideal for runways. Japan quickly developed it as an advance air base to secure the edge of her defensive perimeter. From there, the Japanese strengthened their position by landing some three thousand troops on the north coast of New Guinea at towns called Lae and Salamaua. Those forward positions were so menacingly close to Australia that they created yet another battleground in the Pacific War.

Since February, the Japanese had been executing hit and run strikes throughout the Pacific. With their arrival in Rabaul they could strike at a lightly armed Australian-held enclave called Port Moresby on the southeast coast of New Guinea. It was noteworthy for how far south their military prowess extended. They could reach targets just one hundred miles from the Australian mainland.

Paraphrasing historian Gavin Long, the reason why the Japanese had achieved their objectives so swiftly and at such a small cost in men and equipment was simply that at every level and in almost every category of arms they surpassed their enemies. Throughout the Pacific and down to the Dutch East Indies their naval forces were not only overwhelming in size but also more efficient than those of the European colonial troops.[11] Deploying squadrons based in the former French Indochina, Japan marched down the Malay Peninsula. Supported by naval and naval air forces they assaulted Singapore, the British fortress known as the "Gibraltar of the East." By February 15, 1942, the British surrendered the colony, which it had held since 1824.

Japan continued even further. While consolidating their conquests in the Dutch East Indies, they identified a base the Australians were hastily trying to outfit at Darwin, on the extreme northwest coast of Australia. On February 19 a Japanese Imperial naval force made a preemptive strike and bombarded it.

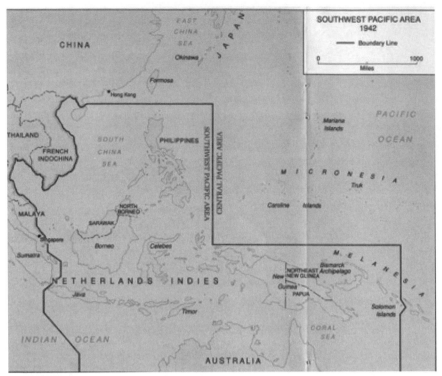

The South West Pacific Area in spring 1942.[12] By this time, Japanese forces had swooped south down through the South China Sea to the Dutch East Indies and New Guinea, threatening Australia.

DWIGHT EISENHOWER, "DRIBLET ASSISTANCE"

Back in 1932, Manuel Quezon, the President-elect of the Commonwealth of the Philippines, asked Douglas MacArthur to undertake for his government the task of developing their army and other defense forces independently of, but in cooperation with, the Philippine Department of the United States Army. But even after ten years of such assistance, the people of the Philippines were hopeless against the onslaught of Japanese forces cascading down from bases in Japan and Formosa (Taiwan).

A war conference in Washington, DC, was convened in December of 1941 to assess how to address the German, Italian, and Japanese aggressions. At this conference, the US agreed with Britain, Russia, and other allies to a

"Germany first" policy, designating the defeat of that nation to be the priority in all war efforts. In coming to this conclusion, the US determined that fighting the European war was the more important because it brought to bear the strengths of three allies—Russia, Britain, and the US—to fight the common enemy there: Nazi Germany. The thinking was that by not supporting Russia and Britain immediately in that fight, those Allies could be split and made vulnerable. Were we to fully commit to the fight in the Pacific first and get back to Europe later on, we would have to face Germany, perhaps alone and maybe with Germany in a stronger, entrenched position. And additionally, an early victory in Europe would release Britain to support us in the Pacific where Britain had important colonies of Australia, Singapore, Malaya, and Hong Kong.

With the attacks on Pearl Harbor and then the Philippines, then Brigadier General Eisenhower was called to Washington, DC, to serve as an assistant to President Roosevelt's Chief of Staff, General George C. Marshall. As early as a week after Pearl Harbor, Eisenhower was asked to report on the American's situation in the Philippines and our capacity to send more support to the already besieged Filipinos. Eisenhower replied,

> General, it will be a long time before major reinforcements can go to the Philippines, longer than the garrisons can hold out with any driblet assistance, if the enemy commits major forces to their reduction. But we must do everything for them that is humanly possible.... Our base must be Australia, and we must start at once to expand it and to secure our communications to it.[13]

The attack on Pearl Harbor moved US industry and manufacturing toward the production of arms and equipment. The training of men began at once. But that ramp up to battle readiness would take time. And anyway, the vast majority of what we did have in men and matériel was to go to fight Germany first. That left the Philippines in dire circumstances.

In his beautiful memoir, *Crusade in Europe*, Eisenhower wrote that in 1939 the total size of the US Army was 130,000 men—with just 45,300 soldiers posted overseas. We had not one armored division (tanks) and had just

1,175 airplanes, mostly hand-me-downs from the World War I era. Our military was so negligible, said Eisenhower, that it had fewer men and less equipment than the Polish Army at the time of the Nazi invasion.[14]

While war had been declared, practically speaking, there was not a lot America could do in the field of battle. A new base, far from Japan, was needed if we were to hold any hope of saving Australia, or if we were to maintain any hope of not being chased out of the Pacific altogether. Even with Pearl Harbor completely disabled, the US would first have to establish and defend a supply line along the various islands and ports from America to Australia. Those "stepping-stones," as President William McKinley once called them, that chain of islands cum refueling stations en route to the South Seas, required runways, docks, warehouses, and defense. And that became the priority in the Pacific—building and defending that supply line.

JAPAN'S CROWNING ACHIEVEMENT

Just months into their campaign, Japan came to surround in conquest the entirety of the so-called Southern Resource Area. With themselves recently overrun at home in Europe by the Nazis, the Dutch were completely unprepared to defend their holdings in the long-abused East Indies colony.

On February 20 the island of Timor was invaded by Japan. The Allies, meaning Australians and some Dutch forces, hoped to relieve Timor via Darwin, Australia, from about four hundred miles away. But the Japanese beat back that support having already bombed Darwin the day before on the 19th.

On March 9 the Dutch formally surrendered the island of Java, giving the Japanese effective control through the longitude of the entire swath of Pacific Ocean corridor running north to south: from Japan through Formosa (Taiwan), the Philippines, and Indochina along the Pacific coast of China; and to Borneo and on to Java in the south seas. The surrender marked the crowning achievement in the Japanese war plan. They acquired the central gem in their newly renamed "Greater East Asia Co-Prosperity Zone" barely three months after their startling attacks on Pearl Harbor.

In many instances the local populations helped the Japanese evict their colonial rulers. Throughout Asia, while apprehensive about a Japanese take-over, the native born population wanted to get the Europeans out. They embraced the anti-colonial theme promoted by the Japanese, "Asia for the Asiatics!" Gavin Long, in writing about the Japanese successes by March of 1942 observed,

> In every area some Asian troops as well as civilian leaders soon changed over to the Japanese side...joining Japanese forces whose destruction of Western power in Asia had the effect finally of releasing the Asian people from western government.[15]

Arrested by Dutch colonial authorities an entire decade earlier, while agitating for home rule, the Indonesian Nationalist leader known simply as Sukarno, for example, was being held under detention when the Japanese invaded. In exchange for his freedom and for his support in pacifying the local population across this vast island group, Sukarno was soon freed by the conquering Japanese. He was allowed to continue to promote his nationalist agenda, hoping eventually to achieve independence, in exchange for collaborating with the invaders. Sukarno did promote pro-Japanese propaganda and he was able to help keep the country united. As such the Japanese were initially welcomed as a friendly neighboring power who had liberated other Pacific islands after hundreds of years of European colonial rule. But, little by little, the Japanese lapsed into the same habits as the Dutch. The local population was conscripted into forced labor to build railways and airfields, to mine and harvest Indonesia's resources; they were forced to ship raw materials and foodstuffs out of the country to feed Japanese soldiers and generally support Japan's war effort. The result was an estimated one million civilian deaths attributed to worse deprivation and starvation than they experienced under the Dutch.

MACARTHUR EVACUATES THE PHILIPPINES

Approved by Emperor Hirohito and implemented on December 7, 1941, the Japanese war plan called for:

1. The neutralization of the US Pacific fleet so as to buy time in establishing and enforcing their own positions throughout Southeast Asia.

2. The seizure of the mineral rich, agriculturally rich Southern Resource Area, comprised of these various European-held Pacific colonies. (These vast resources of Asia were known at the time to include iron ore, flax, coal, chrome, and manganese ore in the Philippines; rubber, tin, iron ore, coal, manganese, tungsten, fluorite, and bauxite in Malaya; and oil, rubber, tin, coal, iron ore, bauxite, copper, manganese, lead, zinc, chrome, tungsten, mercury, bismuth, and antimony in The Dutch East Indies.)

3. The capture of key geographic positions in establishing a defensive perimeter around the Southern Resource Area.

In effect, Japan sought to take for herself the Euro-colonial lands in Asia. To do so, she deployed a force equal to that which the UK currently had spread throughout the entire globe in her colonies from Gibraltar, Syria, Egypt, and Africa, through to India, Singapore, Malaya, and Hong Kong.

On December 8, when Japanese pilots attacked the Philippines, they caught two squadrons of American B-17s lined up at the airfield with a number of fighter planes just preparing to take off. The first wave of Japanese twin-engine bombers achieved complete surprise and destroyed most of the American aircraft. A second bomber strike followed, and then Japanese fighter planes swarmed in to shell the airfield. What was known as America's Far East Air Force lost fully half its planes in the Philippines during the first day of the war. As a reaction to that destructive surge of power, the US Navy evacuated most of its fleet from Philippine waters. By neutralizing US air and naval power in the Philippines within the first forty-eight hours of the battle, the Japanese had gained a position never anticipated by American or

Filipino war planners. And with air superiority ensured, Japanese amphibious landing and ground assaults were carried out against little opposition. Caught off guard, General MacArthur's task became that of maneuvering his remaining men with their equipment to defensive positions. But such complex movements required greater planning and execution. The hasty redeployments caused units to leave behind much of their basic kit, such as food, ammunition, weapons, and medical supplies. This would prove to be fatal in the subsequent weeks. Thus it came as no surprise that, toward the middle of March, one commander estimated the combat efficiency of his troops to be at 20 percent; another reported that 75 percent of his men were unfit for duty.

Over the months of their siege, Japan committed over 129,000 troops and attacked with over 500 planes. Thousands of American and Philippine soldiers were captured and held as prisoners; thousands more were weakened by malnutrition, disease, and exhaustion. Under such circumstances, MacArthur had no choice but to be evacuated, forced to retreat out of the Philippines.

MacArthur was driven from his home and his office; obligated to leave his colleagues and a good part of his life's work in the Philippines. Worse still, he had to abandon platoons of desperate US and Philippine soldiers still fighting as organized troops or fragmented and dispersed as guerilla fighters. With his forces surrounded by the Japanese on March 11, MacArthur boarded a PT (patrol torpedo) boat with members of his family and staff. They traveled stealthily to the southern Philippine island of Mindanao where they met an army air corps plane, which flew them to safety. Resistance held out until the Americans surrendered to the Japanese in June of 1942.

MacArthur retreated to Australia, expecting to be comfortable with US support, far enough away from Japan. But in fact, Australia was in a panic following the unthinkable destruction of Pearl Harbor, the Japanese seizure of Singapore, and the overwhelming of the Philippines, among many other longtime British, French, and Dutch colonial holdings. With that February 19 Japanese bombing of Darwin, the Australians saw the web of Japanese control descending from the north, stretched east to west across the southern Pacific, approaching their homeland.

This was a pivotal moment for Australia. But, since the earlier outbreak of war in Europe, the majority of her own troops were deployed throughout the Middle East in defense of British imperial interests there. Now, with conditions so dire, in January of 1942 Australian troops of the British Army were sparingly moved from positions in Syria and Egypt into Malaya, in a vain effort to try to defend those British colonial holdings. It was written at the time that Prime Minister Churchill had trouble accepting that Australia would insist upon calling her troops home in the defense of their mother country. It was a shocking example of the control the ruling country exercised over the colony in the British colonial system.

When MacArthur arrived, he was of course welcomed heartily as representative of the American commitment to help defend Australia. Government and military planners began to share with him their own desperate defense plans—including the appalling scheme that, when the time came, they might choose to defend Australia from a line east to west across the middle of the country at Brisbane. In other words, the panicked Australians were planning to concede the northern half of their country to the Japanese. That line of defense came to be known as the "Brisbane Line." Their intention was to concentrate their limited forces in an attempt to hold and defend the more heavily populated southern half of the country.

Upon hearing of that perilous plan, and after his own harrowing and failed fight to keep the Japanese out of the Philippines, MacArthur was reported to have been stunned. "He turned deathly white, his knees buckled, his lips twitched."[16] Unable to sleep, he paced in worry all night. MacArthur had not yet come to grips with the thorough military control the Japanese had so quickly achieved in Asia and the South Pacific.

CHAPTER 4

From Civilian to Soldier

In January of 1942 temperatures in Chicago reached minus four degrees below zero Fahrenheit—it was not at all uncommon. With no natural barrier between the city and the North Pole, winds barrel down into the caverns of office buildings, mix with the warmer air off Lake Michigan and create a havoc of snow and ice. Under these conditions Len and the many new recruits made their way to Chicago's Union Station bound for the warmer climes of San Antonio, Texas, over twelve hundred miles from Chicago.

Arriving limp from the trip, the men were facing a new adventure. Len for his part, once settled on base and more than a year after meeting Julia Case, began writing her immediately. A picture postcard of the reception center at Kelly Field, the men's new home, showed it to be freshly carved out of surrounding farm fields, with its little air strip running through the middle. He wrote that San Antonio was the "center of activity for Aviation Cadets." In fact, it became the home to three major air bases: Kelly Field, Brooks Field, and Randolph Field, all specializing in different levels of training and different strategic applications within the evolving fields of aviation.

BASIC FLYING SCHOOL, KELLY FIELD, SAN ANTONIO, TEXAS

The US Army desperately needed trained soldiers to fight. Her enemies on both fronts were highly militaristic and disciplined, black booted and fearless, almost robot-like. One biography of Japanese General Hideki Tojo tells us that in 1919 he was posted abroad as a young military attaché, first in Switzerland, then Germany, learning western ways. He was there to network among the diplomats and weave together support for Japan's political and military agenda. After his time in Europe, his 1922 transit home took him through America. His take-away was that we were a materially strong but spiritually weak country. He contrasted Americans' casual nature against that of the formal Prussian German. Americans, he concluded, were undignified, and he scoffed at their individual pursuit of happiness, in contrast with Prussian communal discipline. An American's easy informality and independent inclinations would be no match, he felt, going against the ascetic samurai spirit and the pride of his own unified countrymen.

Juxtaposed to that, maybe confirming it, even at a military training base, Len's confidence and calm gave the feeling he was launching into a gap year adventure rather than joining an urgent military build up. Upon arriving for this five-week session of primary training, Len wrote enthusiastically that his new barracks were "two stories high, all brand new" and stated, "Classes haven't started yet...[so we are living] the life of Riley." He wrote of "hazing by upper classmen...what a beating!" But then, "uniforms are a knockout," adding mention of a great camaraderie with "the gang here."

With a girlfriend and a loving family of three brothers, four sisters, and adoring parents supporting him, Len felt buoyed. The stresses at home, the burdens of scarcity, the war economy, the depletion of men from their towns were not on his mind.

Throughout his training regimen he strove in his letters home to Julia to place her directly into his daily routine. For example, here is how he outlined his day:

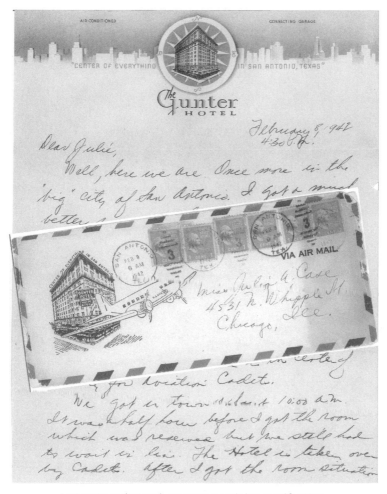

Len's years on the Loyola newspaper made him a prolific writer.

…shave, make up bunks, and clean up for inspection.

By 8 o'clock we are out for morning drill.

At 9:15 we are all lined up in front of the Athletic Director for physical exercise and sport.

At 11:30 we are back in the barracks and preparing for dinner [lunch].

The drilling will later be substituted with classes in ground school...[then,] parading in dress uniforms with white gloves!

Then he adds,

[We] will get rifles when the upper classmen leave.

Our gang of 18 [from Chicago] is still together.

The "rifles" reference points to the key underlying issue that the army was dealing with: coordinating the flow of new recruits with barrack space and food, and the manufacture of weapons and airplanes. There was clearly a major "production flow" problem to be sorted out, for what was being produced was an entirely new army air corps itself.

This was the beginning of cadet training, and only the beginning. While the initial impression may not have conveyed Prussian discipline, the air corps' goal was to recruit and develop the best men in the country—the best physically and the best mentally. While they sought out men with college degrees, they opened the door to others and substituted the degree requirement with standardized testing and problem solving examinations. Cadets would be evaluated for character, strength, and skill. Combined with academic testing, the men were to undergo physical trials. The Air Corps was not necessarily looking for athletes or weight lifters, but rather men with dexterity and fine motor skills, capable of coordinating mind and muscle in the cockpit. The men had to be of such high intellect that they could reasonably be expected to first understand the orders they were given, then also work through rigorous ground school training courses centered around the new and evolving science and technology of flight. So they were tested. The air corps tested the new recruits in math, physics, English, and history, then general aviation knowledge, mechanical comprehension, and reading comprehension.

On February 16, Len sent Julia a picture postcard of a single engine training plane like the one he was using. He wrote that he had five hours of practice in it and that he hoped "to solo this week." The model is called the

PT-19. In use since 1939, the PT-19 (PT for primary trainer) became the first military training plane for most cadets of the era. As at his CPTP school, it was a two-seat airplane for cadet and instructor.

In classroom training, the new airmen were expected to read and then apply lessons from instruction manuals on the particularities and mechanical details of all the airplanes they would fly. At the time the PT-19 was considered a sophisticated aircraft, featuring a slim nose behind a wooden propeller housing a 175 horsepower engine and a low wing (under the pilot, not overhead). It was a big bird. It could reach awe-inspiring speeds of 150 miles per hour. Weighing 1,845 pounds, pilots considered it balanced and comfortable to control for both for takeoff and landing (thanks to its fixed-in-place and widely separated landing gear). Fully fueled, its range was around 345 miles. All in all the plane was double the speed, the weight, and the power of the Piper Cub in which Len first flew at home.

Len's February 1942 PT-19 low-wing training plane. Open cockpits called for the cadets to wear sheepskin-lined suits with their goggles and parachutes. Len Happ photo.

While the plane was otherwise sound, the plywood wings were soon discovered to bend and crack apart in the heat and humidity of southern training bases. This led to demands for all-metal wings on future training aircraft.

With the postcard Len added, "No classes today but plenty of homework...finals at the end of the week on quadratics and plotting...I wish I had your math brain." At the end of those five weeks at Kelly Field tests were wrapped up. Surprisingly, illiteracy and a fundamental lack of comprehension washed many of "the gang" from further training.[17]

GRIDER FIELD, PINE BLUFF, ARKANSAS

A six-hundred-mile train ride via Dallas, rolling gently to the northeast toward Little Rock, took these aviation cadets along hidden lakes and through majestic pine forests to manicured farmlands to what was called an elementary flight training school. Located along the Arkansas River in the heart of the state was the Pine Bluff School of Aviation. Len wrote that they were there "to complete our Primary Course in ground school and flying," which would last ten weeks. While studying the mechanical and operational procedures required to fly new planes, classroom studies included "safety precautions when releasing bombs" and "selection of bombs to be released."

He noted enduring a round of "hazing for misdemeanors," calling it a "Tee Party." After taking a beating, he was forced to run out to, "the wind tee [a wind direction indicator about a half mile out in the fields] and back. It was a beautiful moonlight night, however the mud was inches thick on the fields after a rain." This was quintessential Len Happ: He got busted for "misdemeanors" and was hazed (covered by a bed sheet and punched around), then sent out on a punishing run through heavy mud. But what he really saw and noted in correspondence was "a beautiful moonlight night" and thick mud after a rain. He even stopped partway through his run and reached down into the mud to squeeze it through his fingers in childish joy and wonder.

Here the cadets undertook cockpit, navigation, and aerobatics training both in classroom studies and then in air flights. With anxious concern he wrote that not all cadets were making the grade at this base either, "People washing out of here right and left and no one knows when the ax will strike. It is not an easy life."

Along with his college degree, President Roosevelt's CPTP gave Len a true head start in cadet training. He arrived at Grider already knowing general flight regulations (like *Rules of the Road* for new drivers), fundamental navigation skills, and basic meteorology, such as how wind and weather impacts flight. It also gave him increased confidence because unlike those who were new to flying, he had already made his first solo flight on his way to gaining his private pilot's license: a test and a task that intimidated many.

To dramatize this aerobatic flying, Len enclosed a newspaper article describing a second cadet in as many weeks who "tumbled out of [his] training plane" practicing maneuvers near Lake Dix. The article went on to say that upon falling out of the cockpit, the cadet looked down and saw "an uninviting Saturday afternoon bath in the Arkansas River coming up toward him." To the cadet's relief his parachute opened properly and guided him down to "an unoccupied piece of Arkansas River bottom."

The perception among cadets was that flying was safe and that they were in a somewhat controlled environment where accidents may occur. The air corps did have safety procedures and programs in place. All along the way throughout training, steps were taken to reduce mishaps.[18] Accidents were categorized in two ways: either poor aircraft design (mechanical) or pilot error (which could also result from instructional error). Nonetheless, as the men progressed through their training, flying faster and more complex aircraft, the risk of plane crashes and fatalities was always present.

Before he and his class moved onto another new base, a new airplane model was introduced. Len was chosen as the first among his classmates to test out an AT-6. It was a far stronger training plane, twice again the power and weight of the PT-19. The AT-6 (AT for advanced trainer) featured an all-metal alloy frame and wing for increased strength and reliability. The plane stood eleven feet tall on the runway, twenty-nine feet long, with a forty-two foot wingspan. The new 550 horsepower engine made this aircraft 30 percent faster than the PT-19 at 210 miles per hour. It also covered twice the range (on one full tank of gas) reaching now 750 miles, or nonstop from Chicago to Philadelphia. It was a single-engine plane built for a pilot and copilot both facing forward. And as a training plane it carried no armaments, yet still weighed some 5,500 pounds fully fueled—another quantum leap in size for the men to handle. While modern and advanced, some cadets felt frustrated that flying procedures seemed to change almost every other day. For example, now for the first time the men had to deal with the added feature of retractable landing gear. The new feature made the plane significantly more aerodynamic, cruising with less drag.

All throughout training the men were tested for their ability to think clearly and read directions under duress or conditions of confusion. To probe for these qualities, it was common for examiners to verbally berate, cajole, and harass candidates during written tests. Try as they may, it was found to be difficult to test in training for what was called combat stress or "operational fatigue." The War Department was constantly trying to determine what factors caused fatigue, fear and cowardice. One medic summed up the feelings of many commanders at the time saying, "We must know that any applicant will develop into the type of man we would like to associate with for the remainder of our military service as brother officers"[19]—in other words, no cowards or deserters.

Len graduated from Grider on April 29, 1942, and wrote, "It hardly seems true that I managed to finish here on top," that is, at the top of his class. In fact, his distinction had been recognized throughout: he was allowed to finish his flight training ten hours early because of his obvious competence and his previous flying experience; he was called first to fly the new plane #103 and led his squad's training in flying "V" formations. But in one of Len's surprisingly few references to his own apprehension, he wrote Julia, "God has certainly been with me here more than I ever felt him to be with me before. My most ardent prayers are that in His direction of this Great Catastrophe I may soon be led back to a finer purpose, happy once more with my family and you."

Len's life alternated between periods of longing and loneliness on the one hand and thrilling new flying experiences on the other. All the while, the war, in fact almost the entire outside world, was ablaze in gunfire and bombing, stinking of diesel fuel and death. Len was in his own world, patiently and meticulously following a long training schedule while Japan was marching rhythmically atop oceans of islands and atolls, swallowing up former European colonies as they pressed their war plan forward with Prussian precision.

CHAPTER 5

MacArthur Redraws the "Line"

S itting in quite a hot seat, MacArthur had trouble accepting that actions against Japan in the Southwest Pacific should be limited to defensive ones. He chafed at not being given the forces and equipment he wanted. According to one biographer, he feared that his new base of operations in Australia might be overrun by the enemy just as he had been chased out of the Philippines.[20] In mid-April MacArthur was named Supreme Commander of Allied Forces in the South West Pacific Area (SWPA)—but without any manner of air support to speak of. In May Roosevelt's Joint Chiefs of Staff determined that the security of those various and strategic stepping-stone islands marking the supply lines from America to Australia, were the military priority in the South West Pacific theatre of action.

With that decided, MacArthur moved to cope with the justifiable panic that accompanied his arrival down under. He would not wait for the Japanese to invade Australia proper, and he emphatically rejected the strategy of the "Brisbane Line." He instead proposed to meet the seemingly ubiquitous Japanese threat with the meager forces he had, north of the foreboding and cloud-shrouded Owen Stanley Mountain Range. The natural barrier lumbers southeast to northwest through the heart of eastern New Guinea.

That became designated as his line in the sand; his physical and symbolic barricade against further Japanese expansion.

In late April the Japanese army began probing and flying reconnaissance flights along the wild northeast coast of New Guinea at places called Lae and Salamaua. What Allied forces MacArthur could cobble together were to be deployed near those same coastal towns to harass an expected Japanese landing force.

AN UNCHARTED NO-MAN'S-LAND

In the 1940s, New Guinea was still very much an uncharted no-man's-land at the outer edge of what even the Japanese envisioned as their Co-Prosperity Sphere. But with her rapid victories north to south in the Pacific, it was incumbent upon Japan to defend that corridor with a defensive cordon on her eastern front centered at Rabaul.

In her moving, 1943 romantic history, *New Guinea, The Sentinel*,[21] an Australian author, Isabelle Moresby, wrote of the unexplored paradise that was New Guinea at this time. While she concedes that New Guinea was likely known to the Malays and Chinese, true to her European colonial roots she credits the "discovery" of the island to Antonio D'Abreu, a Portuguese explorer, in 1511. He stumbled upon the island just twenty-odd years after Columbus opened the floodgates now called the Age of Discovery.

Throughout the years 1699 to 1874 the British explored, scouted for raw materials, and charted and named important points around the edges of New Guinea and the surrounding islands. Yet not even by 1940 had the entirety of the island coastline been charted for depths, tides, contours, or barriers. Moresby says that it was only just as World War II was breaking out that gold mining by Australians had started to yield any commercial loads there. A 1991 symposium paper presented by Dr. Henry Frei of Tsukuba Women's University (Japan), *Why the Japanese were in New Guinea*[22], details even Japan's ignorance of, and historic disinterest in, New Guinea. He pointed out how throughout history New Guinea was frequently depicted on Japanese maps as a "peninsula protruding out of north Australia."

Among the more detailed knowledge about New Guinea that does exist are rare diaries of a simple English traveler who made an exceptional visit in the 1870s. The adventurer named Octavius Stone observed, "With so many competitors in the field, it seems strange that, until the last few years, no one should have succeeded in journeying more than fifteen miles inland; a vast area remains unexplored.... It is larger than France."[23] In fact, the island is larger than France and England combined.

Stone noted that the channel separating Australia from New Guinea, "the Torres straits, had not been surveyed, and many hidden reefs and sandbanks not marked on our charts caused the navigation to be one of considerable risk and difficulty."[24] Once on the south shore of New Guinea, Stone and his companions entered the Maikasa or Pearl River, which was a mile wide at the mouth. They traveled on a steam-powered boat, as the first whites to ever make their way inland. Then, "A low line of mangrove trees marked the coast...swamps extending we knew not how far inland...[an] interminable forest of mangrove-trees on either side...[with] the highest land only a few feet above the water line." He encountered natives, "They were perfectly naked, but many of them wore a pearl shell breast ornament...their ears were pierced all round...several wore wigs, like mops, having shaved their heads."[25]

After that, Stone and his party discovered footprints, but no natives; smoke was visible far off in the distance. He described that the "stillness of the scene was almost painful...all as silent as a grave...death like solitude...." After about 30 miles Stone came across a single native in a canoe who was "thunderstruck" when seeing the "great machine" [their steam engine ship]. But, "the faster we steamed toward him, the faster he paddled...he turned back in evident terror, staked his canoe to a bamboo, and ran off inland."[26]

We know today that the peaks of Owen Stanley Mountains are between 11,000 and 13,300 feet throughout the length of the range. But in the 1940s our military map makers and pilots had no such information. In fact, military maps were often dangerously incorrect. Even up to the time of Allied ground actions, one had to use local, native scouts and carriers (porters) to help soldiers navigate the densely thicketed inland terrain, just as Stone did in the 1870s.

In concluding his symposium paper, Dr. Frei explained how New Guinea "gravitated into the fighting orbit of the Japanese Greater East Asia War" because of Rabaul's strategic location near the Americans' line of supply between Hawaii and Australia and because of its proximity to the strategic stepping-stones such as the Solomon Islands, the Caroline Islands, and the Marianas Islands. But perhaps most importantly he found it was to "take Port Moresby and keep the southernmost front active."[27] Active in the sense of supporting the first objective of the Japanese war plan: to buy time in order to establish their positions throughout Southeast Asia and bog down the Americans.

And so it is here, on this completely neglected island, over the course of the next several months, that MacArthur and the Allies in the Pacific were drawn into a series of intense, dramatic encounters—operations launched by the Japanese with the intention of capturing Port Moresby, the only existing Allied base on the island which, due to its location just across the Torres Strait, was nothing less than the gateway to Australia. Losing Port Moresby to Japan could mean the loss of the US supply lines to Australia, and would deal the Allies a crushing blow.

THE THREAT

The US Army Air Corps had been training new cadets in the PT-19 that flew an amazing 210 miles per hour. On one tank of gas it could fly a distance of 750 miles. Today, a normal passenger jet cruises comfortably at about 560 miles per hour and can fly 6,700 miles nonstop, routinely. Advances in modern engine power and communications completely diminish the magnitude of the situation in the Pacific. It is difficult to comprehend the arduous distances, the volume of coal and diesel fuel and other supplies needed in the 1940s to accomplish what the island nation of Japan had established and what it took, in time, for the Americans to establish.

As background, with America's 1917 entrance into WWI the physical distance the troops needed to travel in order to get to the fighting was a considerable obstacle to our military success. From America to any port in France was almost 3,500 miles. The army was faced with the challenge of sending millions of men and thousands of pounds of equipment across the wide Atlantic to Europe. Then, when supplies reached France, the massive, newly created organization called the Services of Supply (SOS) received those materials. The SOS was also responsible for building much of the infrastructure (docks, railroad lines, and warehouses) to forward those cannons, tanks, and men to the front. It was said that the job of the SOS was to do everything necessary so that all that a front line commander need worry about was putting his men in a position to win the war.

In Australia, 24 years later, General MacArthur did not have that luxury. He was constantly scrambling for more of everything and trying to allocate scant resources in a way to stop the energized and experienced enemy. So when military planners told the General that the first priority in the Pacific had to be the build up of the supply chain through these various stepping-stone islands, they were recognizing that it was impossible to supply his base in Australia, in any meaningful way, directly from America. They needed the logistics to haul weapons and soldiers to where MacArthur could put them to good use. The distance from San Francisco south to MacArthur's headquarters in Melbourne was 7,800 miles, more than twice the distance from America to France. With available planes that was a three-day flight. By boat it could take three to four weeks. To that end, during the early months of 1942, for example, an Ohio National Guard unit was sent not directly to MacArthur, but deployed to build up and defend Fiji, while separate army units were sent to New Caledonia, along the route to Melbourne.

Secondly, the supply of war materials was dependent on the capacity of diverse, independently operated manufacturers. The flow of guns, bullets, bombs, food, medicine, fuel, jeeps, plows to pave roads, wires to establish communications, tents, radios, and trucks all had to be coordinated in a useful fashion. Bullets might come through production weeks before the guns, beans might be harvested and canned weeks before forks and spoons were delivered. So as to better manage that seemingly unpredictable flow of goods, bullets had to be warehoused while waiting for the guns, tires had to be warehoused while waiting for truck frames, and such. Fuel had to be sent ahead to these island stopover positions so that ships and planes could be refueled. And that station had to be outfitted with docks as a proper port facility, runways needed to be paved to receive planes, offices needed to be wired for communications and the crews housed and fed. That was the main purpose of these stepping-stones—as safe areas to receive and to move goods (men and materials) closer to where commanders needed them.

It was envisioned that the army could safely ship goods from San Francisco and Hawaii southwest generally through Fiji, the Solomon Islands, and New Caledonia to Australia; and then once there, receive goods, re-group, build our forces, and launch an eventual campaign against Japan. While focusing on the development of that distribution system, what became dauntingly clear, however, was that with their own well-established bases in Taiwan, the Philippines, Malaya, Singapore, and especially Rabaul, the Japanese could easily attack almost any location in the New Guinea and Australia area. And indeed a series of battles were soon fought over exactly that: the American supply chain and the flow of goods to MacArthur.

THE BATTLE OF THE CORAL SEA

On May 4 Japan did indeed send a naval force from Rabaul to sail south via the Coral Sea to attack and capture Port Moresby. With the few ships available to them, the US and Allied forces intercepted this southbound armada. It was suggested that the Japanese may not have known that US battleships were in the area. Over the course of the next few days, in the air and at sea, a crucial battle ensued. Heavy losses were sustained all around and both sides limped back to their respective safe havens. The death toll taken in this, the Battle of the Coral Sea, counts 656 Allies lost against 966 Japanese. For the first time since the war started at Pearl Harbor, the Americans and Allies managed to stop a Japanese offensive, thus saving Port Moresby for the time being.

Rabaul is located on the northern tip of New Britain island. MacArthur used the Owen Stanley Mountain Range separating Port Moresby from Buna and stretching up to Lae, as both the geographic and figurative blockade against the Japanese advance. Kokoda sits in the mountains between Port Moresby and Buna. Milne Bay is located on the extreme southeast tip of the peninsula and faces the Coral Sea.[28] The arrows indicate traditional troop movements, not air strikes.

MILNE BAY

Having survived the very real military engagement with the Japanese during the Battle of the Coral Sea, MacArthur decided around May 25 to "reinforce" Port Moresby in expectation of another attack. He placed a small force of dive-bomber-style aircraft there, protected by antiaircraft guns and a battalion of soldiers redeployed from Australian bases. When they became available in mid-June, he also sent Australian brigades to Milne Bay on the extreme southeast tip of New Guinea. Facing the most logical sea route through the Coral Sea, their mission was to build a forward base there in anticipation of another Japanese attempt from Rabaul on Port Moresby.

MacArthur was anxious to take offensive actions but was severely limited by the troops and material available. A Park Ridge, Illinois, news article reported that one young American soldier named Bill Connor, "had lost all his outfit [kit] while in New Guinea." Apparently, a few basic items were eventually supplied to him by the Red Cross, "but needing shoes and clothing, he had to apply for ration coupons and was given twenty-five coupons, twelve of which went for shoes and four for sox."[29] It dramatizes what biographer Gavin Long stated: the US was still very unprepared for offensive action in the Pacific and MacArthur still "lacked the means" for anything but defensive measures.

THE BATTLE OF THE KOKODA TRAIL

Then, somewhat impetuously, an Allied ground force was sent from Port Moresby north into the Owen Stanley mountain village called Kokoda. From there, MacArthur planned to advance to the north coast and establish air bases from which to attack Rabaul. Such bases would avoid the need to fly over the treacherous, cloud-shrouded, and tempestuous Owen Stanley Mountains. The problem was, the Japanese got there first. After landing fourteen thousand troops at the northern coastal town of Buna on July 21, the enemy marched inland, south, toward the very same village of Kokoda. North and south, in and out of this settlement, the trails are inhospitable and densely tangled by wild jungle. They are encompassed by the even less hospitable, ragged with dense brush, Owen Stanley Mountains.

By July 29 those Japanese troops were themselves in Kokoda. They were on a follow-up operation to take Port Moresby, only this time overland, via what became known as the Kokoda Trail. The rock and tree root tangled footpath is barely wide enough for a single hiker at a time. Dense jungle, streams and mosquito-breeding malaria made any progress along the trail arduous at best. It was the first overland challenge to MacArthur's strategy for defending Australia at a line along the Owen Stanleys. Neither side, through July, in the bloody and gruesome battle of the Kokoda Trail, could claim advantage or progress against their adversary.

THE BATTLE OF MIDWAY

Midway is just that, halfway between North America and Asia on a line of latitude roughly from San Francisco to Tokyo. It is a solitary two-and-one-half acre of rock, in geographic terms, an atoll, that had to have been the most frightening post in the Pacific. At its highest point it is just eighteen feet above sea level. It is hauntingly isolated and disturbingly surrounded by water day and night, located either 3,200 miles from San Francisco or 1,300 miles from Hawaii, depending on which way you faced on any dark lonely night. But Midway was a vital American refueling station for battleships and submarines en route to and from other points in the northern Pacific.

Just a month after the Battle of the Coral Sea, coded messages revealing the details of an immanent Japanese attack were intercepted by the intelligence staff of US Navy Admiral Chester W. Nimitz. Forewarned, his forces overwhelmed the Japanese during the course of the four-day battle. It became a spectacular show of muscle and modern weaponry that killed over three thousand Japanese combatants, compared to the three hundred Americans who gave their lives successfully defending the strategic atoll. Military historians wrote that the US had so much firepower turned on the enemy that Japanese aircraft carriers were sunk even as dozens of their planes circled above. Without alternative landing spots, four thousand miles from the Japanese-held Philippines and running out of fuel, their planes and pilots helplessly crashed into the sea—a horrific fate for the airmen of any nation.

CHAPTER 6

Pioneering Instrument Flying

Cadets playing poker during the 350-mile train ride to Sherman, Texas. Len upper right. Len Happ photo.

PERRIN FIELD, SHERMAN, TEXAS

Saturday, May 2, 1942, Len wrote "...arrived here Thurs. noon after a dull train ride...This is really a military post and no country club like Grider.... Our upper class drills us and administer strict military discipline. We are taught here to take orders so that one day we may be eligible to give them..." He continued, "...we learned how to start the new ships today. Rather complicated! These Vultures cruise at 150 mph...flying and ground school here will be very tough..."

Tough indeed. This new plane was the Vultee BT-13, nicknamed *Valiant* or *Vulture*. Made by the Vultee Aircraft Company of California, the BT designation standing for basic trainer. The BT-13 was used for teaching pilots to fly blind, meaning guided only by the instrument panel, not by signposts or landmarks outside. The cockpit had a curtain that could be drawn closed in broad daylight forcing the pilot to fly, not based on outside conditions, but rather on the various dials and gauges on their instrument panel.

Pilots had to overcome their fears and learn to trust the instruments on the control panel. To assist, the men were introduced to the first "flight simulator," the Link Trainer. The men were to focus on five basic cockpit instruments: altimeter (altitude), air speed indicator, compass, bank and turn indicator (amount of roll/amount of turn), and tachometer (engine speed/revolutions). Sometimes men were blindfolded (on the ground) in order to memorize the location of cockpit gears and controls. Over time a minimum of six cockpit flight instruments came to be mounted on the instrument panels of all air corps training planes throughout the war years, adding an attitude indicator (nose pointing up or down?) to those first five instruments.

Night flying was accomplished in the early history of flight, but usually on a clear night with a full moon and with a series bonfires along the pilot's planned route. By 1942, however, with the new science behind those newly developed instrument panel indicators, a pilot could "visualize" where he was like never before. It became known as "flying on instruments."

As training progressed, some pilots failed to make adjustments to new, faster planes, others were unable to navigate long distance flights and still others could not master the aerial maneuvers that were critical to survival in bad weather and in combat. In fact, during this revolutionary but risky phase of training, many men became disoriented or lost and some died in terrible crashes. Accident rates were four times higher than in daytime training.[30]

And, as if that were not enough, Len observed that, "The new subject Radio and Code work requires plenty of concentration." Indeed, radio communications were also in their infancy. In the early history of flight, ground crews communicated with pilots in the air using colored paddles or flags, much like harbor markers for sailors—as the phrase "red right return" indicates, for example. In 1942 physical, "modern" landline telephone connections were still very limited in availability and uncertain in connectivity. As Len had written, he tried, "all day Sun to talk to mother but couldn't get through. I finally had to send a wire [telegram]." But now, with the urgency of World War II, wireless communication technology was spurred on. New innovations helped make radios small enough to fit into a cockpit. For the first time, pilots had to learn how to send and receive messages using cockpit radios to coordinate first with control towers, later with each other in the air. Eventually radio control towers could manage the various flight paths of multiple aircraft coming in and out of their airfields.

In the margins of one of his rosters Len noted the individual cadets who had washed out, failed in their training at Perrin. Len's list shows that some twenty out of an original fifty-five-man roster had been reassigned at this point, a percentage almost exactly supported in a 2013 study by Marlyn Pierce of Kansas State University.[31] That study reports that it was common to see overall washout rates of 40 percent from the very first cadet rosters to the final phase of training. Those men were reclassified and most often moved out to other air corps duty. There was plenty of need for trained crew in other extremely challenging aspects of modern aviation[32] and these men were able to fill those roles. The primary jobs to which cadets were reassigned were navigator, bombardier, gunner, and mechanic.

Producing a good pilot was time-consuming and expensive. The gruesome conundrum for the War Department was training smart, literate, physically and psychologically fit men knowing that maybe 40 percent would wash out, while calculating back into those numbers new recruits, who would succeed in the training programs and who were needed to replace those killed in combat.

BROOKS FIELD, SAN ANTONIO, TEXAS

Here the surviving cadets began the final nine weeks of preliminary training to become an Army Air Corps pilot, summing up a total of thirty-two weeks of preliminary training in all. The Advanced Flying School at Brooks Field was established in 1917. The original hangar and air ship dock for dirigibles there had only recently been converted for use by modern aircraft. Brooks graduates include Charles A. Lindbergh, the pilot of the Spirit of St. Louis whose thirty-three-hour solo flight from New York to Paris thrilled the world in May of 1927. James Doolittle, who recently led a small group of B-25s from a secret aircraft carrier in the Pacific to bomb Tokyo that April of 1942, was also a Brooks grad.[33] His "raid" was seen as a popular morale boost by a still-stunned nation and a warning to Japan that the Americans were coming.

A REALITY CHECK

Back on the ground, on July 24, the carefree spirit of a gap year adventure gave way to a sobering reality check urged on by the Air Corps: the men were asked to fill out and sign a "last will and testament."

Len was just twenty-three years old. In line, waiting to pick up their forms, the comments among the men must have been grim, punctuated by occasional frat boy, half-hearted attempts at humor to gloss over the truth that in combat many among them would be lost. Breathing heavily, their thoughts might have turned to home, to their fathers and to a last tug on their wrist when they parted from their mothers, maybe regret at not turning back to see their faces one last time. Len's will was officially, if silently, witnessed by Brooks classmates James Wimmer, Burton Goldstein, and Donald Hopperstad, with power of attorney and beneficiary claims endorsed over to Len's father, Honorius. It was a reminder to the entire "gang" that they were training for war, and not everyone makes it home.

Len's Last Will and Testament, 1942.

AERIAL OBSERVATION

Then came more—the excitement of flying a unique type of plane, the Curtiss-Wright O-52 or *Owl*. With it came the demands of learning how to operate yet another aircraft. This observation aircraft stood nine feet tall on the runway with front and back seats for a pilot and a student reconnaissance observer sitting under a forty-foot wing. The cockpit was enclosed in a retractable glass canopy that stretched almost half the length of the fuselage front to back for increased lines of sight to the battlefield. This single-engine plane, with its retractable landing gear, weighed 4,200 pounds empty. It reached speeds of 190 miles per hour over a range of 700 miles. In theater, it could accommodate one forward-facing and one rear-facing machine gun.

Len was singled out for the assignment of flying student-officers from various service branches in their observation training, many of whom had never even flown before. It was a lot, juggling and remembering the characteristics of all these new airplanes, all those dials and flashing lights on the cockpit instrument panel, flying at over 150 mph. And for all that there was still a mission to carry out—spying on the enemy (observation)—before "turning tail" fast for home.

Yet for all his skill and derring-do, Len's file shows that he was human. He was, in a very un-Prussian way, roasted in the *San Antonio Express* newspaper as a "Bonehead." The accident that must have qualified him for the distinction is not known. In the photo he is being handed a bone as being inducted into the "Boner's Club."

For as humorous as this incident may have been, associated with the fear of crashing was the pilot's fear of being washed out of pilot training. Since its earliest days the Air Corps administration accepted that accidents and indeed fatalities in this rapidly emerging branch of service would be inevitable, while pilots were generally rewarded for being courageous and taking risks. But the frequency and the gravity of accidents reached higher and higher levels, at a time when pilots and planes were more and more needed. Extensive investigations began into their causes and possible steps toward their prevention. What generals may not have appreciated was the scale of accidents and fatalities. In this, Len's first year of training, the Air Corps recorded 5,612 accidents, of them 482 were fatal crashes resulting in 1,096 deaths and wrecking more than 1,259 aircraft.[34]

SAN ANTONIO EXPRESS

BONEHEAD—Cadets don masks to meet a new member of Brooks Field's "Boner's Club" as Cadet Capt. Gerald J. Skibbins presents the "bone" to the neophite. The new member wears the bone around his neck until another cadet blunders, then it goes to him. Cadets can get into the club by running their plane into another on the runways, or by landing with the wheels retracted.

The caption reads, "The new member wears the bone around his neck until another cadet blunders, then it goes to him. Cadets can get into the club by running their plane into another on the runways, or by landing with the wheels retracted." Len Happ collection.

CHAPTER 7

The Japanese Keep Coming

Fighting the Japanese had become a game of "whack-a-mole" for MacArthur. In this game you are given a hammer with which to smack the pesky moles as they pop their heads up randomly from spots around the game board. The Japanese seemed to be everywhere in the Pacific now, menacing the eastern half of New Guinea from the north coast at Buna heading down the Kokoda Trail.

To add to his unease MacArthur saw Japan's expansion extending toward various stepping-stones along his supply lines in the Solomon Islands, some eight hundred miles out to sea, due east of New Guinea and the Coral Sea. That island group was a vital link along MacArthur's new supply route, and a Japanese foothold there could also create another angle from which to wreak havoc on Port Moresby. Already feeling vulnerable and incapable of offensive action as he was, the discovery that Japan was building an air base on Guadalcanal[35] was a major shock.

GUADALCANAL

It was unexplored, but what could be seen was overgrown and weed-infested. Much of America's early intelligence about the terrain on Guadalcanal came from missionaries and farmers who abandoned the island at the first sight of the Japanese. While helpful, their information lacked the detail and scope necessary for military assault planning. But it was all the marines had to go on at the beginning. The Americans came to learn that Guadalcanal is 90 miles long and generally 25 miles wide. Its uncharted coral-studded waters complicated naval access to shorelines with no natural harbors. The interior was a re-creation of Kokoda: rock-strewn streams interrupting narrow mosquito-clogged footpaths, which led through tangled jungle in turn broken up by rugged, unmapped, breathless mountains reaching over seven thousand feet into tempestuous clouds. In spite of the fact that the root-tangled terrain allowed for only the most nimble of pack trains, in July Japan was discovered there to be building port facilities and leveling ground for airfields, bristling with strategically placed artillery.

The threat to MacArthur's supply lines, and to Australia itself, was so significant that Washington determined to finally risk offensive action. In fact, some in Washington thought that Australia was in greater danger of being invaded by Japan than the UK was of being invaded by Germany. Thus it became the only time that Washington deviated from the Germany first policy; more planes and matériel were sent. The battle plan amassed tens of thousands of men from both service branches to carry the fight. It required the coordination of both US Army and Navy forces, directing scores of battleships and aircraft. Then, on August 8, 1942, using heavy storms covering the area to their advantage, the US Navy landed marines on a godforsaken beach at Guadalcanal to disrupt and destroy the construction of the growing new Japanese base. The enemy was taken by surprise. Caught off guard by the attack, and having few men at this forward area, Japan had to quickly send a naval task force from well-stocked Rabaul to reinforce her troops there and counter the Americans. Because the terrain allowed for no major troop movements and only sluggish and arduous tank or artillery movement, of Guadalcanal Long wrote, "On sea and in the air, a long battle of attrition had begun."[36]

The strategic value placed on this little island will be reflected in the months invested in bloody combat and the resulting death toll on each side. It would become one of the most grotesque examples of a battle of attrition, as disease and hunger will rival bombs and bullets for responsibility for the ever-accumulating fatalities.

MILNE BAY

MacArthur had also been working to strengthen the Allies' base at Port Moresby amidst ongoing Japanese air bombings. Japanese and Allied forces were still engaged in bloody back-and-forth jungle battles along the malaria-infested Kokoda Trail. By mid-August the Japanese were approaching the summit of the Owen Stanleys, less than one hundred miles from Port Moresby.

During this same time period since May, MacArthur continued to divert what men and equipment he could to build a new airfield at Milne Bay. But as Japan was pouring troops onto the island along the north coast, they discovered this new Allied buildup. In turn, they shifted some of their own troops overland from the Kokoda Trail to attack and interrupt the General's plans. On August 25 Japanese infantry, supported by naval forces from Rabaul, landed about two thousand men at Milne Bay, creating yet another battlefield.

LIMITED RESOURCES

MacArthur remained anxious and frustrated, badly lacking the troops, planes, and ammunition, trying as he did, to defend so many points over such a vast geographic area. For both adversaries, the biggest problem was logistics and supplying fighting men for traditional ground battles through dense jungle and uncharted mountains. The Australians put forward detailed plans for 7,000 Allied troops and 3,900 native carriers (porters) to be deployed into the Kokoda battle. The expectation was to break the stalemate and push the Japanese backwards. Troops were to be inserted by airdrops in order for them to more quickly reach the scene. It was an impractical proposal. In the initial stages of this battle, Port Moresby had just two small transport planes originally built to accommodate not more than twenty men at a time. The Aussie plan was aborted. In spite of the difficult terrain the men went in on foot. Only their limited supplies could be dropped in by air, reluctantly, using the planes available.

As recorded by Isabelle Moresby, New Guinea had barely been explored even by the 1940s. Our own military maps were incomplete and inaccurate—which led to unrealistic expectations of progress and success, even of simple maneuverability. These various battles exposed how unprepared the Americans were. Increasingly, the American brass were seen by the Australian military as "desk jockeys" for not going to the front to better understand the deplorable conditions in which the troops were operating.

Lacking planes was one thing. But the shocking lack of even basic supplies such as boots, uniforms, rifles, and food was another. Then the difficulty the Allies faced in delivering what little they did have led to hunger and disease among the men. In fact the Americans were only just coming to grips with the fact that malaria and dysentery were killing as many, or more, of their men than were the Japanese. MacArthur and his commanders still had much to learn about the facts of warfare in the tropical mountains. Yet, having arrived in March, it would not be until October that MacArthur paid his first brief visit to New Guinea.

MIDDLEBROOK, THE FACE OF WAR

In August of 1942 we begin to gain insight into of the fragile nature of life on the front lines in New Guinea from one of the early American pilots in theatre. Garrett Middlebrook[37] of Crowell, Texas joined the Army Air Corps in July of 1941 when he was twenty-three years old. He flew what was considered a medium-size bomber, the B-25 (nicknamed the *Mitchell* bomber, after the American aviation pioneer, Billy Mitchell). Middlebrook was a machine gunning "strafer" and bomber pilot with the newly formed 38th Bomb Group out of Hamilton Field, San Francisco.

The B-25 was a twin-engine gunship and attack bomber carrying a crew of five, each trained in multiple roles: pilot (who also fired forward-facing guns for strafing), a navigator/bomber, turret gunner, radio operator/gunner, and tail gunner. The men had up to eighteen machine guns at their disposal and carried two to three thousand pounds of bombs. Introduced in 1940, the plane featured a uniquely identifiable tail with twin rudders, one on each end of the horizontal stabilizer. While it could reach speeds of up to 270 miles per hour on two 1,700 horsepower engines, this heavily loaded plane normally cruised at 225 miles per hour over a range of 1,350 miles without using supplemental gas tanks. The famous Doolittle Raid on Tokyo was made with sixteen of these bombers.

Middlebrook kept a detailed diary about his experiences. He became a consummate fighter pilot, focused on and dedicated to, the survival of his squadron mates. In his writing he meditated on life and death. This unique Texan was well-read and periodically referenced the philosophies of different historical figures. He struggled with the moral responsibilities associated with his professional duties, such as killing an enemy who, like himself, was just following orders. His chronicle is written in clear terms about the dire conditions of the American Army Air Corps still only nine months past Pearl Harbor.

With its successful World War I experiences, the American military establishment was very skeptical of the usefulness of airplanes. In fact the Air Service of the American Expeditionary Force as it was called, was demobilized after the Great War. Throughout the 1930s the army lacked the budget for tanks and cannons; the Navy thirsted for new warships. Few commanders expressed interest in aviation. They could not justify funding untested and unproven flying machines. Re-created as a branch of the US Army in the interwar years, the air corps had fewer than 1,800 planes in 1938. Only when the German Luftwaffe demonstrated the impact of uncontested air power did the US begin to build an arsenal of airplanes. But the ramp up was slow. In 1939 just 921 planes were built for the US Army and Navy. Germany produced 8,295 aircraft that same year—and her airmen destroyed all resistance in front of them, leading the way forward for her troops to storm over feeble borders.

With or without the Germany first policy there were few planes available for the Pacific War effort when Middlebrook started. There were few trained pilots. With the Air Corps lacking officers, his commanding officer was a first lieutenant and also just twenty-three years old. What equipment they did have was allocated to enthusiastic young recruits with limited experience and on-the-job training. After training, Middlebrook flew his army-issue B-25 bomber himself, in a small cohort of thirty-two planes, across the Pacific to his overseas base. They departed Hamilton on August 7, 1942, at about the time the marines invaded Guadalcanal. Instructed to fly only by day, with only the most basic of navigational instruments, they traveled first to Hawaii and from there continued southwest across the Pacific to Fiji. They flew alone, for hours across the vast south Pacific, trying to find the little dots of islands where they could refuel. Upon arrival the sight of Fiji clearly disturbed Middlebrook:

> I experienced my first tropical rainstorm in Fiji. As I approached the airstrip, a rainstorm as black as midnight blocked my approach. The cloud looked so angry and the air currents so turbulent that I dared not fly into it…the storm caused us to have two plane crashes.[38]

Low on fuel while seeking a survivable approach to the airfield, two pilots crash-landed in torrents of rain desperately hand cranking their landing gear into place. It took months to repair the planes.

Air corps training evidently failed to filter out some men for character and even temperament. Middlebrook was witness to a group of five planes, from his original thirty-two, impatiently heading out the next afternoon for Australia. The five crews hurried to refuel their tanks and depart early so they could enjoy a bit of nightlife. As those first pilots arrived over Australia, they found the entire coast under blackout for fear of Japanese submarines. It would have been very tough for these new airmen to fly there, arriving at night and on instruments, then identify a blacked-out air base at which to land. The next afternoon, when Middlebrook and his colleagues arrived, they heard news of the five planes.

> In darkness of night the crews of 4 out of the 5 planes had abandoned their ships [bailed out] and parachuted to the ground. The cover on a parachute in one of the planes had been torn open [in transit] allowing the chute itself to blossom out and therefore the crew members did not think it would open properly if used by one

of them when they abandoned the ship....[A] co-pilot strapped himself to the navigator with their two trouser belts and jumped with the one parachute. When the chute jolted open, the belts broke, causing the navigator to fall away to his death.[39]

Thus, in their initial crossing of the Pacific Ocean, the squad lost or damaged seven out of the thirty-two aircraft that originally took off from San Francisco.[40] Two of the planes were damaged by mechanical failures; the other five were pilot errors based on the poor judgment. This is what MacArthur had to work with.

HORN ISLAND

En route to his assigned base at Port Moresby, Middlebrook was first sent to Horn Island on Australia's northeast coast. It is just fifty miles across the Torres Strait from New Guinea. He was there for a brief period to get acclimated to tropical conditions. Upon arriving he reported,

> A small detachment of Australians was camped out on the
> south end. In the center was a large tent where we all ate—or
> attempted to eat. We were entirely on Australian rations,
> but the problem was that they had no rations. For two weeks
> we ate coarse bread, which was baked into large loaves
> and flown in twice a week in one of their Lockheed planes
> from Townsville. Once a day, we were given a spoonful
> of marmalade to spread upon the bread...we lost weight
> and energy; yet we continued to perform our duties.[41]

Even on Horn Island the men were under the threat of periodic Japanese attack planes bombing them. If the pilots saw a yellow flag go up at their control tower, it meant a Japanese air raid was imminent. The pilots then had to scramble and get their planes off the ground and out of the way so as not to leave them exposed to be targeted. Many a night Middlebrook was obligated to sleep under a mosquito net beneath the wing of his airplane. He wrote, "The high command could ill afford to have our few precious bombers destroyed while they were sitting on the ground."[42]

Middlebrook and crew were part of MacArthur's shaky build-up at Port Moresby. Of this barely understood, barely explored island he noted,

> Inland from Port Moresby, a mere 30 miles from the seashore, the mountains rose to 11,000 feet. [New Guinea] was awesome in many ways—its rain forest, cascading rivers and rugged terrain were impressive, but its sheer, vast wilderness was frightening. The boiling mass of clouds overhead was likewise scary.[43]

When they arrived at Port Moresby Air Base, two American fighter planes were in flames. Japanese airplanes had executed an attack just fifteen minutes before Middlebrook arrived. Pilots had been unable to get them off the ground and escape before the bombs hit them. Adding insult to injury, the base had no firefighting equipment. No effort was made to put the fires out. The planes burned to ash.

As we have seen, Port Moresby at this time was also under threat from the Japanese army via the Kokoda Trail. That same day on which Middlebrook arrived, his plane was refueled and loaded with bombs and machine gun rounds. He and his crew were sent out immediately as part of a task force to bomb Buna Airfield. It was known to be a base from which the Japanese were targeting Port Moresby. Middlebrook had expected a pep talk before his first mission. But instead the base commander fidgeted and twitched as he abruptly gave and repeated orders to the air crew, nervously returning his cigarette to his mouth. He believed Japanese ground forces to be just twelve miles away. The mission was to fly up over the Owen Stanley Mountains and further north to the seashore and attack where the Japanese were expanding that base of supplies. Because of the enemy's recent and intense bombing missions on his base, this commander fretted about even more aggressive retaliation on Port Moresby after that mission. He recommended that after hitting Buna, "if they [Middlebrook and crew] have enough fuel," return not to Port Moresby but rather farther away, back to Australia and Horn Inland.

WAR: THE ENEMY, THE WEATHER, AND THE MIND

In September, Middlebrook was already intimidated by the epic weather and emphasized how important it was to be able to fly only by instruments. And that just as aviation cadets were learning at Perrin Field,

> Instrument proficiency was acquired from practice and concentration.…. The clouds were so black against the light blue sky that we could see the boiling, angry currents; this indicated such turbulence that I feared the thought of flying near them, let alone of having to flying through them…. Dark menacing clouds so heavily laden with moisture that I wondered how they could float in the sky, loomed in front of us. We came face to face with our second enemy, the weather, which we sometimes feared more than the primary foe.[44]

Austere and simple, a Japanese Zero fighter aircraft. Photo from US Navy archives.

Middlebrook described one of his first encounters with the Japanese. After successfully reaching the north coast and bombing targets at Buna, he and the others in his small squadron of six planes were met by a squadron of the famous Japanese "Zero" fighter planes, mid-air, scrambled to defend Buna. Throughout the course of the war, almost all Japanese attack airplanes were called Zeros. This single-engine, one-man plane, dominated the Pacific starting immediately with its introduction in 1940 in China and outperformed every Allied airplane in the sky. With this weapon they established what came to be called "air superiority" or uncontested control of the airways; they seemed to appear everywhere. But the model that Middlebrook encountered was technically known as the Mitsubishi A6M2. From a distance it was not much bigger than Len's Piper Cub, but it yet weighed almost five times more. In fact, Middlebrook referred to them as looking like toys. The Zero's height reached just slightly higher than a basketball hoop (about ten feet) with a thirty-nine-foot-long wingspan. Its speed was attributed to its lightweight aluminum alloy frame and the fact that it carried no protective armor plating. Its fixed, low wing (under the body of the plane instead of overhead) required no external support, which further reduced its weight. All in all, a fully loaded Zero weighed upwards of 5,500 pounds including armaments. It carried two machine guns blasting out of the engine and two cannons thundering from each wing. It could deliver another 130 pounds of bombs from each of those wings. Piercing gravity, streaking into the sky, the pilot could climb to 10,000 feet (almost two miles) in under four minutes and stay aloft for seven or eight hours at a time over a range of 1,930 miles. Its understated silhouette could appear out of nowhere, blazing fearsomely at speeds of up to 330 miles per hour.

The B-25's maximum speed was almost 35 percent slower. On the surface, there should have been no contest. The Zero should have been able to shred Middlebrook's plane. The lumbering B-25 was a fifty-two-foot-long target for the Japanese Zero, its wingspan a very visible sixty-seven feet. It weighed almost four times the Zero at 19,500 pounds, empty. At its most vulnerable, at take off, it could carry a maximum weight of 35,000 pounds.

I could do nothing for the first few seconds except sit there and watch them [the enemy planes] while the reality penetrated my mind that for the first time in my life someone was going to try to kill me.[45]

I did not need to see the Zeros to be conscious of the stream of tracers [glowing bullets, the stream of which helped guide the gunners aim] that were...passing by us...I expected our plane to be riddled at any moment since I found it inconceivable that all those bullets were missing their targets.... It was at that particular instant that I was introduced to the debilitating effect of cold, deep fear. I was not prepared for the paralyzing effect that that agonizing emotion had upon me, nor had I yet learned how to control fear.[46]

The 17-ton B-25 over New Guinea. We can only marvel at the technology leap from Len's original 750 lb. Piper Cub. The bombs alone on the B-25 weighed 3,000 lbs. Len Happ photo.

Middlebrook knew the Zero could outmaneuver any plane in the world with dramatic turns and aerobatic rolls to shift direction, altitude and positioning. The B-25's defensive firepower, its eighteen machine guns, were oriented upwards and outwards. Therefore it was most vulnerable to attack from below. That meant Middlebrook had to keep his B-25 low to avoid playing into the Zero's strengths.

Applying tactics learned in his twelve months of training, Middlebrook flew the majority of his missions under one hundred feet to surprise the enemy, to spray machine gun bullets (strafe) at their ground targets, and to drop bombs. This same low-level flying technique would help avoid being attacked from below by the faster fighter planes. Amazingly, by dodging, weaving, and hiding in the clouds, Middlebrook was able to evade the Zero and return to base.

MACARTHUR STRAINS AT THE LACK

With the Japanese continuing to press over land, along the Kokoda Trail into the Owen Stanley Range, MacArthur again beseeched Washington for more men and more matériel. He was told, to "make the best of what he had."[47] For their part, Air Corps commanders in Washington recognized that MacArthur had nowhere to even put new planes or squadrons. His own base was thousands of miles from the battle and Port Moresby was by no means safe.

On September 7 the Japanese operation to take Milne Bay was considered repulsed thanks to superior numbers of experienced Australian forces. While the battle not only demonstrated the Allies' capacity to scramble together an effective defensive force, the success also boosted the Allies' morale and gave the men an indication there might be a limit to Japanese power. The cost to stop the enemy totaled some two hundred Allied soldiers killed and another two hundred wounded, with many going down to malaria. The Japanese lost over six hundred killed with another three hundred wounded.

As noted, senior officers, men capable of interpreting and carrying out General MacArthur's orders, were also in short supply during this initial phase of the war. It was an entirely new type of war being fought. Unrealistic expectations of progress in the field, stemming from ignorance about the conditions of the battleground, were straining relations with the Australians—especially as Australian battalions were still deployed in the Middle East fighting for British interests there. As his senior Air Corps officer MacArthur recruited Major General George Kenney, "an exuberant and confident officer who swiftly won [his] confidence."[48]

George Churchill Kenney was a pioneer flying cadet in 1917 assigned to the US Army Signal Corps serving on the Western Front. He went from there to fly reconnaissance missions along the US border during the Mexican Revolution. In 1920 he was commissioned into the regular army. As an assistant military attaché observing German and Allied air operations in the early stages of World War II, Kenney recommended insightful changes to Air Corps aircraft and tactics. Two years later he found himself on MacArthur's staff in Australia. At the time Kenney took over as head of the Air Corps, his responsibilities covered the only 260 American aircraft that existed in the entire Southwest Pacific theatre of war, "many of them unserviceable."[49]

Given the military demand for all sorts of airplanes, these 260 planes were US Navy-used and battle tested A-24 aircraft. They were shipped to Major General Kenney in pieces to be reassembled in Australia. But, because not all the parts to those 260 planes arrived with the bodies, the Australians were asked to scrounge up and cannibalize what was needed from other planes or outright make the pieces that were missing in order to get the planes operational. Those planes represented the scant 15 percent of total available aircraft that the War Department was ready to commit to the Pacific Theatre. As Long observed, "For the time being, shortages of ships and critical situations elsewhere would limit army forces in the Southwest Pacific."[50]

Again, on September 16, President Roosevelt and the Joint Chiefs of Staff confirmed to an ever-vexed MacArthur that he had all that he was getting for the time being. Two days later, after being recently pushed out of Milne Bay, Tokyo ordered her South Seas forces to positions along the north coast of New Guinea, supported by this seemingly inexhaustible fountain of strength in Rabaul. MacArthur was so concerned about losing Guadalcanal that, by October 31, he prepared a plan to withdraw from the north coast and from all of eastern New Guinea altogether[51]. He was thinking that the "Brisbane Line" might not be so absurd after all.

CHAPTER 8

Forming an Air Corps Bomb Group

Citation:

The Secretary of War has directed me to inform you that the President has appointed and commissioned you in the Army of the United States, effective this date...

Personnel Orders, Number 186 stated that Len was now "required to participate in regular and frequent aerial flights, at such times as [he] is called to active duty with the Army Air Forces.... All orders in conflict with this are revoked." On September 6, 1942 Len graduated as "Pilot" from the Advanced Flying School, Brooks Field, Texas. With graduation he officially entered active service designated with the officer's rank of Second Lieutenant. The men also learned their eventual assignments: aggressive pilots would be assigned to single-seat fighter planes; men with more leadership qualities would be assigned to multiple-engine planes that flew with crew on board. Commissioned with him were flight school buddies who would become lifelong friends, such as Ed Hambleton of Oklahoma, Don Hopperstad from Illinois, Kenneth Hedges from Oklahoma, and Ewing J. McKinney from Texas. They were joined by men who would eventually lead them in battle: First Lieutenant William Pagh and First Lieutenant Selmon Wells.

He wrote enthusiastically to Julia, "[I am] establishing myself in my new quarters—the Bachelor's Officers Quarters…I wish I had the time to tell you all about this new life as an officer. The change is unbelievable. It is a real thrill!"

HUNTER FIELD, SAVANNAH

Len was assigned to the 84th Bomb Group, located at Hunter Field in Savannah, Georgia. Hunter was a new base, specifically built for the war effort. Located two miles from Savannah, it provided classroom training, gunnery ranges, flight simulators and audio-visual demonstration (movies and slide projections). It also had separate clubs for officers and for enlisted men (supporting ground crew and aviation mechanics).

Annual aircraft production totals now exceeded the combined figure of 3,000 planes in 1939. By 1941 production for the army and navy alone recorded 1,770 combat planes added to their arsenals. And another 1,840 military planes were produced that were categorized generally as either transport or training planes like the BT and AT types.[52] Production was increasing at such a pace and became so specialized, that military statisticians could categorize the various new combat aircraft into six groupings by their specialties, such as: small and fast attack planes or heavy long-range bombers.

The planes the men were using at Hunter, however, were still whatever they could get their hands on. Of those 1,840 training planes made in 1941, there was a fight in Washington over who would get them. Hunter got a handful of what were officially called the *Vengeance* fighters, what the men again called *Vultures*. Only, these models were well-advanced from the versions the men used at Perrin Field.

In the classroom and in the air they developed group communication skills. The airmen also practiced new dive-bomb techniques in simulated battle conditions in two new types of Vultee aircraft. But first, they were required to complete the *Questionnaire on A-31 or V-72 Type Airplane* before being cleared to fly. That involved learning the weight of the plane, stalling speeds, air speeds, gliding speeds, dive brakes, hydraulic hand pumps, maximum bomb load, and bomb jettison switches. The final question brought these pioneering aviators back to the sobering nature of their work: "Describe means of destroying [your] aircraft in case of forced landing in enemy territory."

The two planes were interchangeable in that both the A-31 and the V-72 were fit with single, 1,600 horsepower engines for carrying a pilot and navigator/gunner. The planes were thirty-nine feet and nine inches in length with a forty-eight foot wingspan and sat fifteen feet four inches tall on the runway and weighed 9,725 pounds empty. They had the capacity to carry four forward-firing wing guns and two machine guns in the cockpit, with the heft to also carry two internal 500-pound bombs and two 250-pound bombs on wing racks. Cruising at 235 miles per hour, with a maximum speed of 275, they had a range of 1,400 miles when fully fueled. While the planes and their uses were similar, the *Vengeance* was exported to the British Air Force and was designated as the A-31, while the later version was flown by French forces and designated as the V-72. Ironically they were never used in combat by the American military. In the States the planes were mostly used in dive-bomb training or to tow airborne targets for air to air gunnery practice.

After so much training to develop the individual pilot, the men now undertook unit training and group tactical maneuvers. They practiced ordered takeoffs, re-groupings in the air and flying in formation. V-formation flying (like geese) required a pilot to fly with just five feet separating his plane from the wing tip of the next plane over. It was primarily a tactic for mutual defense, a way to protect the group from enemy aircraft en route to the target area. As early as World War I, aviators found that two planes flying together survived more missions and scored more victories than single planes flying on their own.

Once aloft, dive-bomb exercises taught pilots to bomb and machine-gun the enemy positioned in front of their ground forces. It was seen as a support role for American or Allied ground troops advancing on the enemy. On October 28 from Hunter, Len wrote enthusiastically,

Hop and I are now dive bombers and I don't mean maybe. We are assigned to the 84th Bomber Group. It is a relatively new job for the Army but we're doing it now. The ships we fly are designed and used by the Navy and have been used with great success in combat. The Navy uses them from carriers…nice to handle. The ships are single engine but with 1350 horse power—a lot of stuff. The air speed indicator is calibrated in knots as it was designed for the Navy as I said. Miles per hr. are the knots plus 15%.

Just a few years earlier, it was a marvel to get a plane off the ground and land it safely. Now, planes were being built to execute steep dives carrying five-hundred-pound bombs to drop on a given target and then safely pull out of that dive while being shot at by the enemy; pulling up and away to live and fight again. It was a lot of physical stress on both the men and the planes.

Practicing in these single-engine aircraft included the bombing of old trucks and wooden shacks set up for target practice. The men's training was beginning to merge with current practices in the fields of combat. Among the latest battle innovations introduced were "airfrag" or "parafrag" bombs. These were bombs with small parachutes attached, designed to be dropped by low-flying aircraft, from twenty to one hundred feet in altitude. Once activated and released, they floated down and detonated on the first thing they touched. The slow descent gave the pilot valuable seconds to accelerate away from the target so the bomb would not explode directly underneath them or underneath their wingman's airplane. The new weapon dramatized the need for precision flying as the release of the bombs was coordinated with the passing of other low-flying aircraft in one's attack squadron—timed so the pilot behind you does not get blown up.

Pilots found the A-31 difficult to fly as a dive-bomber because the plane felt unbalanced and its large engine made it difficult to see directly in front of them. And while the V-72 was more comfortable to fly, lines of sight were still blocked or impeded by the way the cockpit was similarly set (low) behind the engine. Training accident rates, not due to pilot error, were numerous because of periodic engine trouble. Both Vultees, the A-31 and V-72 types, also had imprecise aiming systems. Reports showed that bombs missed targets by up to one hundred yards. To add to the complications, landing gear frequently collapsed under the weight of the plane upon landing. Meanwhile, new types of planes were constantly being developed or increasingly adapted to new fighting strategies, which forced aircraft builders to react to evolving military demands. Therefore, both of these airplanes were eventually replaced by advanced versions that attempted to correct the various aerodynamic, stability, or performance shortcomings of these earlier models. But new generation aircraft were few and far between.

In the interim Len then wrote,

> The air base here is rather new…"Hop" and I room together in a suite. We are up early in the morning 6:30 A.M. and have to be back in the B.O.Q. [Bachelor Officers Quarters] by 10:30 P.M. We have one night and a day a week off. The country around here is all swamp and river. Savannah itself is 18 miles from the Ocean. The town is booming with 3 ship yards and Army posts. The town of Savannah itself is dimmed and not at all inviting as yet…. Our evenings are very quiet.

By Savannah being "dimmed," Len was referring to blackout measures taken due to the ever-present worry over German U-boats lurking along the Atlantic coast. Just as the Illinois War Council worried about Union Station in Chicago, the Georgia War Council fretted over the very real possibility of attack on their people, their facilities, or on friendly cargo ships at or near the Port of Savannah.

THE 312TH BOMB GROUP

Back in September, Lieutenant Colonel Robert Strauss, at thirty-two years of age, was slotted into the position of commanding officer of the 312th Bomb Group stationed at Hunter Field. Born in Boston and graduated from West Point, Strauss went on to learn his basic flying skills at the same Air Corps Flying School at Kelly Field as Len—only Strauss graduated two years earlier. Soon afterwards, he became the private pilot to General George Patton. Strauss was a man of strong character and an inspirational leader if not a role model. In this new assignment, Strauss would go on to fly with and command this unified team throughout the better part of the war.

The original configuration of the cohort was made up of remnants of other training classes. Within the 312th were now four smaller subgroupings, bomb squadrons, designated as the 386th, 387th, and 388th along with the squadron to which Len was permanently assigned, the 389th. With the formation of that bomb group Selmon Wells was immediately promoted to captain and named commander of Len's 389th Bomb Squadron.

Then in late November yet another new model, the A-36 Apache dive-bomber, was delivered to Hunter. Len wrote,

> Flying this morning and tonight so this afternoon I have a chance to answer some letters. Hunter Field and the squadron surely keep 'Hop' and me on the go…we are in a new squadron, the 389th. We will soon be flying some new ships here. This week the Field got in 5 sleek 'Mustangs.' The ship is the dive-bomb version of the No. American Pursuit 51 [P-51]. The ship is designated now as the A-36…[and] cruises at three hundred miles per hour and should be a new thrill to fly. The big guns are now flying them and we should be flying them soon.

Among the first Air Corps P-51 to reach Hunter Field in Savannah. The original US Navy designation was A-36. Len Happ photo.

This aircraft represents another leap forward in design, endurance, and in aviation technology. Its revolutionary contours were based on experimental (theoretical/classroom) data leading to a trimmed low wing and innovative liquid-cooled engine. The new shape made for less drag from the wings and less drag from the engine configuration, which both contributed to superior speed and range. The A-36 was a single-seat, single-engine bomber. It had a thirty-seven foot wingspan and sat thirteen feet tall on the runway. While bulky, weighing 7,600 pounds empty, it could reach a then jaw-dropping cruising speed of 440 miles per hour.

Newly operational at the end of 1942, this aircraft was considered the precursor to modern jet fighters and competitive with the Japanese Zero, which flew at 330 miles per hour. Besides the speed and weight, it was a quantum leap for the men in so many more ways. For example, the flying range of the A-36 was 750 miles. But significantly, fitted with external ejectable and disposable fuel tanks, it could stay aloft on a bombing mission for 1,650 miles, equivalent to flying round trip from Savannah on the Atlantic coast to St. Louis on the Mississippi River. Fully armed, the pilot had at his reach two nose guns, four wing guns and 1,000-pound bombs under each of his wings.

In just these ten months Len's training planes had advanced from 175 horsepower BT engines to 1,490 horsepower in the P-51, and from training speeds of 75 miles per hour to now over 440.

Flying altitudes also were increased. As a dive-bomber, the P-51 pilot generally started his dive at the lofty altitude of 12,000 feet, and in descent, bombs were released from an altitude of 4,000 feet to 2,000 feet. Recalling the PT-19 with its wooden wings flying horizontally at 130 miles per hour, advances in metallurgy and design now meant the wings of the P-51 could handle incredible stress during descent and when pulling out of dives. This allowed pilots to achieve a dive speed, when releasing bombs, exceeding 350 miles per hour, thus making it increasingly difficult for the enemy to sight and shoot down. As the versatility of this new plane came to be appreciated, it was used as a dogfight style fighter plane as well. The dogfight component came into play in the P-51's use as an escort plane for slower flying, heavier bomber airplanes, like Middlebrook's B-25. As we have seen, those slower planes were vulnerable to attack from the Japanese Zero. Now, the P-51 could escort those bombers to their attack area and confidently defend them from counter attack from the enemy.

Not only were planes in short supply, there was always a lack of even basic soldiering equipment. All throughout 1942 and '43, the Air Corps scrambled to get ahold of all sorts of things to fill simple hygienic needs as well as ongoing combat needs. Military planners waited for gear to be produced so they could parcel it out to the various fronts and training bases. It was not until December 18 that Len received his leather Type A 4 pilot Navigation Case, into which went his instruction manuals, navigation charts, and maps. He also received his most basic fighting kit—"belt, pistol, first aid packet, canteen, blankets, tent and tent poles." For all the exciting and promising advances in technology, America was not quite ready to outfit her men for battle. In every category of need, from canteens to aircraft, the country needed more and they needed it delivered into the fight.

CIVIL DEFENSE, THE FIRST WAR GAMES

Before the publicly neutral US officially entered the war, scrap metal, armaments, airplanes (broken down into sections), and other supplies were sent to aid the UK and other Allies through the Port of Savannah, among other, what were called, debarkation points. Immediately after the war declarations, by January of 1942 in fact, some nineteen Nazi U-boats were found operating in the waters off New England alone. As we have seen since Pearl Harbor, Americans at home were indeed on edge, not only struggling to manage under essential oil and fuel rationing schemes, but also keeping an anxious eye on the seas and skies. By March of 1942, Nazi submarines had sunk seventy merchant ships along the rugged length of the American east coast.

The Port of Savannah was almost completely shut down in 1942 because there was so much U-boat activity in their waters. The Savannah city council made the entire waterfront area a restricted zone to protect it from sabotage. Their ordinances prohibited fishing, consumption of liquor, smoking, explosives, flammable materials, electronics, cameras, and firearms, among other articles within those boundaries—and, as Len had observed, at night a complete blackout was in effect.

As the men gained the competence to fly advanced combat planes, Colonel Strauss led them in practicing the tactical methods that would guide their air combat as a fighting team, learning the techniques and maneuvers to attack and fight as a group. And from here at the training base, the feedback of pilot and ground crews helped evaluate the shortcomings and advantages of all of these new aircraft. Then airplane manufacturers, in a unified and coordinated war effort like none other, worked to implement new discoveries from classrooms, from training bases and from laboratories into their latest models.

The work came full circle. As military requirements continually pushed airplane manufacturers to expand the capabilities of aircraft and to expand the levels of production, those manufacturers needed increasing numbers of qualified engineers and mathematicians (men and women) to work out new calculations and advance technologies in the effort to improve these flying machines. As part of this drive, colleges took up the study of theoretical and tactical wartime problems in the classroom.

It was challenge enough for a dive-bomber to hit a stationary target. The German U-boat, for example, was a moving target. In October of '42 when the 312th was being formed, Mundelein College had Julia working on just these wartime issues—specifically the mechanism required to adjust dive-bombing on fixed targets to moving targets. Julia was photographed at a chalkboard for an article in the Mundelein College newspaper entitled "Interceptor Command."[53] She is shown working on sophisticated equations and diagrams, demonstrating the interception of an adversary's cruiser and the technicalities of a successful hit on a speeding enemy craft.

Julia Case demonstrating the mathematics of intercepting enemy craft. Courtesy of Mundelein College.

Describing Julia as a senior year mathematics major, the article went on to relate how she was working out a "Theory of Equations" meant to solve war problems, factoring such variables as, "Air navigation figures...[and] true air speed...." The article went on to say, "They are learning to determine the time and position for interception of enemy cruisers, by means of the laws of Vector Aviation in a polygon of forces."

RUSH AT SAVANNAH

Civil Defense authorities by chance caught site of an enemy craft operating in the waters of their restricted zone on January 16, 1943. Hunter Field base command was informed by the Coast Guard, and immediately the 312th was asked to assist. They were to locate and destroy what was thought to be a German submarine sighted off the Savannah.

With their stinging memories of the foreign incursion at Pearl Harbor, mechanics rushed to the airfields to prep their planes, watching overhead for what else may be coming. As one man put machine gun ammunition in place, another loaded the last of the bombs in the planes. Simultaneously, zones of responsibility were graphed out by base commanders and pilots were assigned specific grids on the surface map to the north and south of the Savannah River delta. Pilots scrambled their P-51s into position and awaited the radio call to take off from the control tower, wondering if this was a practice drill. As best they could navigate over the featureless open waters, counting seconds and minutes in various turns, their enthusiasm quickly melted into the real anxiety of possibly being shot at by a real enemy with real bullets.

After two long hours staring expectantly into the sea, they found no signs of a U-boat. If there had been one, it was now mysteriously submerged deep in the Atlantic. They never did find a sub that day, but to these young pilots the effort was a rush. It was also their first real-world threat, which they met with a real-world response.

CHAPTER 9

The Battle of the Bismarck Sea

THE AGONIZING ALLIED POSITION

Incessant, expansive, offensive action in the eleven months since Pearl Harbor caught up with the Japanese. They began to withdraw troops from the Buna area to consolidate their vast gains. The Japanese repositioned between 5,500 and 6,500 experienced troops on the northern coast to a more strategically located town called Lae, west of Buna, and moved thousands more back to Rabaul.

Their consolidation led to a period of positive forward momentum for beleaguered Australian troops, who fought their way into Kokoda on November 2nd. The next day they advanced an unheard-of nine miles overland toward the original Japanese starting point on the coast at Buna. So far, this five-month-long Kokoda Trail battle had cost 625 mostly Australian lives and over 1,000 wounded. Exhausted, both the Japanese and the pursuing Allied troops were riddled with disease. The shift in the battle gave more breathing room and flexibility to the Australians and Americans in supplying forces there. But the Allies were still lacking the most basic of supplies and medicines to operate as effectively as commanders wanted in the oppressive tropical conditions.

Meanwhile, the horrendous battle in the steamy wilderness and rock-tangled seas of Guadalcanal was also yielding positive results for the Allies. In October they had secured control of the airfields, but were still engaged in intense fighting around the perimeter to maintain that control.

To the astonishment of the Japanese, the Americans were still pouring thousands of troops into the deadly scrimmage in sand and bush all over the island. In fact, both sides were. Ground troops, midshipmen, and pilots on both sides were arm wrestling over corners of beaches from which they could establish a foothold—gasping, hoping to pave the way for reinforcements.

In mid-November, the Japanese sent a fresh battle group of ships from Rabaul to launch a naval bombardment of the Guadalcanal airfields. Their marines were to then surge forward to once again take control of the airfields. Alerted through intelligence sources, the US Navy limped into position to stop them. The Americans lost more of the few destroyers available to them, sunk in the fight. But they did enough return damage to stop their adversary again. They had done enough to force Japan to cancel this latest offensive. In December, the Japanese decided to abandon their efforts to retake the airstrips and began a long process of evacuating troops back to Rabaul under heavy assault from the Allies.

"MASSIVE ENEMY TROOPS"

The official histories do little to enlighten us on the violence that was raging. In November, Middlebrook was ordered out on an early-morning mission to bomb and "harass" the growing Japanese airbase at Lae. While the term "harass" can be interchangeable with "strafe" (in both cases, firing a machine gun in a sweeping motion across a target area), "strafe" is intended to mean shooting at specific enemy target and "harass" is used to describe indiscriminate shooting at random enemy targets. As his plane approached his objective, anti-aircraft guns started firing back at him.

> Just before our bombs fell, flak started to explode all around us.... Ten bursts of flak exploded on our left followed by a cluster of equal number on our right, and then a number of [these] black puffs burst right in front of us.[54]

Shells shot at an attacking airplane explode, spraying shards of metal called flak. These shards are intended to disable the attacking craft and pilot. The object is not to necessarily to hit the airplane directly, but rather to explode close enough near the ship to seriously damage it. One of Middlebrook's companion B-25s, with their five crew members, was hit directly by flak and went crashing down, right in his view. Then, while dodging and maneuvering to escape the area, Middlebrook's was hit with gunfire by a Zero. But his plane stayed aloft even with twenty-two holes scattered along the side of it. Middlebrook says he was distracted by the downing and certain death of his comrades and almost lost his own life watching them. Snapping out of his daze in mid-flight, he found he had no time to think about them when his life, the lives of his crew, and his plane were in such peril; focus was his only hope of survival.

At base in Port Moresby, through December of 1942, because of the frequent bombing raids by the Japanese, Middlebrook was still sleeping under mosquito netting, on a cot, beneath the wing of his airplane. He determined to sleep as close as possible to his plane so he could more quickly get it out of harm's way when they came. Finally, a tent was made available to him. He recorded in his diary that while the air warning alerts and the frequent Japanese bombings kept him awake at night, he was also highly disturbed by Allied intelligence reports from the Southwest Pacific headquarters. In those reports Middlebrook read the Japanese had,

> massive enemy troops and planes scattered from Korea through China, Formosa and the Philippines, Borneo, the Celebes Islands, Timor and on down to Singapore. Compared to our pitiful little force in New Guinea, their forces seemed awesome.[55]

The modern Japanese military had been developing her skills and firepower in earnest since the 1930s, as their aggression against China advanced. Middlebrook's immediate adversary, the Zero, for example, evolved during that time period. It was so unique and formidable that as Japan's drive for empire expanded beyond China, the plane was found to be highly adaptable to both aircraft carriers and to the unusual terrain and tenuous runways of these various islands and colonial outposts, such as Lae and Rabaul, that dotted the Pacific. Throughout this period in the war, the Japanese were so strong and the Allies were so undermanned and so outgunned that any Allied counter attack must have come as a surprise to the Japanese.

With the chilling comprehension of his vulnerability, Middlebrook worried, "Once the Japs [have] bases on the southern shores of New Guinea, they could attack Australia. I dared not allow my mind to become too overwhelmed…but nonetheless, I could not hold back."[56]

He was right to be concerned. The intelligence reports he read confirmed the extent of Japan's strength. Port Moresby faced down direct attacks from three directions: Guadalcanal, the Kokoda Trail, and the Coral Sea. The base still suffered random bombings almost without opposition from the air; gunfire could still be heard in the direction of Kokoda. Middlebrook feared for his life and dejectedly wondered whether they were fighting an unwinnable war. And certainly a day did not pass that General MacArthur himself re-lived in his own mind the horrors brought down on him in the Philippines, and his frightening evacuation.

JAPANESE REDEPLOY FROM BUNA TO LAE

From January to June of 1943 the battleground in eastern New Guinea lapsed into what historians called a "strategic stalemate," but not inactivity. Each side attempted to reinforce and/or replace losses from these earlier battles focused on Port Moresby and MacArthur's supply lines. Paraphrasing the military historian Edward Drea: neither side had the resources in early 1943 to force any decisive progress, and the various battles seemed likely to continue, as the Japanese hoped, as drawn out wars of attrition.[57]

Shipping shortages (especially due to vessels lost in battle) created logistics and transportation bottlenecks for both sides. The Japanese struggled to replace their heavy losses in naval planes and pilots as they were gradually trying to take control of strategic air bases and ports throughout the north of New Guinea. Fifth Air Corps Commander General Kenney found himself trying to justify additional warplanes from Washington. MacArthur lacked transports, cargo vessels, and landing craft as well as the trained crews to man them. They were still fighting with the short end of the American stick—receiving just an estimated 15 percent of American wartime production.

With the Japanese regrouping their forces and redeploying them, to strengthen their hold over their gains, on January 22, 1943, the Allies took the town of Sanananda, near Buna, thus completely closing Japanese overland access to the Kokoda Trail link to Port Moresby. The long, drawn out battle exacted a bloody toll of some six thousand Japanese soldiers killed, although, probably more than half died from tropical diseases. The Allies lost close to one thousand men. Shamefully, there is no official record of the number of New Guinea "volunteers" and porters—native men and women—killed. Among the wounded on all sides since the start of the Battle of the Kokoda Trail, a staggering twenty-eight thousand were estimated to be dying from malaria, dysentery, and other tropical diseases.

GUADALCANAL

The Battle of Guadalcanal was considered over in February of 1943 when the Japanese completed their evacuation from this area to Rabaul, Lae, and a place called Wewak, located further west, well up along the New Guinea coast. In the end it was a sweltering shoulder-to-shoulder ground battle, which the Allies won. But the cost in lives on each side was again tremendous: overall close to 15,000 Allied soldiers fell dead and wounded versus 31,000 Japanese lost, and over 8,500 of their men sick or wounded.

At that point, more than a year after Pearl Harbor, the southeast corner of New Guinea was somewhat more secure. US Navy actions to halt the Japanese in the Coral Sea, at Midway and Guadalcanal, at a considerable cost to the Japanese Navy, helped clear the waters along MacArthur's supply chain. Port Moresby was only somewhat more relieved of the Japanese threat. But this was just a prelude. The Japanese were still entrenched all over New Guinea, a threat to Australia to be sure, including in a very fortified, almost uncontested position at Rabaul.

THE BATTLE OF THE BISMARCK SEA

North of New Guinea lies a crescent shaped island called by its colonial name, New Britain. It forms the eastern border of a sea known by its colonial name, the Bismarck Sea (for the father of German unification). Rabaul sits on the extreme northeast peninsula of the island. It is in fact comprised of several harbors, which are in turn surrounded by hills. Throughout the war, supply ships set off from Japanese held ports on its home islands. Groups were joined together by ships from Formosa to make up heavily laden convoys in order to fortify Rabaul. At various times throughout 1942 and 1943 it was estimated to house and feed some ninety-five thousand Japanese troops, with upwards of sixty ships at anchor and defended by more than three hundred anti-aircraft guns strategically placed in those surrounding hills. Lacking sufficient planes and pilots, and lacking forward bases that could cover the distance, MacArthur was only able to launch sporadic and minimal harassing attacks against Rabaul.

In late February, sixteen heavily laden ships set out from Rabaul to deliver goods and to deploy soldiers into Lae. They carried 7,000 reinforcement troops, along with fuel, machinery and food, all protected by a naval task force of well-armed battleships. The planned route took the convoy west, somewhat along the equator through the Bismarck Sea, then south towards the Japanese-held north coast of New Guinea. Tropical black and gray storm clouds would normally shroud their movements.

On March 1st, however, this vast convoy was spotted by an American pilot patrolling in a B-24 bomber. He reported their position to his headquarters, whereupon their position was promptly lost again in bad weather. On the morning of March 2 the convoy was again spotted and the aborted attack plan conceived the previous day was reinitiated and carried out.

The B-24 Liberator on patrol over New Guinea. Lon Happ photo.

Because of those almost inconsequential attacks on Rabaul, the Japanese were unaware, or unconvinced, of the growing US capacity to stop such large supply convoys. But, as ground troops had thus far been bogged down in impenetrable forests, dying in arduous battles, the mobility of the air forces, as limited as they were, seemed to be shifting the battles in the Allies' favor. Coordinated by General Kenney, there ensued over the next days a hail of Allied air bombings and strafing on this convoy, the likes of which the Japanese never expected. It was claimed that over the course of these next days, the Allies sank more than twelve transport vessels and destroyed another ten naval fighting ships. Almost all of the 7,000 Japanese troops perished in those transport ships. The very few ships and men who survived somehow limped into either Lae or back to Rabaul.

Garrett Middlebrook was part of this attack force, but not immediately. He wrote in the following excerpts what was actually happening on the seas and in the air. At the onset of the Allied attack he underscored the continuing imbalance in the production flow of war matériel by writing, "We had more crews in our squadron than planes."[58] Thus, he was not part of the first wave of attacks.

While waiting to be called upon, Middlebrook listened to the reports from other pilots of the fighting on the first days of the battle. When his time came, he was ordered to fly as co-pilot in a B-25, as part of an attack group made up of B-17s and a new model, the A-20 aircraft. Freed from the responsibility of flying the plane, he had the opportunity to see "a war drama of great magnitude unfold."[59]

On the day of his attack mission,

> The weather was wet and foul, making it impossible for our planes to get a good view [of the convoy]...Those of us who tried in vain to stop the last convoy from reaching Lae in January, looked with dread and trepidation in having to attack the one which we engaged on March 3rd.[60]

Another new, faster, and more maneuverable type of attack airplane accompanied Middlebrook's group of slower flying B-25s. They served as defensive protection against the anticipated encounter with the swift and heavily armed Japanese Zero airplanes. Middlebrook wrote, "Twelve P-38s followed us closely..."[61] en route to the enemy. The P-38 is unusual for its distinguishing box shape. Propelling the machine some 25 percent faster than the Japanese Zero, its two engines trail boom-like shafts back to, and connecting with, horizontal stabilizers joined at the tail of the plane. Between the two engines sat the pilot in a distinctly egg-shaped cockpit.

The planes flew over the uncharted, cloud-shrouded mountains, completely on instruments alone for fifteen to twenty agonizing minutes—twenty minutes of not being certain if their plane was nose up or nose down, unable to see if they were flying straight or drifting at an angle through storm clouds and hidden mountains. The weather, he wrote, "[while] frightful and sometimes terrorizing, it was also fascinating."[62]

As happened frequently, many of the planes, especially these new P-38s, were unable to find a passage through the weather over the mountains; planes lost complete sight of Middlebrook's group. Lacking the skills needed for instrument flying, the pilots became confused about their routing and failed to re-join the mission after being separated. These were just the formation flying and navigational skills being practiced so assiduously by Colonel Strauss's men back in the States, for example. Inexplicably, an astonishing number of these P-38 Lightnings in various theatres, appear to have been lost in severe weather over the course of the war.

Approaching the enemy convoy from the east, now vulnerable without the P-38s, Middlebrook's air group came to within a mile of the Japanese ships and began to circle in formation. First a group of model B-17 aircraft banked into their bombing dive from an altitude of about 8,500 feet. They soon were being sprayed by machine gun fire from distant Japanese Zeros. At this point, Middlebrook could cock his head in every direction and crane to follow the action. He saw that "Zeros and P-38s were putting on a spectacular show almost directly over the B-17s [in a] dogfight...at an altitude of about 10,000 feet."[63]

It was a desperate experience. The cockpit of a Japanese Zero afforded its pilot a 360-degree view of the air space around him while the view of the P-38 pilot was obstructed by his wings being eye level with the cockpit and the shafts leading back to the tail frame. The experienced Zero pilot could outmaneuver every airplane in the Pacific with its dramatic loops and sharp-turning radius.

Turning to the battle below Middlebrook saw

...the A-20s attack with the viciousness of hornets whose nests had been disturbed [from about one hundred feet off the surface]... we could certainly see [the para-frag bomb, like those Len had at Hunter] explosions into the side of the [Japanese] ship about four or five seconds after the A-20s roared across the deck [with machine guns blazing].[64]

[Our] B-25s dropped 500 pound skip bombs [like flat stones thrown across lake water] and they too, just as did those of the A-20s, exploded four or five seconds after the plane cleared the deck [using delayed-fuse bombs].[65]

I realized with incredible disbelief how terribly effective...machine guns could be. We had then moved closer so my view of the details became better. I watched one of the strafers open fire on one of the moving ships. Long before he dropped his bomb, debris from the ship flew all over the water. I wondered what all the pieces of debris were and squinted harder. My god they were human bodies![66]

According to historian Harry Gailey, "The final and most damaging attack came from the B-25s with their forward firing .50-caliber machine guns striking at individual targets."[67] Indeed, the Americans' guns could reach the enemy ship before the shorter range return fire from the Japanese could reach the Americans'. Middlebrook wrote, "…[our] fire power blew many of the troops completely off the ship while making carnage of the others."[68]

THE COMEDOWN

When Middlebrook and crew came back to base from their role in the bombing and strafing attack, other men were already home celebrating their own safe return. For the most part, as Middlebrook observed, many of the men were matter-of-fact about the killing, but added: "*God,* we had to be tolerant and understanding of each other over there. Each guy got up for the kill in his own way and came down from the kill in his own way."[69]

Middlebrook moved away from the group to better contemplate how he felt about all this. But then, "Being quite aware that it was bad policy to be conspicuous by non-conformity in the Army, I got up and rejoined the party, feigning an enthusiasm I did not really feel."[70]

It took Garrett Middlebrook some fifty years before he could bring himself to write his memoirs. He tells quite explicitly what he did, whom he shot, how their bodies ripped apart; acknowledging blood and death by his own hand. He writes of his ethical puzzles, his internal conflicts, his struggles with patriotism and with human nature as a B-25 pilot. There are official histories of the war in the Southwest Pacific and then there are a few real life and death accounts of fighting and killing each other there. Because it was so unbearable, it became part of the serviceman's DNA to suffer silently and not to talk about what he really did or what he really saw in battle. It would be impossible for others to understand.

CHAPTER 10

Patton's Shadow

DERIDDER, LOUISIANA

Later in February of 1943 the 312th Bomb Group was transferred to a base nine hundred miles west of Hunter Field named DeRidder Army Air Base, not far from the Gulf of Mexico coast and some fifty miles north of Lake Charles. The full complement of the 312th was made up of 142 officers and 1,060 enlisted men. Enlisted men made their way west by train while the pilots flew ahead in yet another model of dive-bomber, the A-24, nicknamed the *Banshee*. It was more than eight times the size and weight of the Piper Cub in which Len learned to fly. This was a two-man dive-bomber, with pilot and gunner sitting back to back, just like those recently delivered to General Kenney in Australia.

Even though it was designated as a dive-bomber, it was for that additional purpose, air support or close air support, that the A-24 was used. The plane was thirty-three feet long with a forty-one-and-a-half-foot-long wingspan and could travel at upwards of 250 miles per hour with its single 1,200 horsepower engine. The A-24 had a flying range of 1,100 miles before it needed to be refueled. Empty it weighed 6,400 pounds, but it was capable of taking off with cargo and fuel weighing over 10,000 pounds. Fully armed, the plane featured two heavy machine guns in its nose and a slightly more flexible and lighter weight machine gun mounted in the rear cockpit. Furthermore, it could be fitted to carry 1,200-pound bombs under each wing and one under its belly.

Len and his comrades were becoming increasingly involved in war games activities. For the first time they practiced close air support of an armored tank division. The men trained in various aspects of mission operations: intelligence gathering and use, communications, and operations to hide American ground activities by smoke-laying diversions. Anxious whispers among the men centered around speculation that their eventual deployment would be to North Africa. And with the Germany first policy the odds favored deployment there. The men had been through five different training schools; DeRidder became their sixth, and the specter of war was becoming increasingly real. After twelve weeks in Louisiana, the next stage of their preparation took them fifteen hundred miles farther west.

THE MOHAVE DESERT

In those sweltering summer months temperatures reached 120 degrees. It was no country club vacation. They were baking in a kiln called Rice Army Airfield for desert training and war games. They spent twelve weeks sleeping on sweat-soaked cots in stale canvas tents getting acclimated to sweltering heat while working through their combat readiness exercises. Even their food and water were the packaged frontline battle rations, powdered and dehydrated foodstuffs as given to the troops on the parched sands of Morocco, Algeria, Tunisia, and Libya.

Rice Army Airfield was hidden away in the Mohave Desert well east of Los Angeles on the Arizona border, some fifty miles northwest of Blythe, California. The base was once commanded by the then Brigadier General Patton where he prepared forces in modern tank versus tank warfare methods. He and his 2nd Armored Division led the Western Task Force that took Casablanca, to begin the expulsion of the Nazis from colonial French North Africa back in November of 1942. After months of training at multiple bases, whatever doubt the men of the 312th had as to their ultimate deployment must have been put to rest by this move to Rice.

The sun radiated such heat that the men sometimes found metal vehicles, tools and even the airplanes themselves were too hot to touch. While

incubating in the cockpits of their model number A-24 aircraft the men had
to remember the proper sequence of manual, in-cabin levers to pull, buttons
to push, and pedals to depress in order to make the machine work properly.
As a navigation training mission, Len was ordered to transport replacement
parts from Rice to the Advanced Single-Engine Pilot School at Luke Field,
Phoenix, Arizona. Without GPS or radar, the navigation of flight paths,
directional angles, altitude, time, and distance were to be figured out manu-
ally by the twenty-four-year-old pilot. Len smoothly mastered the course in
just under forty-five minutes in clear skies, heading out west, then banking
east-southeast in choppy air over the dry mountain wilderness to Phoenix.
But as he lowered the nose down for his final landing approach he could
not see that men in the control tower were frantically shouting, waving
their hands, and jumping up and down. The radio operator yelled into his
mouthpiece, trying to warn the novice pilot. He then shoved it away from
his face in frustration as he watched Len, at over one hundred miles per
hour, pancake onto the runway. Bursts of dirt and smoke flew into the air,
enveloping the A-24 in swirling gray clouds of grit. The plane bounced up
above the loosely woven veil of debris, then hit the ground with another
jolt and skidded out of control, sparks spinning all around. Len's head jerked
one way, his shoulders another. For several eternally drawn out seconds Len
arched his back and jammed on the brakes. With his right hand he reached
for the rudder flap and strained to keep the plane skidding straight. As the
ship lost energy it came to a breathless stop wedged between two parked and
perfectly unscathed planes. With that, Len inhaled deeply, released the air
from his chest, unlocked the muscles in his hands, and let go of the wheel
as his shoulders tumbled forward. Reaching for the crown of his head, he
felt it to be in one piece and leaking only perspiration. He was both relieved
and dejected, nervously happy to be in one piece but wondering about the
damage sustained to his government-issue plane. Loathingly aware of what
happened and scowling at himself, he also started preparing himself for the
browbeating to come from his commander.

Once the mess was cleaned up, Len was obligated to collect his thoughts
and write a formal report of the incident.

At approximately 15:30, PWT, I was on my approach leg, wheels up and locked. The propeller hit the runway before I was reminded that I had forgotten to lower the wheels...Damage to the airplane consists of center section, propeller, and probably engine damage.[71]

According to the incident report filed by Len's commanding officer, Captain Selmon Wells,

On July 31, 1943 Leonard W. Happ, 2nd Lt., Air Corps, was scheduled to fly to Luke Field, Phoenix, Arizona. He departed Rice Army Air Field at approximately 14:45 and proceeded to his destination. Upon arriving at Luke Field at 15:30, he proceeded to land with his wheels up and locked. He did not have radio contact [with the control tower]. There was no mechanical failure.[72]

After many long months of air combat training, in multiple classrooms, learning the specifications and then the flight testing of so many different types of aircraft, Len had so much on his mind, such as speed (throttles), angle of descent (flaps), "attitude" of the nose (instrument panel dial), and so forth, that on this occasion he simply forgot to put down his retractable landing gear (by cranking a heavy lever to the right of his cockpit seat). And in this particular mission, he had no radio in his cockpit because it had been removed in order to fit more boxes of replacement parts for the good men of Luke Field. Therefore, the control tower personnel monitoring his approach, one after another screaming at him to lower his landing gear, could not reach him to alert him to the oversight. Imagine a wartime pilot operating a 5,500-pound airplane some 10,000 feet up in the clouds. World War II-era movie directors loved creating dramatic, desperate scenes of harried pilots facing the flashing lights of the cockpit instrument panels with engines choking and sputtering outside. With all those dials spinning and lights flashing, the instruments were inevitably telling pilots that something was going dangerously wrong—that somewhere in that blur of blinkers and needles adjustments needed to be made to stay aloft—*now!*

The pilot way up in the air had left and right horizontal wing flaps (ailerons) for steering and to maintain the plane's altitude, and a vertical tail flap (rudder) to keep the plane flying straight. Then, all of those gears and levers had to respond, not to curves or bumps in the road, but to unpredictably shifting gusts, or worse yet, blinding and disorienting clouds. And make no mistake, the whole point of their flying was to then grab another set of controls, hurtling forward at the breathtaking speed of 250 miles per hour, open bomb doors under the belly of the plane, keep flying straight, and then grab another set of controls to release the bombs onto the target.

Throughout that summer of 1943, these attack pilots of Colonel Robert Strauss's four bomb squadrons, were juggling all that and more. Upon approaching their destination, the pilot separated from the formation and, in carefully timed succession, dove down at the right time, dropping a bomb on a small dot of a target thousands of feet below. Desert objectives included piles of rocks with white circles painted on them or abandoned old cars. Using only hand-eye coordination, pilots turned their attention from flying and looked down into a scope focused on the ground and calculated the optimal moment to initiate destruction of their prey. Once the payload was dropped, with the ground racing up toward them, the pilot had to immediately pull out of the dive, defying gravity's pull, to accelerate skyward.

Since a large part of their mission was to give ground support to army troops, pilots observed and sometimes even trained in the tactical use of tanks to better understand their movements, speeds, and vulnerabilities. To give their rear-facing gunners practice for aerial combat, a twin-engine B-34 mid-range bomber would tow a target into the air and the pilot would have to chase it down. When in position, the gunner took control of his weapon, aimed and repeatedly fired at the bobbing target.

It was a challenge remembering the intricate functioning of various prototype planes. The airmen expressed concern, for example, that an earlier model known as the A-31 had weak landing gear. According to aircraft engineer and air force historian Lawrence J. Hickey another early model, the A-35

[had] an ineffective aiming system [that] could cause bombs to miss their targets by as much as 100 yards. Moreover, the plane's poorly designed landing gear could result in washouts if the gear collapsed on landing.[73]

On one particularly hot day that summer, Colonel Strauss led a group of pilots in war games flying again in the recently developed A-24 model air planes. They practiced in full gear, attacking mocked up "railroads" and important "enemy" supply areas, destroying their targets with fifty-pound sacks of flour standing in for real bombs. Other pilots that day, including Len Happ and his mates Ed Hambleton and Ewing McKinney, were sent to pick up new, state-of-the-art P-40 aircraft from the School of Applied Tactics in Orlando, Florida and fly them back to Rice in California. Len wrote, "I was one of 25 lucky pilots, drawn by lot, to go to Orlando, Florida, to check out in the P-40s and bring one back to the desert in California where we were training."[74]

In his navigation case, Len kept a document entitled, *Flying Characteristics of the P-40 Type Airplane*. The first lines of the description referred to it as "a fast, easily controlled, modern, airplane. It is aerodynamically clean and will perform on equal terms with any airplane in the world below 15,000 feet. It is the first all-steel aircraft."[75] It was the latest generation of military aircraft. The P-40 was a single-seat (one man) "pursuit and ground attack" plane which flew comfortably at a blazing 360 miles per hour; to be used primarily to escort and defend heavier, slower-flying planes against enemy threat.

It was to be used both as a dive-bomber and to "escort" slower and more vulnerable bombers. In a combat mission, flying a given route from base to the enemy position, the P-40s were to fly with and defend, heavier, slower-flying Allied bombers against counter-attack from faster enemy aircraft.

Air Corps officials were learning that the A-24, with its speed reaching just 250 miles per hour, was not performing well tactically against enemy planes in battle. For all of its shortcomings, the A-24 could maintain a steep dive angle, making it much more difficult for enemy ground fire to knock out of the air. The P-40 was only capable of shallow dive angles when dive-bombing. Therefore, new attack strategies were devised to take advantage of its superior speed while adjusting for its shallower attack angle. The shallower attack dive, at a forty-five-degree angle to the ground, came to be called "glide bombing" …which meant that there was that much more to remember and practice.

Once comparisons were made, Air Corps officials finalized a decision to discontinue use of the two-man A-24 in favor of the one-man P-40—nicknamed the *Warhawk*. Moving from the two-man A-24 to the single seat P-40 also meant that fifty-six of the group's gunners were no longer needed. They were reassigned out to other bomb groups.

The file copy of his six- page *Pilot's Proficiency Examination* on the P-40 airplane instructs, "Mix control back into idle cut-off and then to auto-rich; check instruments for desired temps and pressures; transmitter frequency; prop safety switch; prop selector switch; flaps; cooling shutters; normal cruising fuel consumption…" Throughout his training, again and again, Len flew new machines, with new technical specifications, in new ways. He loved learning and mastering the advanced planes, but it was a lot of new information to absorb.

Days into training with the P-40, in those oppressive desert conditions, Len was cited for dangerously "irregular activity" when the plane he was landing at Rice Field popped a tire and went into "a violent left ground spin." According to Len's *Statement of Aircraft Accident,*

> Upon contact with the runway, air-speed between 90 and 100 mph,
> I became aware of left flat tire. The ship started in an arc'ed-path to
> the left, increasing to a left ground loop. At about 90 degrees around,
> the left gear buckled. The prop and left wing hit the ground, as the
> ship settled to a stop approximately 160 degrees to left of landing
> heading.[76]

The base operations officer concurred: "Apparently the left tire blew out either on landing or takeoff…"[77]

There were the usual pilot errors in training exercises and other learning curve irregularities found with all aircraft. But after close monitoring, it was soon discovered that the tires on the P-40 wore prematurely in desert heat. As Air Corps veteran Russell L. Sturzebecker would later write, "One of the major problems in maintaining the P-40 was the critical situation regarding tires. Generally a set of tires on the landing wheels exhibited severe wear after less than a half dozen landings."[78]

Thinner layers of rubber on the tread of this new model were determined to be the cause of the premature wear. Among the many shortages created in wartime America was that of rubber. Worldwide the largest suppliers of rubber to America included the British colony of Malaya and the Dutch East Indies, both of which had already fallen (early 1942) to the Empire of Japan. A third supplier, the Belgian colony of Congo, was then under the control of Nazi Germany. Those hostile powers ceased selling rubber to American tire makers. As a result, factories were increasingly, and it seems perilously, making due with less rubber.

As the war progressed, local Civil Defense committees across the country rallied to fill the need for basic raw materials such as rubber. They initiated massive schemes for recycling and collection such as, "SALVAGE DRIVE FOR OUR COUNTRY"[79] and, "CLEAN OUT ATTICS AND BASEMENTS IN SALVAGE DRIVE."[80] The increased production of war materials combined with the loss of foreign suppliers meant the home front needed to recycle raw materials to keep production going.

> We urge YOU to check your home THOROUGHLY and save every bit of scrap you can. Here are some of the materials which our country NEEDS and NEEDS QUICKLY... Lead – Aluminum – Brass – Bronze – Copper – Zinc – Iron – Rubber – rags – Old Clothing – Tin – Newspaper – etc.[81]

In urging everyone to join the "Salvage for Victory" campaign, Illinois Governor Dwight Green, for example, reminded his constituents that "salvage is our only hope to keep production of consumer goods at even a minimum level."[82] Such rallying cries were widely heard and heeded across the country.

Salvage drive brochure 1942.

For as bad as Len's accidents looked, they were common. Throughout training, at high speeds in new planes, there were accidents, sometimes fatal accidents. Colonel Strauss's 312th Bomb Group alone suffered six crashes across the months of these various training exercises, killing seven officers and one enlisted man, while practicing in six different fighter airplane types. Reconciling himself to the losses while referring to yet another, the *Vengeance* type of aircraft, 312th pilot Tommy Overton wrote, "[it] was a real challenge to the young, inexperienced pilots and crewmen to master the peculiarities of the aircraft, for both the flying and the maintenance demanded a great deal of determination for the men of the 312th."[83]

(G397B-788P-AABHF)(1-10-4 3-4P)V72 AF851

Landing gear periodically buckled and collapsed in those early airplanes. Here, a Vultee-72 crashed during training. Len Happ scrap book photos.

Pilots accepted that, even under the best of conditions, theirs was a particularly hazardous profession and that death was a possibility any time they flew. As a result, each one developed his own internal coping mechanism. These young fliers used terms like "hardening" their minds to accidents and not fearing or worrying about death. In Len's *Statement of Aircraft Accident* report above, he outright stated a pre-flight concern that he knew "the brakes [on that P-40] were weak prior to take off." Yet he confidently took to the skies anyway.

LEAVE

It had been a long period of intense training. On May 18 Colonel Strauss granted Len a five-day leave in San Francisco effective the following day. During this time Len was able to get word to Julia and congratulate her on her graduation from Mundelein. He had been away for the second half of her junior year and all of her senior school year. Missing her graduation was just one of the many prices they both paid being in a wartime relationship. He was proud of her active college career and accomplishments. From the fall of 1939 as a freshman playing basketball to her graduation that spring of 1943 as class president, Julia was cited and photographed upwards of sixty-three times in her school newspaper, *Skyscraper*. Their lives before and during Len's training remained closely bound. His friends were dating Julia's friends, her sisters knew Len's friends, and tying this whole clique together was their Catholic upbringing and education. The highlight of the graduation ceremony was Julia's nomination to the Kappa Gamma Pi National Honor Society of Women's Colleges.[84] She was a popular and dynamic group organizer and throughout the war Julia continued fundraising for the Illinois (College) War Council for the purchase of war bonds.

SALINAS

Ready or not, on Friday, August 13 of 1943, sequestered and maybe ignorant of current events in the war, the 312th training program moved again. From the oppressive heat of the Mojave Desert they were sent to Salinas Army Air Base, Salinas, California, where they were bathed in the cool breezes coming off Monterey Bay. At this point the men knew their training was basically over and were anxiously asking about their deployment. While waiting for further instructions the group was put through various calisthenics and runs. For nine weeks the men put the uncertainty out of their minds as they grunted through basic survival and soldiering skills, like throwing hand grenades, crawling on the ground under gun fire, and climbing cargo net ladders. After that they just waited, fighting boredom and stress, speculating continuously about French North Africa, unaware that General Patton had begun his campaign through Italy.

A year ago at Brooks, knowing the realities of flying new airplanes, a sobering truth was brought to the men's attention when they were obligated to sign a Last Will and Testament. Here at Salinas, as the men prepared to embark for combat, they were given another heavy reminder that not everyone would come home from war. Based mainly on statistics from the European Theatre, US Air Corps crews were experiencing upwards of a 25 percent loss rate[85] in combat actions. Such cold statistics were needed to determine the production flow quantities of pilots and planes needed to maintain troop strength. The men were brusquely instructed to sign over a power of attorney to their designated loved one. Should something happen, should one become disabled, wounded, or otherwise incapacitated, who would settle their final affairs? Who would decide for them? Standing in line, waiting to sign, Catholics could imagine ornately dressed priests and mystical funeral services. One might almost hear the clanging sound of the chains as they struck the censer out of which choking incense billowed. Pilots breathed heavily as their thoughts turned back to close calls they had in their training planes. Len, for example, might shiver as he remembered the cracking shock of his propeller hitting the runway in Phoenix when he failed to lower the landing gear of his A-24. His face might redden with apprehension remembering the uncontrollable, violent spin landing in the brand-new P-40 at Rice. The men could not have known these were child's thoughts compared to the violence that awaited them overseas.

Perhaps reflecting in solitude on his mortality, Len pensively designated power of attorney to his father, Honorius. Once signed, the solemn and dreadful document, foreshadowing the unknown and unknowable, was notarized with appropriate dignity by the firm G. L. McCarthy in nearby Monterey, settling never-before-contemplated horrors. Should something happen, Honorius would decide for him.

Len's Power of Attorney to settle is affairs in the event of his demise.

And plenty of things had happened already, hadn't they? Sad examples would revolve again in most men's minds—friends killed in training, squadmates, comrades crashing, floundering, dying. Even just recently there were accidents, including a horrific midair collision involving two P-40s over the blue ocean southwest of Salinas. Both pilots managed to bail out, but one died of hypothermia in the icy waters of the Pacific. A week later, a P-40 crashed at Stockton, California, killing that pilot. The 388th Bomb Squadron alone suffered six deadly crashes over the course of these various training exercises, killing seven officers and one enlisted man, all practicing in different types of fighter airplanes, fighting with bags of flour, unopposed by enemy fire. Even Len, in his bookkeeper's mind, could calculate from experience something like 20 percent of airmen lost; oddly comparable to both the percentage Middlebrook's group lost in their initial flight over the Atlantic to Australia and to the War Department's loss rate. Certainly any crash made the pilots more apprehensive and cautious. But after an accident they simply wanted to move on and get back to their normal existence and needs, which were most often eating and sleeping. It was not until after the war that the sobering facts were summarized. In that current year alone, 1943, the Air Corps experienced over 1,775 fatal accidents in training exercises, causing an astonishing 4,200 lives to be lost and 3,850 aircraft destroyed.[86]

CHAPTER II

Turning Point

The Japanese dominated various ports throughout the north coast of New Guinea. While the Kokoda Trail battle had been declared over only on March 25, there were still many pockets of Japanese devilishly spread throughout the country. The enemy was roaming menacingly between Milne Bay on the island's eastern tip and Lae to the northwest.

As March wore on Navy admirals complained to Washington about the defensive stalemate and "inactivity" since the robust battle on Guadalcanal. MacArthur, of a similar, unsettled mood, was again told by Washington to make do with what he had. For their part, Japan was trying to keep some base in the Solomon Islands. Guadalcanal was a costly loss for them, but other islands held promise as outposts to help defend Rabaul and their southern perimeter.

MacArthur was most uneasy about Rabaul, which loomed above him literally and figuratively. On April 13 Japan again sent a bombing mission to harass and test the defenses of Port Moresby. They most frequently sent three planes at a time, sometimes as many as six. Middlebrook wrote that well into that spring of 1943, and in fact, "for the first year of his duty in New Guinea, the enemy bombed the Port Moresby area at least three nights out of four."[87]

From Japan, troops and supplies kept pouring into New Guinea as they adjusted their positions. They linked roads and supply lines along the north coast to the growing port town of Wewak. On July 2, the Australians reported enemy forces were growing in numbers northwest of Lae at place called Nassau Bay near the Huon Peninsula. MacArthur again implored Washington for more help. Washington continued to stress that they could not send supplies or reinforcements that would compromise the campaign against Hitler in Europe. But indeed, seeing growth in industrial production at home, the Joint Chiefs of Staff felt confident enough to at least plan an eventual Allied counter-offensive in the Southwest Pacific.

President Roosevelt met in August of 1943 with British Prime Minister Churchill and other Allied heads of state at a conference in Quebec City known as Quadrant. In Quebec the Allies once again sorted out priorities for the defeat of Nazi Germany and how it would be ultimately carried out. The Joint Chiefs also agreed that with more trained men ready and more materials soon to be delivered, the Allies needed to push the war faster. They noted that any more stalemating or battles of attrition (as at Guadalcanal or the Kokoda Trail) and they would lose the support of the American people for the war; they sensed the public was anxious for the war to be ended, on both fronts, as quickly as possible with minimal loss of American lives.

The Joint Chiefs of Staff confirmed Pacific area responsibilities, giving naval commands to Admiral Chester Nimitz[88] based at Pearl Harbor, and army commands along with a detachment of vessels, such as troop carriers for maritime landings, to General MacArthur in Australia. Since Pearl Harbor, Nimitz had been successful enough in securing American lines of supply from San Francisco, that just a few weeks back on July 20, MacArthur felt secure enough to move his headquarters one thousand miles closer to the war front, north from Melbourne to Brisbane.

Their first objective under this new command structure, was control of New Guinea, including the seizure of the islands encircling Rabaul. To do this, action was proposed in three phases: first, Nimitz was to take strategic points in the Solomon Islands, on the northern edge of the Coral Sea; second, MacArthur was to take control of the southernmost Solomon Islands; and lastly, MacArthur was then to take Rabaul and adjacent positions around the north coast of New Guinea. To that end, within a week, Allied air raids were again initiated on Rabaul.

Following here is a New Guinea Area map 1942–1944.[89] From the extreme southeast corner of New Guinea to its extreme northwest corner is a distance of some fifteen hundred miles—equivalent to driving from New York City to just beyond Fargo, North Dakota. Rabaul is found on the northern tip of New Britain Island. Guadalcanal is found in the extreme lower right, at the eastern edge of the Coral Sea.

THE HUON PENINSULA

From mainland New Guinea, the closest point to New Britain Island, on which Rabaul is located, is the Huon Peninsula. The waterway separating the peninsula and New Britain Island is called the Vitiaz Strait. This strait connects the Bismarck Sea to the Coral Sea and was therefore vital to Japan in supplying her forces in eastern New Guinea. Japan's main outposts for defending the Vitiaz Strait surrounded the Huon Peninsula. Those outposts included the garrisons of Lae, Finschhaven, and Saidor. In order for the Allies to control the straits and eventually neutralize Rabaul, these positions first needed to be taken out.

Middlebrook was impacted directly by the Quadrant initiatives to accelerate the war effort, and there was a new intensity to his duty. He started flying almost daily missions at this point, over great distances into hostile territory. On August 14, he was part of an attack on a town called Salamaua. He bombed and strafed in close air support where Allied ground forces were battling Japanese. In addition to his normal responsibilities, he was also ordered by an Aussie (Allied) commander to stay low and hit collateral targets "of opportunity" after his mission was complete. He was explicitly told that the Chinese workers brought in by Japan to build roads and haul goods were "collaborators" and should be treated as enemy combatants. Middlebrook was obviously conflicted by this, to the point of contemplating insubordination. He was deeply troubled by this commander for ordering the targeting of innocent Chinese workers. He recognized that the Aussies

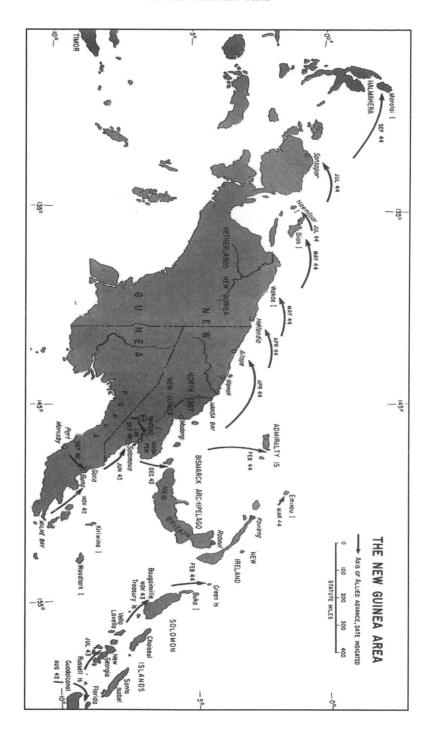

feared for their lives and the survival of their country. But Middlebrook had a more tempered and ethically based point of view. Chinese workers had been conscripted to do work in overseas colonies by the Europeans for generations. To Middlebrook they were not pro-Japanese; they were forced labor. It was a disturbing order for him and he struggled with it even while in the cockpit.

On August 17 Middlebrook was assigned to bomb Wewak, approximately five hundred miles from Port Moresby. His B-25 was built to fly that distance and back, but not against the buffeting winds and the cockpit-rattling storms that sap fuel over the Owen Stanley Mountains. The assignment was among his most hazardous, dramatizing key points upon which all aircraft manufacturers were focused: cruising speed ("normal" flying speed) and range (flight distance on one tank of gas). To accomplish his mission, first of all, Middlebrook had to fly over the unpredictable and stormy mountains at a dizzying sixteen thousand feet; and secondly, he had to be prepared to be chased during the mission, at maximum speed, by much faster enemy Zeros, both of which demand extra fuel. To that end, Middlebrook's ground crew jerry-rigged supplemental fuel tanks into the rear of the B-25 at a place that temporarily blocked one of the plane's turret guns. As fuel was spent those supplemental tanks would refill the original tanks in his wings by way of an electric pump. But once drained, or in any event before they arrived at their targets, the improvised tanks were to be jettisoned in order to regain access to the vital turret gun.

When the several squadrons of planes took off for this mission, the weather was so bad that the fighter escorts (again P-38s) and almost all other planes, aborted the plan and returned to base—except for Middlebrook. When he arrived at the target and was lining up his approach, he wrote that he was,

> conscious of my responsibility to my crew and asked myself what right I had to destroy their lives by carrying out a mission everyone else had abandoned.[90]

Timid pilots did not live long in our deadly game of air combat at 20 feet [off the ground]. We were not afforded the luxury of a second chance because our first mistake was also our last venture.[91]

We were eighteen miles, three minutes and twenty seconds from that awful moment when bombs and bullets would be launched from our planes causing death, agony, torture and destruction to the Japanese, while streams of death-seeking firepower would come toward us from the Japs on the ground.... Any person who pretended (and some did) that he did not feel cold, penetrating fear at such a time was either abnormal or he was an outrageous liar.[92]

It was recorded separately that this air attack mission on Wewak hit and destroyed one hundred airplanes that were on taxiways or parked in their staging areas. And that extra fuel got the B-25s out and back, through the expected hazards. But, after the mission, in fact now after fifty-five combat missions, Middlebrook wrote, "I felt depression and I worried over the new emotion." He questioned his "emotional stamina"; he noted that he was getting tired and his buddies were feeling it too. Middlebrook was twenty-four years old at this time and had been in combat for thirteen months. Over those fifty-five missions he had seen many friends, mentors, and enemies killed—all innocent in his eyes. The patriotism, pride, loyalty, and enthusiasm with which he entered the war were gone from his voice. By this time he was fighting the Japanese just to do his job, to stay alive, and to keep the others in his plane alive.

The following day, on August 18, Middlebrook was again ordered back out on the twelve-hundred-mile-round-trip mission, using supplemental gas cans, to bomb Wewak. The pilot made this experience sound like attacking a hornet's nest with a stick. The Japanese put up a furious defense by both land-based gunners and by the famed Japanese Zero aircraft, diving and attacking the slower but low-flying B-25s.

In that strike the Allies destroyed another twenty-eight Japanese planes.[93] But the mission also resulted in the unfortunate shooting down and ditching at sea of Middlebrook's beloved, longtime commanding officer,

Major Ralph Cheli) and his crewmates. Confused with fear and fatigue, the crew survived their crash only to be picked up, out of the sea, by the Japanese and taken to Rabaul as prisoners of war. The loss and anxious uncertainty over the fate of these men tormented Middlebrook for years. Some time after the war, he undertook to uncover just what happened to these men. He found the Japanese themselves recorded that these particular prisoners were killed, pathetically, "by our own [Allied] planes during the devastating attacks we rained down upon Rabaul in November and December 1943."[94] Middlebrook wrote that on each August eighteenth for the next forty-five years, he and his former crewmates stopped, paused for a moment of silence, to remember those young men, their devotion to duty, their unselfishness, and their patriotism.

On all of these missions, planes were to fly, sometimes one group of three planes after another, in sequence (in waves) during a bombing run on a target. On August 29 Middlebrook attacked another Japanese coastal enclave called Alexishaven, a staging area and town north of the Huon peninsula, north of Saidor. He dropped delayed fuse bombs, which exploded approximately three seconds after detonation. Middlebrook lamented that one of the newly arrived replacement pilots blew the timing (like Len and his mates had practiced at Savannah) and attacked too closely behind his squadron leader. "His aircraft was torn apart by the concussion of one of our 500 pound bombs."[95] It was yet another heartrending scene that embedded itself in Middlebrook's memory. But he had to repress these memories lest fear creep in that would cloud his judgement or cause him to be incapable of acting decisively.

The grind wore on. Another convoy of cargo ships was discovered en route from the Japanese-held Philippines bound for Wewak on September 2. Middlebrook was ordered to bomb it when it arrived before the Japanese made much progress unloading and distributing the contents. That marked his fourth twelve-hundred-mile-round-trip mission to Wewak in two weeks.

GUSAP, NADZAB, LAE

Japanese forces, dispersed along the northern New Guinea coast since early 1942, were now regrouped in concentrated strategic centers like Rabaul, Finschhaven, Madang, and Wewak. Supplies for these troops and new war machinery were still flowing in, despite the destructive interruption from the Bismarck Sea battle and the Allies' various harassing air attacks. Ground forces pursued withdrawing Japanese troops, giving the illusion of progress by Allied forces in battle. But in fact, Japan was simply redistributing her forces, contracting, according to the *West Point Atlas of War*, its "defensive perimeter to gain time for rebuilding."[96] They were succeeding in their plan to bog down the Americans in order to consolidate their territorial gains.

Since the early days, MacArthur sought to draw his defensive line for the protection of Australia at the Owen Stanley Mountains. The Japanese redeployment gave Generals MacArthur and Kenney the opportunity to establish air bases on the north side of that natural barrier for the first time in the war—and with which they could show the War Department they had the necessary installations to take on more squadrons. Allied ground troops first identified an unoccupied and somewhat open area in the Ramu River valley called Gusap, where they cleared away tall, thick grasses to establish a runway and space for housing and command centers. Located sixty miles southwest of Lae, the new base was a strategically positioned point from where General Kenney's fighter planes could better reach Wewak without continually facing the deadly flight up and over the mountains.

With the Middlebrook bombing raids of mid-August and early September, Wewak was temporarily crippled. This allowed General Kenney some freedom to add a second air base called Nadzab, in the Markham River valley even closer to Lae. Both new "forward" bases were linked operationally to Port Moresby (itself still under periodic bombardment from the Japanese). Unlike the spring of '42 Kokoda Trail plan to air-drop men and supplies into the battle, which was scrapped for lack of planes, by September 5 of 1943 the Allies finally had the aircraft and the confidence to air-drop regiments by parachute into Nadzab, with reduced fears of being harassed from the air or counter-attacked on the ground. Again, in this area the jungle was so densely tangled it was impossible for any large unit to drive in or march in. Resupplying the base by ground routes would be virtually impossible; it could only be done in any practical way by air.

On a day of notoriously bad flying weather, Middlebrook was one of "a 302-plane operation which supported and defended the drop of 1,700 paratroopers...into the Nadzab opening of the Markham Valley twenty miles northwest of Lae."[97] First, Middlebrook in his B-25 was to strafe and "clear" any Japanese in the area where the thick jungle hid possible enemy troop positions. So thick in fact, the Japanese could not see and were largely caught off guard by the aggressive thrust forward. Then, ten minutes after Middlebrook finished his run, in a "spectacular display," as an official military account described it, C-47s filled with hundreds of American paratroopers emptied into Nadzab within five minutes.[98] After the drop, Middlebrook was to circle the paratroopers for one hour and destroy any enemy troops which might surprise them at the most vulnerable time of their drop—when the men were recovering themselves on the ground and gathering in their chutes. Almost undetected, a group of Japanese had scurried up a gnarled vine- and bush-infested mountainside to hide themselves on a ledge. From there they were reporting by radio back to their command center on the paratroopers' landing. During the course of his patrol, Middlebrook discovered and methodically "took out" that scouting party of eight Japanese soldiers.

FINSCHHAVEN AND CONTROL OF THE VITIAZ STRAIT

Again, the Japanese withdrew their troops, this time from Lae, to redeploy them at Finschhaven, a well-stocked garrison on the tip of the Huon Peninsula. By around September 16 Lae was considered to be completely in the hands of the Allies.

To confront Allied ships entering this sea lane, about 3,000 Japanese troops from fortified jungle ridges guarded over the sixty-mile-wide gap that separated New Guinea from New Britain Island. This high ground overlooks the entire coastline and out across the straits. And this strategic strait, the Vitiaz Strait, flowing east to west along the north coast of New Guinea, was MacArthur's gateway to the Bismarck Sea, and blocking it was essential to isolating Rabaul. From an offensive perspective it was the most expedient passageway to supply, from Australia or Port Moresby, the Allied troops progressing further west.

Australian troops arrived near Finschhaven on September 22. Fighting again bogged down into a series of gruesome back-and-forth thrusts. By the end of September, reinforcements numbering another four hundred Japanese soldiers joined the battle. Two weeks later the enemy launched a combined ground and amphibious counter-attack. Australian infantrymen beat back the ground attack, but in the early morning darkness of October 17 another barge full of Japanese troops got ashore. Australians attacked the fortified ridgeline again and again, isolating and destroying pockets of Japanese resistance one at a time. Over the next six weeks of fighting the Japanese counter-attack was eventually broken. By late November the Japanese had sacrificed at least 5,500 men in this losing battle.

MADANG

When Port Moresby was the hub of Allied air power, such as it was, Wewak was developing the potential to become another Rabaul. As General Kenney's force grew, he had the capability to neutralize it. But in order to do that, MacArthur determined an intermediate objective, which was to knock the Japanese out of Madang, an important port town, known to have a deep water harbor, about halfway back south of Wewak in the direction of Gusap. The game of whack-a-mole had become a more complicated one of chess. After Finschhaven, the Australian Army undertook operations against Madang. But for MacArthur to effectively strike at Madang, he had to send an Allied amphibious force of troop carriers through the Vitiaz Strait. Thus, to protect such a movement of Allied troops, Southwest Pacific headquarters first ordered the seizure of yet another enemy air and naval base on New Britain called Arawe, some eighty-five miles on the other side of the straits from Finschhaven.

MIDDLEBROOK ROTATED HOME

The expansive Japanese air base at Wewak awed General Kenney and his 5th Air Force. They were unsettled by the fact that their side was highly outnumbered in men and matériel. The Japanese had been receiving new warplanes and crew seemingly daily. It was estimated that a formidable one hundred thousand Japanese troops and three hundred new combat planes were stationed at Wewak. At about this time Middlebrook heard word there were soon to be new pilots and two more squadrons joining his bomb squadron. He picked up a hint that the few pilots who started the war "in uniform" were being rotated out and that a new, fresh generation of pilots were coming in to take over.

The Air Corps and the War Department were concerned about maintaining combat readiness among men very likely suffering from combat fatigue and diminished effectiveness. Having been in action for more than a year, airmen were found to "wear out" sooner than enlisted men, but no one could explain why. There were official guidelines in place to protect pilots. Depending on the commanding officer, the criteria for being rotated off the front lines were generally having flown forty to sixty missions, combined with the pilot's number of months in combat. The range of missions depended on the type of plane and sorties flown. The policy to rotate pilots and crew off the front lines came to be known as the "Commanders' Choice" policy. The seemingly arbitrary word "choice" was of key importance because it made all combat rotations contingent on maintaining troop strength.

Just as General Kenney was about to receive more arms and planes, he was troubled by the fact that he was obligated to rotate some of his experienced air crewmen off the front lines. The Germany first policy had kept his force so tenuously small that the General protested, burnout or not, he could not follow crew rotation guidelines without crippling his squadrons.[99]

The historian Long confirmed that in the fall of 1943 some seventy-five full air groups were deployed to Europe; thirty-five groups were sent to the Pacific to build up General Kenney's force. It was a humble start to this next phase of the New Guinea war. A bomb group, such as the 312th, normally consisted of three or four squadrons of twelve to sixteen airplanes each, thus totaling upwards of some ninety-six aircraft of the same type and function. American arms production and trained personnel were now streaming steadily out of assembly lines into the various bases and camps in battle zones around the world. Sources show that in 1943 the growing US aviation industry produced an amazing 24,650 combat aircraft plus 22,225 of what were categorized as "support" aircraft—transport planes and diverse training aircraft. The numbers seem to hold true: 13 percent (due to Germany first) of 24,650 aircraft gives Kenney his 3,300 planes in 35 bomb groups. The remaining 2 percent would have been delivered as transport planes. As a result, when those units started to arrive in mid-October, General Kenney was in a position to send out 300 to 400 aircraft just to bomb Rabaul, compared to the pathetic Allied total of "some 260 aircraft, many of them unserviceable"[100] sent to Australia when he was made commander of the 5th Air Force.

Middlebrook received word that he would be "grounded" and that his combat service would end in November. It was the first sign "on the ground" that the long-awaited, new cohort of fully trained American servicemen would be entering battle. General Kenney was loath to send anyone home. But his subordinate commanders must have persuaded him otherwise. The pilots of Middlebrook's generation were being replaced by enough post-Pearl Harbor-trained men that troop strength was not diminished and battle objectives could be comfortably addressed.

Middlebrook flew three more missions: two against Finschhaven and one against Cape Gloucester (on New Britain). During that mission, already fighting fatigue and mental exhaustion, he coldly recorded witnessing another colleague shot out of the air: his fuel tanks took a direct hit, burst into flames and the plane crashed into the sea. It added to the continuing emotional pain Middlebrook was trying to bury.

Already in July of 1942 the Army Air Corps implemented its first policy to address pilot combat fatigue and it was called the "One Year Tour."[101] As its name suggested, the policy stated that air crewmen (including gunners, navigators and bombardiers) could be sent back to the States upon completion of one year of combat duty. But, their replacements had to arrive in theater one month before those scheduled to return could depart. In and of itself, that policy suggested that Middlebrook was eligible to return to the States in August—possibly. But, with a shortage of trained manpower and the Germany first policy, it was that much more difficult to get replacement crews in the Southwest Pacific Theatre. And a commander had to maintain the fighting strength of his unit first and foremost. If at this point in 1943 General Kenney had implemented the "one year" policy, he would have depleted his forces and certainly MacArthur's advance across the Owen Stanley Mountains would have been greatly jeopardized.

Middlebrook had flown his 65th combat mission. Ultimately grounded on October 10 and scheduled for rotation out, he was asked to remain at his base for another month to orient incoming pilots to some of the unusual characteristics of flying in sweltering New Guinea. This was another element of the policy, and a priority for the Air Corps: men with experience in combat overseas were critically needed to train new crews, and their expertise was also needed to develop better aircraft and equipment.

Completing that final requirement, Middlebrook departed New Guinea in mid-November as a passenger on a C-47 transport plane to Townsville, Australia. From there he found passage back to his next assignment training new pilots in navigation back in the States. Garrett Middlebrook's generation, the first wave of American fighters after Pearl Harbor, saved Australia; they stopped the initial burst of Japanese energy from streaming any further south. In spite of the fact that commanders in Washington and General MacArthur were at odds about the assets needed to get the job done, the men got the job done. MacArthur's line at the Owen Stanley Mountains was held. Port Moresby was protected; the supply lines from America to Australia were secured. While still under severe threat, the forbidding terrain and men like Middlebrook thus far shielded MacArthur from the cascading forces of the Imperial Japanese war machine.

CHAPTER 12

Into the Unknown

CAMP STONEMAN

Another four painful weeks elapsed before the 312th packed their gear once again. On October 24 they moved with trepidation to Camp Stoneman, in Pittsburg, California on San Francisco Bay. This was the end of the line; the end of their training and the end of their gap year. The many new air groups now coming through the training facilities and production factories created weeks of delays. The delays created more boredom, more anxiety about their individual readiness to fight, each still unaware of their role in the war strategy. Again they were put to march and hike and climb cargo netting...and wait.

Stoneman was one of two large west coast staging areas and embarkation ports. Strict security was enforced, reminiscent of the civil defense regulations at the Port of Savannah. So they sat in monitored secrecy. No cameras, no radios, no electric razors, no flashlights were allowed on this base. The men were instructed about censorship procedures and were reminded that all calls, telegrams, and letters could be edited. Enemy collaborators were watching. Dreadfully, excruciatingly slowly, the men sat, alone with their thoughts, as this final week passed. And, again, they were put to march and to climb cargo netting...and wait.

THEN QUIETLY GONE

Late on Halloween night, October 31, at a foggy, blacked out, and guarded dock, the 312th felt their way to their pier of embarkation. It was too late to plan an escape, or to revisit any bail-out option contemplated after joining up; and the death penalty was the understood consequence for desertion. Finally, it was their turn. Russell Sturzebecker was among the men there that cold night and he wrote that "each man [boarded while] trying to come to grips with whatever degree of uneasiness he felt about the future."[102] Officially past midnight, now November 1, it was All Souls Day. The feast day was once known as the Commemoration of the Faithful Departed. Secretly, silently they sailed from San Francisco on a ship leased from a Dutch concern called the SS *Nieuw Amsterdam*. They were buffeted by the incessant winds in the harbor. With heads tilted upwards, eyes gazed through fog at the blacked-out and foreboding majesty of the Golden Gate Bridge now separating the men from their homes and loved ones. They had no idea where they were headed. In the overnight darkness, the bridge faded in the distance with the men, uncomfortable in eerie new surroundings, shivering on deck.

After so many months of practicing and training, they were off to face the only test that ultimately mattered: combat. Colonel Strauss's 312th Bomb Group, which counted 155 officers and 1,019 enlisted men, now ominously included nine extra pilots to cover the anticipated first month's "combat attrition." The men may have been innocently and only generally aware of the coming danger, but military planners well knew what was ahead. The army calculated that a ghastly fraction of more than two pilots in each of the four bomb squadrons would be killed early in action, not "washed out" for not making the grade, but killed.

The anxieties of real army life were weighing upon the men. Their boat was a rich and overflowing target. Besides the four squadrons comprising the colonel's cargo, the ship was jammed with heavy artillery guns and various military vehicles. It was also crowded with a staggering total of 8,500 officers and enlisted men from various branches of the growing military, plus 600 Dutch maritime crewmen responsible for operating the vessel. Yet, it was supplied meagerly with field rations allowing for just two meals per day for each soldier during the transit. It was speculated about with certainty that if the Japanese could sneak up on Pearl Harbor, they could easily sneak up on this old freighter. Reinforcing that fear, the men were ordered to participate in emergency procedure drills, to be used should they be attacked at sea.

The men noted that as the ship traveled further south, the wind gusted harder and louder, pushing up waves and clanging down heavy rain. The ship rolled hard under their feet. Len was now the furthest he had ever been from his accounting job at Bermingham and Prosser and the bar of Chicago's Edgewater Beach Hotel—with no lifeline home. As their ship sailed in wide open seas, to who knew where, the final passage for Len from the civilian life he knew and loved to his new military life could not have been more obviously marked: he "celebrated" his twenty-fifth birthday on November 5 sweating it out with the other 8,500 guys squirming with the fear of being found out by a Japanese submarine. The next day, Saturday, November 6, the men on the *Nieuw Amsterdam* delighted at the crossing south over the equator. One of the more artistic men on board even created and distributed a certificate bearing the image of Neptune to memorialize the crossing. Here they were cooled by the Southeast Trade Winds, but November is the start of the rainy season when the downpour becomes 30 percent heavier than in October. What had been a nervous, uneventful voyage, was being christened with churning cross-currents of angry weather. On Thursday, November 11 they passed west over the International Date Line, another first. Most of the men never dreamed of seeing San Francisco, much less crossing equators and international date lines. As they sailed, now completely vulnerable and exposed, unescorted, rollicking out in the middle of the Pacific Ocean they crossed into a new time zone and into tomorrow—they were instructed to reset their watches: nineteen hours ahead of California time.

On November 14, the men marked two restless weeks at sea, justifiably sick of cramped spaces. They again were led through sluggish fitness exercises and dubious emergency procedure drills. Men swayed as they scurried along, arms jolted outwards for balance, shoulders lurched right, knocking into other guys, feet stepping quickly to stay upright in the narrow corridor of gray overhead pipes and portals. On deck the rain was reported to have beaten down like lead bullets, thumping and splashing; the freshwater gathered and flowed across the surface of the ship in sheets. Torrential winds screaming along the deck, grabbed the water and twisted it like dough into the surging salt waves spilling over the gunwales. Their deployment had been held secret and they could determine very little as to their heading from the watered sign posts of the endlessly rolling waves of the Pacific. Certainly the sun still rose in the east, but none of them could read any more than that from the utterly featureless trail before them.

At attention and shivering now in a disagreeable tropical rainfall, according to Sturzebecker, they were for the first time informed of their destination. An announcement, unencumbered by code-speak, squawked out of loud speakers: "S - Y - D - N - E - Y." At first it sounded really welcoming: a land where they spoke the same, familiar language, where men could eat regular food and easily encounter attractive blonds…but questions soon began and skepticism emerged. While maybe not yet associating Australia with New Guinea, they would have known of the grisly South Pacific battle scenes at Kokoda and Guadalcanal. One such scene from 1943 appeared in a popular glossy magazine showing three dead American soldiers on the beach at Buna, for example. It was used, in part, to help inform the public about the war in New Guinea—the very sound of the name was grim, like the hollow roll of drums. Such images shocked readers who had been ignorantly distant from the war and what their boys were doing "over there."

War Department image released to the national press corps from Guadalcanal, 1942.[103]

THE NIGHT SKY

Word spread among the men of an impending stopover in New Zealand. On a night of calm seas, standing below warm southern skies contemplating the distances and their loneliness, the men could arch backwards and for the first time marvel at the constellation called the Southern Cross. Its pattern figures on both the Kiwi and Australian flags. There they stood as young men, the uncertainty of war before them, the wonders of God's universe above them, and the world they loved most behind them. As a boy Len took great interest in the night sky. He learned to pick out the Big Dipper, the Little Dipper, and in the winter he could see Orion cross the heavens overhead. While learning to fly at night, he looked into the dark unknown in hopes of orienting himself by the North Star over the vast Texas plains. It must have been a wonder for the men to peer into a different realm from the blacked-out deck of their ship, out into another corner of God's universe, feeling small on planet Earth. It was a humbling perspective on the world, which no one at home could share with them.

The ship stopped in Wellington. After the long and cramped voyage, the men were paraded through the city's streets in military order to announce that the Americans had arrived. They were fed in town, on real chairs at real tables with real food, by New Zealand's finest. They were then regrouped, roll-called to attention, and marched smartly, if not reluctantly, back on ship (lest anyone consider extending their stay unofficially). Military supplies were dropped off; other goods, such as fresh fruits and vegetables, were loaded on board. The *Nieuw Amsterdam* was refueled on the 16th, and continued on.

SYDNEY

Passing through the Tasman Sea, the men came face to face with the awesome southern continent, Australia; raw, new, vital, and strong. On the approach it could look like an immense sea wall, outstretched arms holding back the Pacific itself. They docked at Sydney on November 19 and boarded trains for a twenty-minute ride to a way station, a "camp" at Warwick Farm. In 1798 the Imperial British forced indigenous inhabitants out of the area in order to "settle" disobedient Irish political prisoners. In 1943 it was a thoroughbred race track.

Upon arrival in Sydney the 312th officially became part of the 5th Air Force under the command of General Kenney. The mission of the 312th was now made clear. They were there to give air support to Allied army ground forces in New Guinea—a mission for which they had so frequently practiced. Their deployment initiated the confluence of the long-awaited surge in men and materials needed to commence offensive action in the Pacific War. In fact, they were fortunate to travel on a heavily loaded transport ship, with American rations, as compared to Middlebrook's lonely thirty-two-plane bomb group of a year earlier, and his pathetic dollop of Ozzie jam each day.

BRISBANE

How big is Australia? After a forty-hour train ride north from Sydney on November 20, the 312th enlisted men arrived at Camp Moorooka, located outside of Brisbane. Strauss, Happ, and the other pilots flew ahead as usual. The area was taken from the Indigenous people and "settled" by the Imperial British in 1823 as yet another penal colony.

Neither Len nor the other pilots had seen a P-40 for more than a month. The first time any of them admired the craft was when they were picked up at the School of Applied Tactics in Orlando months ago. It had been another new model of airplane with new power and new performance features. Now P-40s were being transported by sea to Brisbane in sections where they were reassembled into sound fighting machines. Pilots stayed for several days, flying them at nearby Eagle Farm Airfield, testing the working mechanics and verifying their readiness for the fight. Hopefully the tire supplier had added an extra layer of rubber since Len's debacle at Rice.

As Brisbane has a subtropical climate, located in what meteorologists today call a "tropical cyclone risk area," the men were instructed to defend themselves against yet another enemy: malaria. It was discovered early on that Europeans were not particularly well-suited physically to the tropics. German plantation owners in their colonies in Africa and New Guinea, for example, needed protection from this mosquito-born parasitic disease in order to survive. To this end they learned to use a tree bark extract called quinine as an antimalarial drug. With the loss of her African colonies as part of the World War I Armistice, Germany was obligated to buy quinine from the Dutch East Indies. By late 1941 there were some thirty-seven thousand acres of cinchona plantations on the island of Java producing about twenty million pounds of bark a year, from which quinine was extracted. Following the conquest of the Dutch East Indies by the Japanese, the Allies were forced to rely on South American sources of quinine, but that production was very limited. A procedure for manufacturing imitation quinine was developed in 1944. But until then the Allies had to rely on a man-made alternative, the synthetic antimalarial called Atabrine. Among its possible side effects was the mild yellowing of teeth and skin. Malaria was another sign that they were entering an entirely foreign, inhospitable, and unknown world.

PRIMEVAL NEW GUINEA

The 389th squadron left Brisbane on December 4 by a northbound train for the 825-mile trek to Townsville, a bustling city of 30,000 people located astride the Great Barrier Reef and the Coral Sea. When MacArthur was fleeing the Philippines, and the Australian government was contemplating the Brisbane line, an estimated 20 percent of the population (6,000 people) was said to have voluntarily fled this northern outpost in panic for safety in the south. Once Townsville evolved into a military staging area for the war effort, the Japanese made it a point to prove they could reach the port facilities there, bombing them in late July of 1942. Undaunted, military bases and airfields were built as well as air raid shelters and even World War I-style battle trenches to prepare for the fight. The city became a major logistics hub for the US Air Force in the Southwest Pacific Theatre.

Crossing the equator, the International Date Line, then landing in Australia dazzled the men. On December 11 the 312th finally departed Townsville, on board C-47 transport planes. Throughout the flight, 675 hair-raising miles, they were shaken by ghostly tropical winds and buffeted by unnatural gusts en route north to Port Moresby, where they arrived six weeks after departing San Francisco.

Shaking their groggy heads and blinking their damp eyes, the men soon stood emotionless in a humid, flat clearing strewn with thickly bladed grass, swatting ferocious bugs. The flat clearing was called a runway. It was bound by rugged mangrove forests, pierced by barely discernible narrow, root-tangled footpaths and pitted dirt roads. The men were further disoriented by an overwhelming muddy smell in the hot, fetid air that caught in their nostrils. In the distance were foreboding cloud-shrouded mountains, which intimidated the pilots.

As Stone would have found them. From Len Happ photos, New Guinea 1944.

The New Guinea Len and his mates encountered was in many respects remarkably unchanged since the days of Octavius Stone. The explorer's 1875 diary was written just forty years before Len's birth. In it, Stone described a hot day in which clouds gathered, the breeze cooled, and winds increased. He sailed in storm-tossed seas, crossing the Torres Strait between Townsville and Port Moresby. It was intended to be a day-and-a-half transit to their destination. But the current became so strong that they were pushed twenty miles east, in the direction opposite their destination. He wrote, "All that night we hammered away due in the face of a heavy sea." The prevailing weather system in December is known as the northwest monsoons, which portends a seasonal change in the direction of the wind followed by heavy rains. Facing such winds, Stone's party was still miles away from their destination, farther than when they started. With large outcroppings of rocks in the water, "not an inch of progress" was made. Stone's crew was unable to anchor and they "passed the night in the utmost suspense." A violent gale blew. They endured "sudden changes from calm to tempest,"[104] struggling three and a half days in the storm before they finally reached their destination.

Unimaginably farther from home than ever, the Americans began to sense the vastness of this primitive land. They were bewildered in this god-forsaken new world, twitchy nervous about what lay before them in the bushes, struggling to make sense of what they saw. Local people peeked out from the brush unsure what they themselves were staring at, or what was staring back at them, suspecting they might be hostile.

It was a primitive world and the men were there to fight an invading enemy, being not exactly sure who. It was just as Stone noted in his day,

On our first arrival, some of the natives, both men and women, came off in canoes in hopes of selling their body ornaments...None are entirely naked, though they wear nothing more than a strip of bark or a fringe.... Their hair grows long and frizzy.... The features of the lighter among them are the most regular and pleasing, and they seem more intelligent and industrious. Physically speaking they are muscular and athletic in appearance, but somewhat slightly built, and low of stature. [They wear their hair] frizzed out into a light airy mass, [and their average heights are] 5' 4" for men and 4' 11" for women.[105]

We came across the remains of a fire and the bones of a kangaroo, of which the natives probably dined. The shelters are used as temporary dwellings, people roving from place to place...while they stay to hunt game.[106]

As Stone would have found them. Len Happ photo, New Guinea 1944.

Stone found houses scattered irregularly along the coast, with sloping roofs and the floors raised three feet above the ground, made of sticks and poles framework. Stone learned that fever and ague had been inadvertently introduced into the island, "and many natives died of measles, which had unfortunately been introduced into the country through [European] missionaries."[107]

As would a pilot, Stone also paid close attention to the extraordinary weather, with its drastic swings, monsoon rains, and fierce winds. He wrote that in November it was 110 degrees in the shade at midday, 76 degrees in the morning and evening times. But the nights were cool, "you need a light blanket. The hottest month is February...."[108]

The French postimpressionist painter Paul Gaugin had also been compelled to capture[109] the trepidation of his experiences with the unimaginable weather in the South Pacific. In a 1903 treasury of anecdotes he remembered, a quite exceptional storm had just been making the most terrible ravages...bad weather, which had been gathering for several days took on threatening proportions. By 8 in the evening it was a tempest.... The enormous trees, which in the tropics have few roots, and in a soil that has no resistance when it is once wet, fall to the ground with a heavy thud.... The gusts shook the light roofing [made of cocoanut palm leaves] and rushing in from all sides, prevented me from keeping a lamp [fire] burning.... Towards 10 o'clock a continuous noise.... I could endure it no longer...outside...my feet were in water...I was in the midst of nothing more nor less a torrent...[110]

Moreover,

The mountains [here] form a wall...at these points all the water of the upper plateaus come down in an almost perpendicular torrent. The houses, where one has no money, are lightly built and a mere nothing turns them upside down.... The Island of Taoata has just been ravaged by a frightful tidal wave which has torn up enormous blocks of coral.[111]

Primitive people, primeval weather, mysterious unexplored rivers, otherworldly grasslands, and mountains bound by tormented seas. This was the primordial world into which the men of the 312th arrived. There was a vast virginal horizon before them, unspoiled by human ambition, uncluttered by gaudy monuments. Permeating everything was unforgiving natural chaos, assorted unmatched reptiles, hideous beasts in mosquito-infested jungles beneath a haunting, unrecognizable, and tempestuous sky. It was like a construction yard: infinite unsettled groupings of scattered raw materials left by God from the aftermath of the storm of Creation.

CHAPTER 13

From Huon to Hollandia

When MacArthur was first recovering from being chased out of the
Philippines early in 1942, the dividing line between Japanese power
and Allied defenses was fairly wide and clear. The sheer size of New Guinea
and the uncharted, swarthy terrain left many Allied military men not knowing the best way forward to achieve their missions. Japan's base at Rabaul, in
the north, was a major threat to Australia and an almost indomitable fortress
on the edge of the defensive perimeter around Japan's Southern Resource
Area. On the south coast of New Guinea the Allied base at Port Moresby,
conversely, was by no means a stronghold. It simply provided Australia and
the Americans a good starting point for establishing their own defensive
line. Located at a relatively safe distance from the main population centers
of Australia, it served to keep the advancing enemy at arm's length. Various
thrusts forward were made by the Japanese, resulting in deadly, stalemated
skirmishes all over the New Guinea coast and throughout the surrounding
islands. Men were dying, painfully and slowly, as much by tropical disease
as by enemy fire. It was exactly the war that Japan desired when drafting
their war plan—one which would bog down the Americans to give Japan
more time to dig into and defend her supply of natural resources. All of this
brought the War Department to believe that it could take until 1947 or 1948
to defeat Japan.

MacArthur was finally able to establish air bases north across the Owen Stanley Mountains at Gusap and Nadzab. This gave the War Department the justification they needed in order to allocate him more weapons and men. Thus, as Middlebrook was finishing his tour of duty, General Kenney was designated to receive thirty-five new bomb groups for the Southwest Pacific. Len's arrival in theater represented a second and much more ambitious phase in the war: the long awaited confluence of industrial might and trained men that America was to bring to bear on the conflict. Once in theater, Len was no longer oblivious to, or outside of, the blaze of the war as his correspondence suggested. Now his bomb group was writing the history. They created the fire and violence necessary to push the Japanese backwards.

After waiting so long MacArthur and Kenney immediately applied a new combat tactic to overcome their enemy. Uniquely founded on robust air power, it came to be known as "leapfrogging." The intention was to accelerate progress in the war using repeated, punishing air attacks, not ground or naval offensives, to neutralize distant enemy enclaves. They would cut the enemy's supply line, then send in the Allied ground forces to "clean up" those specifically targeted ports or airfields. They thus abandoned the idea of traditional sweeping tank- and artillery-led land movements which in this theater continually devolved into lengthy jungle skirmishes. Once neutralized, those outposts allowed the Americans to leapfrog ahead and to cut off the next outpost further up the supply chain, closer and closer to the Japanese mainland. With the mobility of strong air power, the new strategy envisioned expending less time and manpower compared to conventional ground warfare. Increasingly less frequently would troops be required to slog through the muddied and tangled foot paths, from battle to battle, pulling their gear great distances, to try to capture a Japanese-held enclave. While such battles would still occur, they were lesser battles compared to the main offensive actions conducted by General Kenney's 5th Air Force.

The first new thrusts forward were to concentrate Kenney's pilots against those Japanese defenses at Finschhaven on the Huon Peninsula. They advanced across the Vitiaz Strait on to two points on New Britain Island: one at Arawe on the southeast coast and a second called Cape Gloucester on the southwest coast. That strait, once vital to Japan's supply, was now needed to move MacArthur's follow-on troops and supplies.

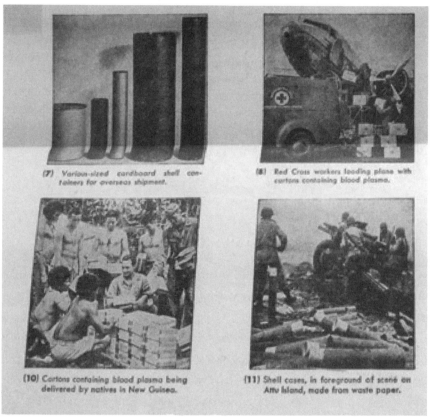

(7) Various-sized cardboard shell containers for overseas shipment.

(8) Red Cross workers loading plane with cartons containing blood plasma.

(10) Cartons containing blood plasma being delivered by natives in New Guinea.

(11) Shell cases, in foreground of scene on Attu Island, made from waste paper.

The war effort at home made possible fresh munitions encased in lightweight recycled paper canisters. The myriad civil defense programs were indispensable to the fighting men. (This image was excerpted from a promotional Civil Defense brochure titled *From Waste Paper into War Weapons.*[112])

SHARING WITH THE 49TH

The freshly arrived 312th pilots spent their first days getting acclimated to their new world by flying missions from Port Moresby over the mysterious fourteen-thousand-foot-peaks of the Owen Stanley Mountains. At the time of the Battle of the Bismarck Sea, Middlebrook had noted that there were more pilots than airplanes in his bomb group. That was true at Gusap in December of 1943 as well. After a week of making adjustments at Port Moresby and getting some flight time in the unique weather, Len and the rest of his comrades joined with another unit at Gusap Airfield and shared the use of their planes. They flew "patrol and escort missions in P-40s in the company of the 49th Fighter Group,"[113] gaining valuable knowledge on the local battle conditions.

Len's heart raced as he crossed the mountains fully alert, navigating on instruments and in awe of the natural beauty and terrible ugliness of it all. He had been to many airfields by this point. Gusap was pathetic and raw: a bare strip of mud in an otherwise dry, flatland of clay, plowed and rolled over many times to iron out the bumps. Good-naturedly he thought there could be similarities with one of the runways at Savannah, starved of surrounding vegetation and a kind of soft gray-brown in color. But try as he might, he could compare it to nothing he had ever seen before. The unfamiliarity caused him to pay closer attention. Located in the Ramu River valley, Gusap was bound by the Finisterre Mountain Range to the north and unexplored jungle to the south.

The men were so close to the fighting they had trouble distinguishing between shattering and booming thunder and the growls and hail of artillery bombs exploding nearby. Gusap, they found, was menaced like Port Moresby by almost nightly "red" alerts from Japanese bombing raids. To the new arrivals like Len, the gap year training ease was shaken completely away by the enemy's pervasive targeting and the evil atmosphere in which they were then living. In many ways, every move they now made around camp was at first with head down, cautionary and defensive. They had to force themselves not to flinch and cower at the crack of a tree branch. Slowly they became accustomed to the fact that, through no fault of their own, other men wanted to kill them. They were on the front lines now.

Over the next several weeks alongside the 49th in their first combat missions, the men hung on every word the experienced pilots offered. In spite of formal preflight briefings they were not clear where the missions were taking them and how they were expected to get across what they could only guess were mountains. Frequently all they saw before them, from east to west, was a solid black wall of clouds across the entire panorama. The timely interaction with the 49th helped settle pilots into their new base and teach them how to deal with the storms from both the enemy and from nature.

SHAGGY RIDGE

For months the Japanese had been establishing colonial outposts unopposed on the north coast of New Guinea. Now, the 312th was being used to bomb them out and cattle drive them back up to Japan. By applying their training, the thud and puff of their sacks of flour now became violent demolition and the reverberating anarchy of real bombs. The widespread offensive actions for which MacArthur had been waiting were at last initiated by the Allies on December 15. For example, just north of Gusap, the Japanese were building a supply road from the north coast down to a base inland at a town called Bogadjim. Protecting that road was an entrenched Japanese force in a five-thousand-foot-high outcropping called Shaggy Ridge by the Allies. From that imposing vantage point the Japanese monitored the road works with strategically placed machine gun bunkers.

Flying with the 49th, part of the 389th Squadron flew dive-bombing missions to make impassable craters along the enemy's road works and then circled back to strafe those Japanese positions on the ridge itself. Aussie troops then assaulted the road works from the ground, trying to force the Japanese out of the area. The difficult jungle and root-tangled terrain caused the battle over this ridge to drag on until the last Japanese positions were destroyed some weeks later in January.

ARAWE, KEY TO THE VITIAZ STRAIT

Since September MacArthur had been whittling away at control over the Vitiaz Strait. Now on the afternoon of that same December 15, covered by the greatly reinforced 5th Air Force from the sky, Allied ground forces sailed north across the strait from Finschhaven to establish a foothold at the coastal town called Arawe on southwest New Britain Island. By the time the Allies began landing troops, the Japanese counter-attacked from both Rabaul and Wewak air bases. For the next several days, the Allies withstood furious enemy air counter-offensives that especially focused on MacArthur's naval transport ferrying reinforcements through the Vitiaz Strait. Japanese planes machine-gunned and bombed Allied boats to shreds and turned back many of the troop ships. In addition, two Japanese infantry battalions of 1,100 men each advanced on Arawe and dug in just up the coast, beyond newly established and fragile American encampments.

WEWAK

Japanese coming from Wewak in the west were preparing to head east in counter-attack missions against the Allies at Arawe. Other pilots of the 389th were directed to bomb and strafe that base, to kill enemy fighters and destroy their equipment.

Leading the 389th pilots was Major Selmon Wells. Wells entered flying school at Randolph Field, Texas in December 1941 after Pearl Harbor. He then received his pilot wings from Foster Field in Texas. Upon graduation he, too, was assigned to the 312th, as a First Lieutenant, at Hunter Field in Georgia, where he and Len met. By the time the 312th reached Rice in California, he was made Captain and here in New Guinea, promoted to Major.

As flight leader, Wells took off first from Gusap to lead the squadron west to Wewak. Len was designated as his wing man. After checking his instruments, and going through his preflight checklist, Len pivoted onto the runway, and took off. Circling to the east, gaining altitude, he merged into formation with Wells. After a third pilot merged, Wells had the group of three planes head northwest, inland over the Ramu River, along the edge of the even less charted Bismarck Mountain Range, and eventually cross the Sepik River for the 325 miles, a one-and-one-half-hour flight, up to Wewak. The country over which they flew, Len noted, was of immense natural strength and bordered by muscular shoulders of billowing clouds. Their "flight" of three planes, wingmen on either side of and slightly behind Wells in a triangle formation, was one among several such "flights" of planes on that mission, all in formation like migrating geese.

Through the turbulent clouds, the men could see that the Wewak base and port facilities were humming with activity that day. With the attack procedures initiated, speeding downward, their heads and necks forced backwards, Wells's men had to trust their training and summon their confidence because before they opened their bomb doors, flak from the many Japanese anti-aircraft guns surrounding the base started to explode all around them. Black watercolor dabs blotted the sky irregularly as enemy gunners tried to estimate the velocity and altitude of the descending planes. The men's instinct was to veer off and climb away but Wells simply steadied his plane forward and lined up along his path to the target. Len followed. He could feel the vibration from the bursting flak. Sticking with Wells's flight path he gripped his control column (like a video game joy stick for steering) and focused only ahead, praying to God that he was invisible. Screeching lower and lower, Len's P-40 raced down to earth. Flak burst black, but well behind him. It was all happening so fast, his heart was in his throat. The Japanese scrambled to recalibrate their guns and their timing. Len counted the seconds in descent. The bursting flak sprayed broken shards of metal, multiplying its capacity for destruction. He had no time to react. Not being distracted from his flight plan and following long-practiced procedures was his only hope of survival. The Japanese got another fix on the incoming plane but not before Len released his bombs and flashed out of sight. Trees underneath were whipping past, then he nosed up. He left the target area, gaining altitude as quickly as he could, then headed south again to regroup with Wells. Peeling away, Len extended his left hand across his body, reaching for his shoulders and torso, breathing heavily. Feeling no damp areas of blood, he assured himself he was in one piece. Accelerating away, fear dissipated slowly like sweat in a cold breeze.

Wells's actions on this mission were particularly recorded because after the attack sequence, on the anxious trip back to Gusap, he discovered and caught up to a squadron of five Japanese fighter bombers headed for American targets in the east. Wells signaled his intention to the other members of his flight group before initiating his attack. As the Japanese bombers attempted to evade Wells, one was separated from his formation. Len stayed a distance behind Wells scanning the skies in order to defend him, as was his role. In his faster P-40, Wells singled out the separated enemy bomber, now weaving an irregular, evasive flight path. The long reach of Wells's machine gun fire burst upon the enemy bomber. Len witnessed the eruption of mid-air destruction while anxiously scouring the air for Japanese Zeros.

At Gusap Air Base, Major Selmon Wells. Above him on his plane, a row of bombs, marking his number of combat missions. Barely visible above that, the image of a Japanese flag commemorating his "kill." The several patched-up areas cover bullet holes where he had been hit by anti-aircraft fire. Len Happ photo.

The event surprised Len for the sympathy he felt for the Japanese bomber pilot as his plane hurtled into the sea. He was outmatched by the speed of Wells's P-40 and the power of its guns. Like Middlebrook before him, it was an emotion Len had to bury. Wells had just saved countless Allied lives by shooting down that plane. The event was recorded as the first air-to-air kill for the 312th Bomb Group.

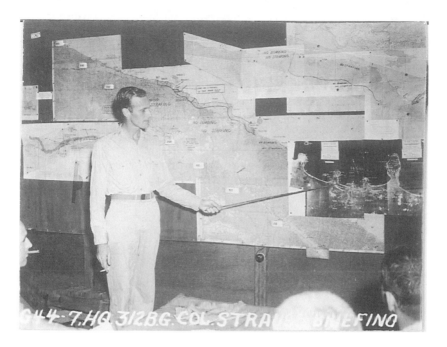

Colonel Strauss describing targets and assignments to the pilots for an upcoming mission. Len Happ photo.

Back at base, as Len sorted out his various thoughts about the exhausting thrill of the mission and the aggressive threat of death, he learned that the tail of Ewing McKinney's P-40 was shot up by gunfire during his mission to Shaggy Ridge. Pals since their days in Savannah, Len was particularly happy to see him alive. With the experience of air combat and the up-close killing, Len was very sober about (and grateful for) the good fortune that kept McKinney from the fate of the Japanese pilot brought down by Wells. Len and McKinney had made it back to Gusap; and from then on they both knew uniquely what it meant to survive their missions.

CAPE GLOUCESTER

Intelligence reports on enemy positions and Allied objectives were used to draw up specific battle orders and missions that were sent out from General Kenney's headquarters. Back at 312th's headquarters Colonel Robert Strauss also had intelligence officers assigned to his command. Operations officers would use that intelligence to help plan missions in detail and assign responsibilities among the men of their bomb group. Together they would take General Kenney's orders and translate them into specific missions on specific targets at specific times with specific pilot positions. (Who leads? Who is on wing? Who trails? Who needs a rest?) All missions would be coordinated with troop movements within MacArthur's overall plan for that time period. After the mission the operations officer would prepare formal summaries of the results.

While the battle to take Arawe was underway on the south end of New Britain, the Allies organized maneuvers to seize a Japanese airfield at Cape Gloucester on the far northwestern end of New Britain. Because strong defenses were found to be concentrated at this airfield, the US Marines landed on an undefended beach about six miles to the east of it on December 26, 1943. Some of the 312th were sent across the Vitiaz Strait to participate in the bombing and strafing of Cape Gloucester, employing their often practiced skills of firing on enemy ground troops that lay ahead of the advancing US Marines. In response, the Japanese sent counter-attack planes from both Rabaul and Wewak. They managed to inflict significant damage on a part of the Allied amphibious assault force by sinking one naval destroyer and damaging many other support ships. But US Marines wrested control over the airfield by December 29. These multiple aggressive actions by the Americans were not even possible just a few short months ago when MacArthur had to do everything possible to scrape together a defense of Port Moresby. Now that MacArthur had the weapons, he was capable of deploying them on multiple fronts.

ON THE FRONT LINES

The new men were beginning to distinguish between the sounds of different bombs and the different motors of airplanes. The pilots for sure knew the sounds of flak bursting in the air, and they knew the burst of mortar shells landing so near that they could feel the ground tremble. On January

5, the distinct sound of Japanese Zero engines sent everyone scurrying for cover. Suddenly five Japanese fighter planes appeared overhead and scared the devil out of the men as they strafed Gusap.

In support of MacArthur's objectives, across the vast north coast of New Guinea, the American pilots were fighting and pressing as Middlebrook had done. Len's missions consisted of P-40 dive-bomb and strafing missions flown against targets all along the north coast, at Wewak, and at places called Dumpu and Hansa Bay. Paraphrasing what Len wrote early on in Savannah, this flying was now really "the business and for keeps." He was assigned missions on multiple occasions to attack remaining enclaves of resistance at Cape Gloucester and Finschhaven, then to initiate new offensives, targeting the enemy troops and equipment at a place called Madang, a supply chain link to the south of Wewak. On January 8 a group from the 312th, in punishing repetition, returned again to strafe the persistent Japanese efforts to establish the Shaggy Ridge road to Bogadjim. Len was becoming more confident of his piloting and the support of his squadron mates. And as the days passed, he became increasingly immune to the atmosphere of war that so disturbed him when he arrived. He less often noticed the putrid stench around him; the constant odor of the mud and rain, the diesel fuel and motor oil were less intolerable to him.

It was an extraordinary life he was living, as the war was in fact becoming less of a mystery, more of a lifestyle, if one could call it that. On January 15, another five Japanese planes made several strafing passes over Gusap. Heavy rains had many planes grounded and vulnerable. These attacks killed four base personnel while damaging several P-40s and C-47 transport planes. Also on the 15th, the 388th sustained yet more tragedy as Captain Glen Carhart, Jr.'s P-40 was shot down. His body was retrieved and he was buried in a military cemetery near Nadzab Air Base. Throughout this period (mid-December through mid-January, 1944) Colonel Strauss personally led seventeen missions over these same targets with his men; Len, too, averaged about one combat mission every other day.

THE NEW A-20 TYPE OF ATTACK AIRCRAFT

Then, in mid-January, the 312th pilots were sent back to Port Moresby. Once again they were to undertake new training, this time in the new production A-20 model aircraft. The P-40 was a single-engine, single-seat (one-man) dive-bomber that normally operated from an altitude of one thousand to ten thousand feet. The A-20 was a two-man, twin-engine bombing and strafing plane. For mission safety and surprise attack, it was normally flown at one thousand before it cruised down to attack from as low as twenty feet off the ground. By flying low, it could not be easily sighted by land-based gunners, nor targeted from below by the faster Japanese Zero aircraft. Antiaircraft gunners could hardly see, and had less time to react, when the A-20s came roaring over the horizon at treetop level. The surprise and the sudden noise of the engines was frightful in and of itself, much less the violent weaponry it carried.

Back at about the time of the Battle of the Bismarck Sea in March of 1943, the first A-20s were being tested in theater. Middlebrook's words at the time were, "The A-20s were fast and maneuverable, sleek and pretty. They were flown by a two-man crew, the pilot and the gunner. The pilot strafed, flew and bombed. I always envied those guys."[114]

At first, lacking A-20 training planes, the 312th flew the similar B-25 type aircraft, already based at Port Moresby, in order to experience the size and weight of the new planes that were coming. After classroom studies on the different features of the A-20s, their first training flights with that plane included cargo pickup and delivery runs to Milne Bay and to Townsville, Australia. Pilots eventually flew down to Townsville as a group in C-47s to pick up their new A-20s.

The A-20 pilot was in effect pilot, copilot, navigator, bombardier and, nose gunner. With his right hand on the steering wheel, his right thumb pressed a button to release bombs and with his right index finger he fired machine guns placed in the nose of the plane. His left hand worked the air speed and other flight control throttles while his feet managed the rudder pedals. His gunner was behind him, in a swivel seat, manning what were in effect twin machine guns mounted below a clear bubble turret. It was a lot to learn for men who had been cutting their teeth in battle with a single-engine, one-man attack fighter.

Thomas Dobrowski (left), Len (center), and assistant crew chief Kenneth Tennyson (right). Len Happ photo.

The men were then assigned their own A-20s and their own crew chiefs, who kept the planes in optimal running order. Their gunners, on the other hand, were assigned alternately to pilots at mission briefings, not teamed with a specific pilot. From this point forward in combat, Len would almost exclusively fly the plane he named *Little Joe* after his youngest brother. Staff Sergeant Thomas Dobrowski acted as his crew chief. Immediately, each time after Len returned, Dobrowski would retune and repair *Little Joe*'s engine, patch any bullet holes, and make sure every detail of the aircraft was functioning properly in preparation for Len's next mission.

SAIDOR

To further exploit the anticipated success at Finschhaven, the Allied army received orders back on December 17 to capture Saidor, just north up the coast from the Huon Peninsula. The operation would serve to sever a link in the Japanese line of retreat to the northwest, thus trapping the remaining enemy and making them more vulnerable. A base at Saidor would also protect eventual Allied shipping through the straits.

With the remnants of Japanese forces trapped, yet still engaged in battle over Arawe and Finschhaven, an Allied amphibious fleet set out from Finschhaven to land, against little enemy opposition, some 175 miles north up the coast at Saidor on January 2, 1944. With that successful advance, the Allies could now claim virtual control of eastern New Guinea from the original fragile base at Port Moresby to Milne Bay and up to the Huon Peninsula.

The battle over Arawe was considered stalemated until a rare maneuver in this jungle battleground was executed. Brought ashore by landing craft from Lae were rare Allied armored tanks, which drove the Japanese from their trenches on January 16. By February 24, key areas in western New Britain in general, and the Vitiaz Strait in particular, were under Allied control. It was the first major objective achieved in the new thrust of battle since mid-December of 1943. MacArthur could now claim to have a "forward" staging base for a plan to knock out that seaside logistics center at Madang. Success there would serve to weaken the defense of Wewak and solidify Allied control of both sides of the Vitiaz Strait at Saidor. The Allies' achievements were now making Rabaul increasingly more difficult for the Japanese to resupply.

SELF-INFLICTED WOUNDS

The personal and camp life adjustments to be made in this otherworldly environment of tropical warfare caused the losses to mount for the 312th. Time and again, weather and disease, now combined with the unfamiliar characteristics of the new A-20s, killed 312th pilots and crewmen. On February 4, Second Lieutenant Chester Rimer of the 386th mysteriously crashed into the sea off of Port Moresby, taking three onboard soldiers with him, in a brand new A-20. Then too, some men were slow to realize that they were fighting against mildew and filth as much as against Japanese guns. Len was privately incredulous that in spite of heavy rains, thick mud, mosquitoes, dengue fever, and malaria men were not taking their Atabrine at mealtimes. Some of them simply distrusted the drug or otherwise failed to appreciate its value. As a ghastly example of nature's threats, on February 9, Sergeant Thomas Hughes of the 388th died of what they called cerebral malaria. On February 16, the 386th lost Private First Class Molan Ivosevic to circulatory collapse, as his body just gave out. These were men with whom Len had been living in close contact for the past twenty months. From sharing jokes in classroom training to cursing while climbing cargo netting, from uproars in dining halls to laughs in movie theaters, they were men with whom he crossed the broad Pacific in the name of duty, and with whom he shared plans to return back home to live out their American dreams. Len prayed for the souls of the departed while bottling up his disappointment and frustration. He was sickened to think how natural this was all becoming, how accustomed he had become to death. He found there was precious little time for grief or moral contemplation as Japanese planes continued to harass from above.

American supplies continued to flow into the Southwest Pacific Theatre. By order of the 5th Air Force Bomber Command dated February 19, Len was ordered to ferry aircraft out of APO 922 (Townsville, Australia) to APO 929 (Port Moresby) with Major William S. Pagh (commander of the 387th), Second Lieutenant Ewing J. McKinney, and First Lieutenant Kenneth Hedges among others. They were bringing in more A-20s. The 312th Bomb

Group soon became known as the Roarin' 20's, as they now flew exclusively the A-20 model aircraft in combat.

During this same time period, violent equatorial winds gusted and rain pelted the Southwest Pacific just as Paul Gaugin and Octavius Stone had once described. This same raw, untamed and dangerous weather caused, on February 21, more tragedy for the 388th Bomb Squadron. First Lieutenant Anthony Hartley, flying a B-25 with six crew plus passengers, was swept away without a trace. They were traveling above the same tormented Coral Sea over which Len had just flown. Then a second group of Colonel Strauss's men, in transit back to Townsville, was overcome along the same route: one member of the 387th, three of the 388th, and one of the 389th were lost to fierce, tempestuous winds—not gunfire from an enemy plane, not anti-aircraft flak from below. And again not a trace of their planes was ever found in the depths of the vast seas. The repetition of losses dulled the senses of the surviving comrades. Soldiers, human beings, just ten weeks into this complex theatre of war, were already emotionally numb to the violent deaths of close friends. Their lives were diminished by the loss of men on whom they most relied for their own protection and survival. But their reactions were nothing more than brief prayers and bottled grief. They had to keep their heads about them. They were under constant threat.

THE BISMARCK ARCHIPELAGO CAMPAIGN

There were no longer clear, traditional battle lines in the Southwest Pacific Area. "Leapfrogging" their way forward, every advance the Allies achieved (Lae, Finschhaven, Arawe, Saidor) left isolated but armed Japanese forces in the jungles behind the lines of those advancing troops. The expectation was that these Japanese would be cut off from their supply lines and eventually be captured or killed by trailing Australian ground forces in "mopping up" missions. But the jungle's mysterious, boggy terrain, which was a death trap for both sides in Buna, Kokoda, and Lae, now served to shelter some of the enemy from these new offensives. Japan was still coordinating action with her troops to the east of Allied positions. The vanguard of MacArthur's troops advanced further westward, where humidity streamed down the mountains like sweat off a boxer's brow. And some of these Japanese troops were still being supplied, or redeployed to other of their strongholds. It was as if the whole area was a vast interlocked checkerboard of overlapping battlegrounds.

As MacArthur and his staff searched for ways to accelerate the campaign to knock out Rabaul, they may have wished to replicate sweeping historic ground battles involving great troop movements to overrun the enemy strongholds. But this was increasingly proving itself to be an air campaign. The jungle and mountains of New Guinea made normal troop movements with equipment virtually impossible. Unlike images, say, of General Patton motoring flat across the treeless sands of North Africa, the Pacific Theatre generals saw that advancing and resupplying the troops in the jungle was a nightmare. They came to find that all of the new ground troops and land-based weaponry, tanks, and artillery, for which the Allies had been waiting, and which were now arriving, had to be used in smaller platoons, in smaller strikes, through tangled jungle pathways or put to sea to sail around to approachable landing areas. Those early New Guinea battles in the Coral Sea and at Guadalcanal dramatized the value of the sea lanes, on which both sides were dependent, for troop and equipment movements to the various stepping-stone ports. But it was these missions from the air that cleared the way for traditional ground forces to land by sea and finish the conquest.

Alarmingly, well into February, Allied intelligence reporting held that constant reinforcements by sea put the strength of Japanese Rabaul at over ninety thousand men. But it was becoming increasingly clear that the taking of Rabaul was no longer essential. It could be cut off from fresh supplies and left behind to wither as the Allies continued to leapfrog forward. This realization led to the development of the campaign to do just that: cut Rabaul off from her supply routes back to the Japanese mainland in the north. The capture and control of Finschhaven, Arawe, and the straits between them, combined with the development of the base at Gusap, laid the basis for what became known as the Bismarck Archipelago Campaign.

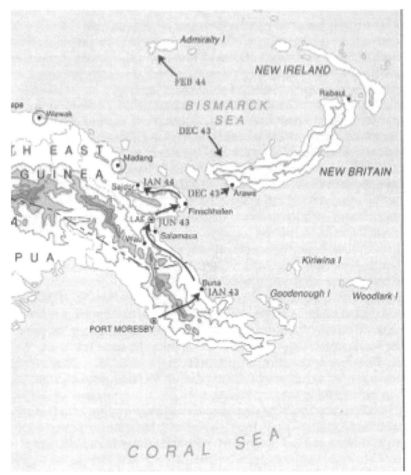

Finchhaven sits on the tip of the Huon Peninsula. North past the Huon peninsula is Saidor. The channel between Finschhaven and Arawe is called the Vitiaz Straits. It links the Bismarck Sea with the Coral Sea.[115]

Over the next several months, two prongs of Allied strategy began to take shape: first, Admiral Nimitz from Pearl Harbor in the east attacking westward through the Marianas Islands, north of New Guinea, in the direction of Formosa (Taiwan); and second, MacArthur and the 5th Air Force attacking along the north coast of New Guinea and through the Bismarck Sea, then northward to the Philippines. Every advance forward by these two forces made it increasingly difficult for the Japanese to resupply their garrison at Rabaul.

ALEXISHAVEN

After so much effort concentrated on targets around the Huon Peninsula and the Vitiaz Strait, a new series of missions began on February 25. These missions extended the arc of the Allies' coverage when Colonel Strauss led the 386th against a port town called Alexishaven. Lying some 150 miles to the northwest of Gusap, it was a distance equivalent to flying from Seattle, Washington, to Portland, Oregon. En route his squadron was tasked to also "sweep" or scout the straits for any Japanese, and destroy them, in order to keep the area enemy free. The distances to these new targets were similar to the more northerly points at Arawe or Cape Gloucester.

During a strafing drive at some twenty feet off the ground, Colonel Strauss was jolted in the engine by Japanese anti-aircraft fire over Alexishaven. It was a desperate situation. At such a low altitude, and trailing a ribbon of black smoke, a pilot's options were limited. Taking the plane to a higher altitude could buy him time, but also expose him to further enemy attack. Strauss managed to evade further anti-aircraft fire and coax his plane over the scattered, vegetated shoulders of the mountains and home to Gusap. Like McKinney, Strauss was one of the lucky ones.

During the last four days in February the four squadrons of the 312th flew a revolving door of seventy-one sorties into the quadrant immediately to the north and west of Gusap. Missions were directed against the multiple, scattered, coastal targets just beyond the Huon Peninsula, such as airfields, supply areas, and oil tanks hidden in the brush. At every turn they endured and survived return fire from machine gun and anti-aircraft gun emplacements. On February 27, the 386th flew missions to clear the way forward for Allied ground troops moving in to occupy the area around Alexishaven. Japanese supplies nonetheless continued to pour in. On February 28, the 387th returned to attack: first one of those isolated enemy groups back travelling along the Bogadjim road, then more pounding to soften up Alexishafen.

The new month started with catastrophe. Edward Hilbert, a civilian representative of the Curtiss-Wright airplane manufacturing company visited Gusap to evaluate airplane performance and to report back to the factory on suggestions to possibly improve them. Previously, Hilbert, in today's terms, had been "embedded" with the 312th at Rice in California where he compiled reports on his company's P-40. Living as he did in the States, his only knowledge of war was through newspaper and magazine reports written by journalists hundreds of miles away. According to the historians Lawrence Hickey and Michael Levy,[116] "[Hilbert] wanted to fly a combat mission before returning to the States." Assigned as flight leader on an A-20 mission, Group Operations Officer Thomas Templeton with Sergeant Marlin Nelson were designated to carry Hilbert on a hot mission over Alexishaven. On March 1, flying no higher than 200 feet off the ground, "big black puffs" of flak exploded around Templeton and he was shot out of the air. His plane hit the ground and exploded into "a very large orange fireball" consuming the three men—the 312th's first A-20 shot down in combat.

LOS NEGROS AND THE BISMARCK SEA

Since establishing the air base at Gusap, Generals MacArthur and Kenney had been methodical in identifying, and relentless in knocking out, strategic enemy strongholds with the goal of cutting off Rabaul. Key enemy positions such as Finschhaven, Saidor, Arawe, and Cape Gloucester were laid to waste and/or brought under Allied control, thus driving the Japanese from the Vitiaz Strait. The Bismarck Sea lay before them, where at distant points, north and west, were long-established and heavily occupied Japanese bases and logistics centers.

In the far northwest corner of the of that vast expanse of water, the Allies arrived unannounced on February 29, 1944, on the island of Los Negros, in the Admiralty Islands group. The initial troop landings caught the enemy completely off guard. Intelligence personnel concluded that the majority of Japanese defenses were facing the opposite side of the island. But two enemy infantry battalions, a transportation regiment, and some naval forces turned out to be so well camouflaged that the low-flying Allied reconnaissance planes had not detected their presence. With those once-hidden forces, the enemy fought back during unusual nocturnal counter-attacks.

The Allies countered by pouring more reinforcements onto the island. After a further three days of pounding attacks, the Japanese struck hard throughout the night of March 3 and into March 4 and nearly succeeded in overcoming the surprise offensive. By daybreak on the 4th the worst of the fighting was over. The Allies prevailed by killing an estimated 750 enemy troops, while suffering the loss of some 60 of their own. On March 5 MacArthur broadcast the Los Negros mission's success.

The Japanese had been insinuating themselves in and around the Bismarck Sea since early 1942. With industrial production of Yankee war matériel now flowing, over the last many months MacArthur's troops began to establish themselves in the archipelago. And as Admiral Nimitz continued to make similar progress from east to west in the island groups to the north of the Bismarck Sea, sea lanes to Rabaul were becoming increasingly sealed off. While Rabaul and other points remained under Japanese control, they were becoming surrounded. And indeed, as the Allied war planners intended, they were being cut off from future supplies. In the future the Admiralties (Los Negros, and soon the Island of Manus) could provide the Allies with logistical bases of their own, and important port facilities from which to continue on plan. A road to Japan, via the next strategic stepping-stone, the Philippines, was presenting itself.

THE MISSING

Calamity, in this scurrying rush up the coast, caused the 312th to pause. Colonel Strauss sent out a force of eight A-20s to attack a Japanese infantry position at a place called Kulau Village on March 13. He also designated a second group of planes to bomb an airstrip at Alexishaven. Ken Hedges, an Eddy, Oklahoma, native who had been with Len's 389th Bomb Squadron since its inception at Savannah, was to lead the second mission. With their duties carried out, the return flight brought both squads home via Alexishaven in a southeasterly direction down the Ramu River. An official pilot report states that Hedges's group of seven planes started to climb over the massive thirteen thousand-foot-Finisterre Mountain Range located on their left, in a direct line to the Markham River valley and Gusap. But horrendous typhoon weather blinded them. Ten to twelve thousand feet was understood by the pilots to be the upper limit of safe performance for these planes. Therefore, knowing those mountains were ahead, shrouded with impossible weather, Hedges plotted a course to avoid certain catastrophe. In doing so, three of the seven planes became frighteningly separated from the group. They were last sighted in the air southwest of Saidor barely a half hour from their base at Gusap.

In a report filed by the operations officer, based on interviews with the flight leader and other mission survivors, the loss of the three planes was "evidently due to bad weather." In the same report, then Major William Pagh admitted to not having any other information about circumstances along route. In other words, since the area was known to be crawling with Japanese, they could have been shot down. But Pagh felt it most likely that the terrible tropical weather suddenly overtook the three planes and no one saw them again. Coldly, for statistical purposes, they were missing in action.

As Stone would have found them. Indigenous New Guinea men in 1944. Len Happ photo.

This by now tight brotherhood of pilots was not going to give up on the three lost crews. The possibility that the six missing men might be alive frightened them even more than their deaths. The unexplored jungles; the unidentified swamps filled with leeches, snakes, and crocodiles; primitive, unpredictable villagers, with whom they shared neither a common language nor culture; and of course desperate Japanese soldiers, all made the men anxious to spare the lost crews this fate by rescuing them as soon as possible.

Major Pagh's report stated that when it was clear the three planes were not returning to base, Colonel Strauss sent Lieutenant McKinney out with eight A-20s to look for the planes. When they arrived in the area where Hedges last saw them, McKinney's group broke into two subgroups to search different areas over land and over sea. Weather permitted them to scour their areas for two hours. Three hours after McKinney's group took off, Strauss had Len take seven A-20s to scour different areas where Hedges might have drifted. After just about two hours, Len's group also came home empty-handed. Over the course of the next few weeks, as planes were available, the men continued to sortie out into the wilds to look some more. And all groups passing through that area were formally instructed to be on the lookout for the missing men. Prayers were said privately. The profound mystery of their fate was never resolved.

LEAVE

In the interim, by the insignia of a single silver bar, without ceremony Len Happ and Ed Hambleton were promoted from second lieutenants to first lieutenants by command of 5th Air Force Lieutenant General Kenney on March 1. Two weeks later Major Selmon Wells formally appointed Len to the position of Assistant Operations Officer. An extract from the United States Army Air Force official history of the war reads:

> 1st Lt. Leonard W. Happ (0-663723)—"Hap" is a native of Park Ridge, Illinois. After graduating from Loyola University, he became associated with Bermingham and Prosser Co. as an accountant. Flying

for the army became his destiny in 1942 and in October of that same year joined the 389th Bomb Squadron. Lt. Happ is a sincere, conscientious worker and has had considerable success in his present capacity.[117]

Bermingham and Prosser Paper Company in Chicago sold paper mill paper for the book printing and stationery industries. According to his military discharge papers Len described his civilian occupation as, "Accounting Clerk for wholesale paper concern. Kept double entry system; checked payables and receivables, assisted in preparing trial balances." A January 1919 trade advertisement reproduced here states:

We make a specialty of
ALL GRADES OF BOOK PAPERS

LIGHT WEIGHT BOOK PAPERS
Coated and Uncoated

BERMINGHAM & PROSSER COMPANY
Chicago   •   Kalamazoo   •   New York

Members New York Master Printer's Association

The extract was authored by Major Wells in consultation with Colonel Strauss. Wells was known to be a strict disciplinarian and a stickler for detail.

In this new assignment, carried out after his day job of fighting the war, Len joined with the commanding officers and the operations officer to decide, plan, and assign pilots, gunners, and aircraft to the next day's missions. The team determined the attack strategy, approach (flight path), targets, ammunition to use and the return to base of the bomb squadrons. Len collaborated heavily with the group's intelligence officer, Leonard Dulac, in order to detail out the mission responsibilities their superiors required. Additionally, on an ongoing basis, the air force evaluated its men for combat stress or "operational fatigue." Operations officers thus also prepared field reports that gave an account of the health and morale of the fliers in their units. These reports evaluated pilots for their continued efficiency by rating their levels of fatigue, fear, and motivation. Back in the States, these reports contributed to case studies designed to improve the way the air force training personnel judged the potential for success or failure of pilots then moving through their programs.

Intelligence officer Lenny Dulac clarifying the air mission against Hansa Bay (far right, center). Len Happ photo.

With that, on March 19, Len was granted seven days of leave and off he went as a passenger on a C-47 via Port Moresby to Sydney, Australia. He came back to Gusap to find that the paperwork for his promotion to First Lieutenant had come through "by command of General MacArthur" himself with orders signed by Brigadier General L. S. Ostrander.

The work of an assistant operations officer was shown in an April 1, 1944 document authored by Len, marked "S E C R E T." It is a combat evaluation report[118] that discusses concerns about pilot errors while strafing. The concern stems from the fact that these A-20 missions were carried out at such low altitudes. The problem was that increasing numbers of planes were being damaged either by trees, through a failure to climb out of their dives in time, or from low level debris from blow back created by bombs dropped by the previous pilot. Both were indicative of poor piloting and undisciplined formation flying. In the report, Len recommended that pilots be urged to not simply focus on their targets, but to see ahead and plan out how they were going to increase their altitude and rise out of the target area after completing their raids. Ominously, his report also discussed "problems with the A-20 fuel system," which gave the pilots inconsistent readings on the level of their remaining fuel. It foreshadowed dreadful tragedies in forthcoming missions.

With such a dramatic increase in activity by the 312th, attacking and bombing all over the coast and islands, there was also increased misfortune. Records from Octavius Stone's time tell of two men traveling with him who were shipwrecked on the New Guinea coast in stormy weather in 1872. Those men told Stone, "Fifteen from [their] ship were drowned and fifteen were killed by natives [when they reached shore]."[119] As with the recent loss of the three planes flying with Hedges, in such emergency situations the Air Force wanted pilots who parachuted to safety, for example, to be able to communicate with locals who could help them survive in these remote jungles.

"Doc" Walsh (left), a local native (center), and Len (right) practicing their new language skills. Since malaria was such a scourge, Gen. Kenney undertook a study to determine which uniforms would serve best to deter malaria. He found that long trousers and long sleeve shirts reduced malaria by 80 percent compared to the shorts and short-sleeved uniforms worn by the Australians. Len Happ photo.

To bridge the culture gap at Gusap between the locals and the American servicemen, that same "secret" report acknowledged that flight crews were being instructed in Pidgin English so they could better communicate with the local population.

HOLLANDIA

With the establishment of the Gusap air base right on the front lines of battle, on a single day General Kenney had the capacity to bomb, from east to west, Madang, Alexishaven, Hansa Bay and Wewak. And as Len was soon to demonstrate, they could reach Aitape, another enemy enclave on the coast, further west still. In light of the successful air attacks from mid-December to March 1, President Roosevelt's Joint Chiefs of Staff issued new battle objectives: to take and occupy the northern Bismarck Sea island of Manus (next to Los Negros), to take and occupy a Japanese coastal New Guinea hub called Hollandia by April 15, and to take and occupy the large southern Philippine island called Mindanao by November 15, 1944. In addition to this breathtaking plan, MacArthur was to prepare for a strike, by February of 1945, against the large island in the northern Philippines called Luzon, on which the capital city, Manila, is located. If MacArthur were not to progress on the Joint Chiefs' schedule, it could mean that he would not lead the troops liberating the Philippines—a thought the general was loath to contemplate. Above all, since being chased from the Philippines in March of 1942, MacArthur longed to return and liberate them.

Back in mid-January 1944, American intelligence discovered that the Japanese were resupplying Wewak from staging areas at Hollandia. For the longest time this port town was well outside the flying range of Allied combat planes. The distance from Gusap to Hollandia is about 550 miles, 1,100 miles round trip. Factory specifications stated that an A-20 cruised at 280 miles per hour with an estimated range of about 950 miles. It would make for an unattainable target. Such a nonstop mission out and back to base would take about four hours. Notwithstanding Len's memo concerning the unreliability of the plane's gas gauge, General Kenney contemplated squeezing more out of the A-20s. He believed that that strategic hub was likely reachable.

Following those intelligence reports on Hollandia, Southwest Pacific commanders detailed plans for the seizure of the base and airstrips of Aitape, 400 miles from Gusap. While still some 150 miles short of Hollandia, it was within the A-20's comfort zone. As a preliminary act in the campaign, Len and colleagues in the 389th were directed to begin a series of harassing missions against Aitape. These assaults were further intended to test the plane's range and evaluate the men's success over this distance. At the same time they were to intended to look sporadic and random so as to not give away the Allies' ultimate intentions. And they did indeed demolish many Japanese aircraft on the runways there.

Throughout February and March, the 312th was also bombing and strafing airfields and supply depots spread throughout the coast, from the Huon Peninsula west to around the Wewak area. Since these bombings began to weaken Wewak, the Japanese in turn began to cautiously move their men and equipment further away to the northwest, to Hollandia, expecting to be placing them out of range from American bombers. And that presented MacArthur with a new dilemma. He was inadvertently causing the Japanese to reinforce Hollandia.

Therefore MacArthur devised a plan to create a diversion intended to hold in place an estimated ten thousand Japanese army troops in the Madang area, and keep them off balance regarding what the Americans' intentions were. MacArthur intended to fake an Allied invasion near Madang (about two hundred miles from Gusap), in order to mislead the enemy into keeping her troops in place there—and not redeploy them to Hollandia. On March 12 a stream of Australian troops laboriously reached to within thirty miles of Madang via tangled inland routes, simulating a traditional ground offensive. At about the same time a number of US troops landed on the nearby coast by sea, staging an attack from another angle. Days later, the two groups were able to join as a combined force and advanced from the south on Madang. The Japanese took the bait and interpreted this force to be part of a greater Allied plan to battle forward by way of traditional ground combat to attack Madang. And that was MacArthur's hope.

As that battle raged, three weeks later, on April 6, MacArthur's theatrics continued. He ordered that more troops land at nearby Hansa Bay some one hundred miles northwest of Madang, giving the impression of moving to surround that base. Strong opposition from the Japanese was expected and intelligence reports confirmed that enemy troops were indeed concentrating to confront the Allies there. Japanese fighters were transferred from Hollandia back south to Wewak, as reserve troops for the Madang battle. MacArthur's fake campaign on Madang was working. It created the perfect scenario for a leapfrogging maneuver to fulfill his original directive. The Americans would leap past heavily garrisoned Madang to take the now less protected base at Hollandia. It was a risky operation in unpredictable New Guinea.

In the melee, on Thursday April 13, Len was once again ordered to strafe enemy encampments at Tadji Plantation and then to bomb the airstrips at Aitape. His gunner on that mission, Nathan Adler, recorded in his logbook that the experience was "rough." Images of Middlebrook's horrific experiences come to mind. Over Aitape the *Little Joe* approached its target from maybe twenty feet off the ground; anti-aircraft guns blasted back at her. Having delivered her payload, she darted up and away from her final target, clearing the surrounding treetops and out of the chaos—or so the men thought. Deadly black shells detonated all around in clouds of flak. Travelling at 280 miles per hour, gravity clutched at the men, tugging them backwards in their seats. As the A-20 rattled skywards, an explosion suddenly shattered the pilot's windshield into Len's lap; iron charred shrapnel and broken glass scattered into the cockpit. With no idea what further damage the *Little Joe* endured, for two anxious hours the harried pilot coaxed the machine back to base through constant gusts and storm. Miraculously, they themselves landed unscathed. Adler claims they "missed being killed by inches."[120] It is impossible to work out how they avoided death.

HOLLANDIA—THE TRIPLE PLAY

Since well before Octavius Stone's 1875-era visits, Europeans have found New Guinea's tropical climate to be dangerous. It is hot and humid all the year round. The average temperature on coastal plains exceeds ninety degrees Fahrenheit, and even in the higher mountain regions it can exceed eighty degrees. Located just south of the equator, the area's relative humidity is quite high, reaching 90 percent—difficult on men and machines. On an average summertime afternoon in Len's native Chicago, humidity was usually at an already highly uncomfortable and sticky 55 percent. This year-round heat and humidity, from seas to mountains, combined to create treacherous conditions.

And then there is the rain. Extreme variations in rainfall are tied to monsoons. At Gusap, for example, it rains on average twenty-two days each month from June through October, and close to eighteen days per month November through March. The variation comes in the volume: during June through October it rains 460 millimeters per month (over eighteen inches), while between November and May it rains 304 millimeters per month (almost twelve inches). For comparison, the United States National Weather Service at the time showed the wettest recorded single month ever in Chicago was August of 1885 when 286 millimeters of rain fell. And that record was not exceeded for 69 years, when in October of 1954 some 306 millimeters fell.

The western and northern parts of New Guinea experience the most precipitation where monsoon clouds gather in the equatorial seas and collide into the Bismarck Mountains, drenching the coasts. The clouds then thunder eastward, still heavy with moisture. Such typhoons commonly develop in New Guinea and cause heavy damage, including flooding, road erosion, and the clogging of rivers and estuaries.

The frequent non-combat-related misfortunes, the retraining of pilots, and the bringing in of fresh A-20s in February and March 1944 highlighted the grave risks to pilots flying in these wild, tropical conditions, while pushing the war further and faster. Even an experienced New Guinea pilot like Garrett Middlebrook frequently found, "As I approached the airstrip, a rainstorm as black as midnight blocked my approach. The cloud looked so angry and the air currents so turbulent."[121]

With the Japanese fooled into preparing for the continued, traditional, town-by-town Allied slog up the coast toward Madang, MacArthur anxiously ordered a massive knockout blow against Hollandia. Washington's deadline for taking Hollandia was ticking past. He was desperate to surprise the Japanese and leapfrog hundreds of miles further up the coast—by far his biggest leap forward yet. Len himself wrote, "It was a very important mission...because it was the final blow in the campaign known as MacArthur's Triple Play. The Triple Play was by-passing Wewak, Madang and Aitape [to take out Hollandia] which the Japs never expected."[122]

In that same correspondence, drawing on knowledge gleaned from the squadrons best intelligence reports Assistant Operations Officer Len Happ further described, "It was known we were going to operate [the A-20s] in the upper limits as far as gas and mileage were concerned. In addition, the weather forecasts were marginal."

On Sunday, April 16, at 07:00 a.m., Colonel Strauss briefed his men on the attack mission against Hollandia. The assistant operations officer would have designated who flew for the 389th, in what "flight" of planes and in which positions. To keep up MacArthur's diversion, Japanese in-harbor shipping was also to be bombed at nearby Hansa Bay that same day by other squadrons. The overall coordinated attack mission included other squadrons from multiple Allied bases in the region, totaling an estimated three hundred combat aircraft. Len wrote, "In fact the whole damned 5th Air Force and 3rd Attack" was in on the show (referring to the 3rd Attack Group of light bombers then based in New Guinea).

At this point in the war, the 5th Air Force had reconnaissance planes and crews trained specifically to fly weather routes ahead (hours ahead) of missions to determine the suitability or risk for flying. Len evaluated those intelligence reports with Lenny Dulac and shared his counsel with Major Wells and Colonel Strauss. It wouldn't be pretty. From the start of the mission crews could see bad weather building. And by now they had the experience to know that if it was bad in the morning, worse was to come from thunderstorms, which commonly broke on Gusap in the late afternoons and evenings. Compounding their anxiety, as Len wrote, was the location and length of their own runway.

The short strip ran almost perpendicular to the direction of the valley, and pilots had to contend with crosswinds blowing across the runway. Furthermore, the runway ran from the edge of the foot-hills out towards the valley. Pilots landed almost dive-bomber style from the precipice of the hillside. And they rarely took off towards the ridgeline, regardless of the prevailing winds.[123]

In other words, on a normal day, pilots had to descend steeply from the hills and fly through perpendicular crosswinds, which blew through the length of the valley, in order to land. On a normal day the pilots fought winds that gusted across that landing strip, constantly buffeting their take-off and landing runs and causing them to drift dangerously off course. On this Sunday, it was looking even worse than normal.

With the details of the mission explained and responsibilities delegated, the men left the operations tent, traveled down to their planes and prepared to take off. Winds jostled their aircraft as they sat in their cockpits await-ing their call from the control tower to proceed. Before "passenger rights" became a thing in modern day commercial civilian aviation, it was a com-mon frustration to board a plane, only to then have the pilot announce a delay that kept passengers sitting there, cooped up, on the runway, some-times for hours. Unbeknownst to many pilots on this Sunday morning, as they sat with their engines idling away, the mission was being reevaluated at headquarters due to the bad weather. Indeed, they were being delayed from their scheduled takeoffs as the brass argued with MacArthur about the via-bility of the missions in such weather. Fuel was being wasted as planes rum-bled in place, awaiting their "go."

Once the mission was authoritatively reconfirmed, planes continued to sit on the runway, burning fuel, waiting for a break in the clouds and final clearance from the control tower. Len wrote, "The weather forecasts were marginal...but we all took off because of the importance of the mission." Many pilots did not take off until eleven a.m.—a highly unusual four hours after their briefing meeting.

With the go-ahead given, off they flew toward Hollandia, bouncing low over the mountains and jostling above rain forests, in radio silence—a five-and-a-half-hour round trip, if they were lucky. They flew mainly by sight, or dead reckoning, over now familiar landscapes without modern GPS, some two hundred to three hundred feet off the ground to avoid detection. It was rough going out, and long.

Of the over two-hour flight to their target, Len wrote, "I was leading a flight of three aircraft. We were to drop 500 pounders with a B-25 loaned to the 389th Bomb Squadron and then hit the deck to strafe." (A-20s could carry a load of just over 24,000 pounds, the B-25 up to 35,000 pounds). In other words, they were to come in low and drop their bombs first. Then they were to loop back and return to the target to strafe, from 20 feet off the ground at a controlled 280 miles per hour. The targets were the enemy's anti-aircraft gun emplacements, supply areas, and parked airplanes.

Len's *Little Joe* in action over New Guinea.[124] One can see why military historians say the Plane "bristles" with armaments, guns protruding from the nose and from the gunner's bubble above, behind the cockpit. Bombs are stored in the belly. Len Happ photo.

The attack on Hollandia completely surprised the Japanese. Three hundred new planes on various runways were destroyed before they even got off the ground. Not one Allied plane was lost to Japanese counter maneuvers or anti-aircraft fire during the raid. However, within minutes after the raid there came trouble. As Assistant Operations Officer, Len had reported with uncomfortable insight on the unreliable A-20 gas gauge. Now, in tempestuous weather and after tarrying on the ground so long before the mission, he wrote, "The problem came when we all tried to get back to our respective bases, in our case, Gusap, with minimum gas and deteriorating weather."[125]

As the men knew by now, the unforgiving jungle over which they flew took no prisoners. The mountains they hoped to avoid either hug the shore line unpredictably from the water's edge, or rise up whimsically thirty miles inland, boiling like lava, surging three, five, eight, to beyond eleven thousand feet in height. The foreign mesmerizing beauty of the impenetrable granite was compelling to the point of being hypnotic. Rain forests below, drained by rushing convulsing rivers also drew the men in. And fear reminded them constantly that within that vast wilderness other natural enemies lay hidden—a grasping mesh with writhing, clinging pests and encroaching fluid diseases.

With sheer survival now at the top of their priority list after the bombing raids, the pilots reassembled their squadron formations and headed back to base. However, while they were engaged in their attack, a monstrous tropical storm had grown between them and their home base, Gusap. Intense equatorial heat ignited the mountains, bringing them to a steamy boil. Thick clouds rose and spilled into the valleys. The mass overflowed, inflating itself north to south, frothing across the island. After dodging the hail storm of Japanese flak, the pilots banked into a dark gray dragon of a storm, menacingly roaming with them, swiping at them, moving with them toward Gusap. They were on the west side of demonic, clawing weather, following it eastward. Len looked ahead but could see nothing but the darkness of night. At that moment "the whole damned Fifth Air Force and Third Attack" were terrorized, believing themselves to be flying in a vice grip between torrents of vicious rain and howling wind. The pilots knew by then that storms along that coast moved from west to east, and they concluded that they were either in the center or on the western edge of the storm. Along the Bismarck Mountain Range the storm drew moisture from the humid jungle and dumped it into what the men considered natural mile markers: the Sepik and Ramu River valleys. But the storm blotted them out.

Disoriented in the gurgling, turbulent clouds and low on fuel, many pilots lost their way, consumed in the grasp of the weather, never to be found again. Len knew of the potentially faulty gas gauge on his A-20 and fought like the devil to maintain calm and fight through the storm. In the journals of mission survivors are phrases like "a solid wall of weather" and "the sea was whipped into white caps by the wind." With the massive tropical storm blocking their return route home, Len and his squadron mates experienced exactly what Middlebrook had written of his missions a year earlier, when he described those turbulent clouds and "angry boiling currents," stating that he was frightened to fly near them, let alone through them.

In such circumstances, facing such weather, pilots were taught neither to fly through it nor under it—and in those days they couldn't get much above it (no oxygen). So they sought alternate routes around it, but to no avail. Early on in his tour of duty, Middlebrook stated categorically that the weather was as much of an enemy as the Japanese. Complications to blind instrument flying were multiplied by the twisting, churning weather. According to a lone newspaper account of the mission, published years later, poor visibility prevented the pilots from seeing the other planes in their formation. Citing interviews with pilots who survived the Hollandia mission, the article said planes became separated and in most instances pilots and crews were alone and on their own.[126]

While avoiding the upper peaks of the mountains where slate glistened purple like a fighter's bruise, Len glanced at his fuel gauge—it was heading toward E. In the mixing, swirling vortex of storm, wind, and rain, he had a flashback from training: it was of an examiner screaming at him and insulting him, inches from his face. That situation occurred during one of their flight school tests in an attempt to rattle the young cadet. The incident validated Len's own steadiness and cockpit demeanor under duress. While stressed, he had confidence in his ability to block out what was unnecessary and to think clearly in this horrific weather. On this frightful occasion, many pilots became disoriented and crashed into mountains or lost themselves out at sea. For other, fortunate pilots, survival of the five-hour mission would take up to seven hours.

Some forty years after the fact, and with the comfort of hindsight, Len drew upon his memory and wrote that

It became a little chaotic but Colonel Strauss was leading the 312th so we all felt safe. There came a point as I remember it when the Colonel gave instructions to head out on one's own if he wished [unprecedented permission to break formation]. Well, the options were not too many. The first option was to head for the northeast coast of New Guinea and down to Finschhaven and Saidor. This option was taken by most of the single engine aircraft with less gas than we had left. However, when these ships arrived at Saidor, the air was filled with empty gas tanks and aircraft were landing on the mat from both directions, too low on gas to go around ["go-around" in the sense of circling the base in another attempt to land].[127]

Len continued,

What occurred on Saidor comes to me first hand from a close friend of mine from my home town of Park Ridge, Illinois. He was in the Illinois National Guard, 32 Division, and had come to New Guinea via the Kokoda Trail. Before the mission on the 16th of April, I had flown up to Saidor several times to visit Bill Connor…he was in the tower getting a first-hand view of this chaos.[128]

The confusion from weather and low fuel forced some pilots to find places to down their aircraft safely elsewhere. According to that same article from *The Transcript* newspaper (Norman, Oklahoma), "[Experienced] pilots reported that some planes just disappeared. Others crashed into the mountains or into the sea.[129] Len noted,

Colonel Strauss took an option that saved my life and the lives of 16 other pilots. Strauss was leading 16 other aircraft in a loose formation—all looking for that hole in the clouds in the upper Ramu Valley just north of Gusap. Well, as I recall, [Ken] Hedges was the first one to announce on radio that he saw a hole in the clouds through which a view of the upper Gusap River became visible.... Well, let me tell you. At about that same time that hole became filled with A-20s headed for that glorious river. I remember being one of the first through that break in the clouds.

Moments later, I was sitting in my aircraft *Little Joe* at the end of the runway completely out of gas. My gunner by the name of Adler was out of his seat in a flash and alongside of me praising the Lord.[130]

Len kept a picture of Julia in his wallet. The seat of his pants was soaked with perspiration. He dug the wallet out, removed Julia's picture and kissed it, thinking, "We made it."

In the end, the storm's toll was devastating: the loss and destruction of thirty-seven US aircraft with their gunners and pilots. And many of the aircraft are to this day unaccounted for. It was known as the biggest Allied operational loss (as opposed to combat loss) in the Pacific War. According to *The Transcript*, "After landing, Ed Hambleton's crew chief checked the tanks of *Je Reviens* [his plane] and told his pilot, 'Lieutenant, the only gas you've got left is in the carburetors.'"[131] Pilot Lee Anderson's crew chief measured sixty gallons still remaining in his ship, *Lak-a-Nuki.*

At MacArthur's headquarters the Triple Play was considered a great success and a week later American troops landed at Hollandia almost without opposition. Another Allied army unit simultaneously landed against light opposition at Aitape. In this grand leapfrogging maneuver, MacArthur had split the enemy's defenses on New Guinea. Dependent on resupply from the sea, a large portion of the Japanese Army in the east (caught in the Madang fake) was now isolated and helpless, left to live on whatever supplies they had or could forage in the inhospitable jungles. In conjunction with control of the island of Los Negros back on March 5, the Americans had cut Japanese supply lines to their bases in New Guinea by their now virtual control of the Bismarck Sea.

In the immediate aftermath of the Allied troop landings, it was found that there had been over seven thousand of the enemy in and around Hollandia. It was discovered that most were logistics personnel, service technicians, or men assigned to communications units. Not more than one in ten of them even carried a rifle, which reinforced the assumption made by Japanese commanders that they were positioned a safe distance from Allied air power. Caught unawares, badly outnumbered, demoralized, and ill-equipped for battle, those Japanese that could, fled into the jungle in hopes of reaching friendly outposts 150 miles to the northwest.

After his part in the Battle of the Bismarck Sea about a year earlier, Middlebrook wrote of stepping aside from the party celebrating the success of that mission. As on more than one occasion, he admitted to having been lost in ethical battles and swimming in remorse. Similarly, it was this desire for a peaceful corner away from the constant swirl of war that would have driven Len to become the Assistant Operations Officer in the first place. It gave him some refuge, more time to himself. Better quarters, perhaps, certainly meetings and responsibilities, but more time to think and write, and less time pretending to celebrate.

While the men in his squadron kissed the ground and hugged each other, still shivering with panic and relieved that they emerged from the chaos and rot of certain death, Len would have quaked and quietly made his way to his wooden desk. He was tasked with writing up a mission report, detailing the performance of the machines and men; to summarize the intelligence by quantifying the destruction. Writing was therapy too. As the months wore on, Len learned to compartmentalize: he knew the effect of his actions—the bombs and strafing—"intellectually," but would not admit to considering the dead Japanese. His real self was just not capable of killing. He remembered months earlier when Wells, for example, shot down a Japanese bomber—not a pilot, not a Japanese man, per se, but a plane. Anyway, it was better not to think about it.

As at Buna and Finschhaven, and in fact throughout the whole of New Guinea, Australian soldiers would continue to do battle against those various pockets of Japanese forces long after the Americans had moved on. While the Americans advanced, the Australians were to take control of areas the Americans had bypassed, like Madang, mopping up the last of the Japanese resistance—still numbering in the thousands. What became known as the

Bismarck Archipelago Campaign would formally end for the United States in November of this same 1944. By the end of the campaign, fully developed American supply bases were completed and were operating inside of Japan's defensive perimeter in support of subsequent Allied operations.

At Gusap a Memorial Day Mass was hosted by Chaplain Clatus Snyder, and prayers were said for the then-revised total of thirty-one men who died and the sixteen men then considered missing in action. This memorial service was unique to the 312th. It is only in their histories and in their memories that the tragedies of this Black Sunday are recorded. In no other history of the New Guinea Campaign is there even a brief reference to those tragedies of April 16. Even in the many and gruesome ground battles, from Kokoda to Guadalcanal and the Coral Sea, theirs was a very high number of casualties for a single mission. Yet there is no other mention of it outside of the 312th. With the 5th Air Force and MacArthur pushing the war further and faster, they barely had time themselves to pay tribute to these fallen comrades. It was such a profound tragedy that, decades later, Len himself wrote, "Somehow, I could never understand how it was that this mission did not receive more publicity."[132]

CHAPTER 14

The Vogelkop Peninsula

Hollandia marks the halfway point along the immense north coast of the country that stretches 1,500 miles from Milne Bay on the Coral Sea in the southeast to the Vogelkop Peninsula and the Halmahera Sea on its far northwestern edge. That is more than twice the distance from London to Berlin. With a broad harbor, Hollandia served the Japanese as a distribution center for aircraft and supplies, located well inside their defensive perimeter—or so they thought. Some said at its peak the air base at Hollandia was nearly as powerful as Rabaul. It was so far within Japan's military web and so far away from Australia and Port Moresby that the Japanese had considered themselves safely out of range of US bombers. Taking Hollandia marked a milestone in the war to liberate Asia from the Japanese. For as far away as it was, it was positioned at the gates of their Southern Resource Area— the main Japanese objective for going to war—starting with New Guinea's Vogelkop Peninsula.

Japanese fleeing into the interior characterized the effects of MacArthur's leapfrog strategy. Throughout the war, the Australians discovered and attacked Japanese Army forces behind the advancing Allied lines. Back on April 12 for example, enemy troops were found to be within about twenty miles of Gusap. On April 20, the town of Bogadjim and the Japanese road through Shaggy Ridge to Lae had only just fallen to the Allies. On April

24 Madang fell to the Australian Army, who pursued fleeing Japanese troops miles into the jungle. Then, further north and west, on April 25, Alexishaven fell to the Aussies. And five hundred miles up the coast, on April 26 the Allied armies, pinching Hollandia from the north and south, joined together to enclose the base and rooted out the remaining resistance—just four days after the initial US troop landings.

The Japanese threat once reached Port Moresby. The style of warfare to fight them off, from Kokoda and Guadalcanal to the taking of Finschhaven in early 1944, epitomized battles of attrition. Japan's plan to buy time and wear the Americans down had been succeeding. An estimated twenty-four thousand Allied soldiers died, some seventeen thousand of which were Australian troops. All of that fighting over eighteen months, all the casualties and death, moved the battle lines in the Allies' favor just two hundred miles from Port Moresby to Lae. And much of that so-called progress was simply due to the Japanese repositioning of her troops, strengthening her defenses.

When the 312th arrived and the 5th Air Force was finally strengthened, the results came quickly. The statistics are amazingly clear: the progress made from Gusap to Hollandia, while costing upwards of nine thousand Allied air and ground losses, moved the battle line over five hundred miles in those first four months of 1944 alone. Kenney's pilots, trained to fly a support role for conventional ground troop movements, were now the vanguard leading the charge, and the troops followed in support of MacArthur's new strategy.

Located too far from their source of supply and now isolated to the point of starvation, Rabaul had failed to hold the Japanese defensive perimeter. Using air power to pry open the path ahead, MacArthur was breaching that perimeter and cutting off the Japanese from their homeland source of supply. At the same time, he was linking together his own supply chain of stepping stones from Australia westward across New Guinea and the Bismarck Sea. And on Black Sunday MacArthur's Triple Play came to epitomize the wisdom and daring of the leapfrog strategy made possible only by devastating air power.

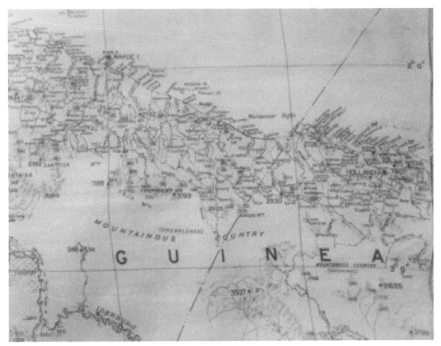

Wakde to the west (upper left) and Hollandia to the east (middle right) on Len's silk emergency survival map with vast areas vaguely marked "Mountainous Country (unexplored)."

FURTHER, FASTER

The Allies, now advancing quickly, had very limited knowledge of the Hollandia geographic area. An attempt to land a scouting party before the April 16 attack ended in disaster when the party ran into hostile locals who informed the Japanese of their presence. And the American pilots, flying missions in this sector of New Guinea, were using maps with vast swathes of the landscape completely blank, marked "unexplored."

Following on the April 22 troop landings, during the rest of April and the entirety of May, the 312th was engaged in "scrubbing," that is, strafing and bombing the vast Hollandia/Aitape and Wewak/Madang sectors. Because their planes could reach jungle enclaves where the army could not, the 312th was deployed to work backwards as it were, killing as best they could, the retreating, scattered remnants of Japanese Army troops, their numbers reaching into the thousands. Their missions targeted supplies and communications, including roads and bridges that could be used to facilitate various enemy regroupings, at places called Tadji Plantation (east of Aitape) and Dagua Airfield (west of Wewak), among others. On May 27, for example, Len led a flight with nine A-20s of the 389th to strafe Japanese troops gathered at a supply area named Wiriu Plantation southeast of Wewak. The men were to then bomb anti-aircraft positions at Boram Airfield, also near Wewak. In all of April, Len's 389th Bomb Squadron flew a total of sixteen combat missions, dropping 776 bombs. In May that number jumped to twenty-four missions over the thirty-one days of that month, dropping 1,237 bombs.[133] That is a lot of dangerous and aggressive flying as the 312th's five-hour missions were still all flown out of distant Gusap.

In May 1944 the men were awarded the Asiatic Pacific Theatre service ribbon for meritorious combat service against the enemy within the Asia Pacific Theater.

Hollandia would need to be made habitable for the arriving Americans. The bombing of Japanese airplanes, the demolition of supply areas, the cratering of the runways (to render them unavailable to the enemy for escape), made the base unusable. The work of moving the destroyed enemy aircraft, resurfacing the runways, moving the demolished trucks, and generally rehabilitating the base for the Americans began immediately. This work also included the construction of new headquarters from which General MacArthur would eventually conduct the next phase of the war.

Also at this time, Len was promoted to Operations Officer, dropping the "Assistant" designation. Within a week after its capture, by May 2, the airstrips at Hollandia were capable of accommodating C-47 cargo planes. In addition to combat duties, the pilots were called upon to deliver men and supplies for the reconstruction effort. Len wrote,

I flew a C-47, brand new with leather upholstery which was assigned to the 389th BS [bomb squadron] as a fat cat [cargo] ship. I flew it many times and have some hair-raising stories about it in weather, etc. on the route to and from [depots in Australia at] Townsville, Cairns, etc.[134]

The Hollandia area was judged to be secure by June 6. By the end of September reconstruction would come to include the army's largest overseas hospital facilities, partially supplied by the "tons and tons of quinine [the anti-malarial drug] and other medical supplies"[135] captured from the Japanese when the base was swarmed over by US troops.

WAR TACTICS EVOLVE

Because of the uncertain terrain, the strung-out locations of the enemy and the significantly increased Allied air activity, the American pilots coordinated closer two-way communications with Australian ground forces. The Allies agreed to special symbols, to be made out of any available material, rocks, tree branches, ripped-up parachute fabric, that could be made into big street signs. These signals to pilots overhead were a way to identify their ground positions or to coordinate attack routes and bombing runs. An arrow => indicated the direction in which troops were travelling,

L L L was the code that meant their ground operation was completed. The pilot above would tilt his wings side to side to indicate "message understood" or he would circle above to indicate that the message was not understood. Another innovation was implemented to better communicate to ground troops after the conclusion of a bombing and strafing run. In this instance an airplane would release red flares to indicate to the ground troops that they could resume their activities.

Starting in May, new types of missions for the A-20s were also introduced using different weights of bombs, dropped from higher altitudes. The A-20's combat success had been proven at twenty feet off the ground up to an altitude of one thousand feet, attacking fixed and known targets. Now, the newer bombs were to be dropped from five thousand feet upwards on more dispersed enemy platoons, hidden supply areas, and bridges. However, the military historians Hickey and Levy point out that the A-20 lacked an appropriate scope with which to identify a target from those heights.

Quoting a combat evaluation report written by Len on June 3, medium altitude bombing was an "unsatisfactory" way to use the A-20. He first stated that that the procedure would improve if the pilots had the A-20 with a plexiglass nose for bombardier operations. He then pointed out that there was often a time lag between when the B-25, with its heavier load, dropped its bombs and when the A-20s followed up. Len found that that lag resulted in "inaccurate coverage of [the] target." His conclusion was that when a B-25 was not available and an A-20 led the mission, there was no way for flight crews to check bombing accuracy from that altitude.[136] At those speeds and new altitudes, after the bombs of the first plane exploded, they could not see the detail of the target they were supposed to bomb.

Len at his roughed-out wooden desk as Operations Officer, 389th Bomb Squadron. He was twenty-five years old at the time. Len Happ photo.

WAKDE ISLAND

This was war. For all of the success the Americans enjoyed since the Quadrant Conference or the arrival of the Len Happ generation of pilots and weaponry, the Allies had advanced only halfway up the north coast of New Guinea. The taking of Hollandia allowed no luxury of boredom or apathy. General MacArthur's and General Kenney's attention immediately turned farther west. As such, "further, faster" came to mean moving not just the battle lines, but moving entire air bases farther westward. Doing so pushed the limits of our planes' endurance and their capacity to continue this strategy of leapfrogging deeper into enemy territory.

Good airfields with long enough runways that could handle the heavy size and variety of US Air Force aircraft were few and far between in the Southwest Pacific. Taking these prime airfields from the Japanese and reestablishing them for the 5th Air Force became MacArthur's primary objective. The Japanese bases on islands called Wakde and Biak became the next targets. But these bases, further west and north along the coast, were positions that the Japanese had early occupied, thoroughly supplied and into which they had dug themselves deeply—being on the edge of their Southern Resource Area. Bombing raids against Wakde by the 5th Air Force's A-20s began on April 28. Then after almost three weeks of softening up the enemy, and under air cover from those A-20s, Allied ground forces leaped the 125 miles farther west themselves and on May 17 hit the beaches to fight to secure this valuable airfield. The army landing forces met with heavy fire from concealed machine guns and mortar. Their missions were made all the more risky as they were carried out at long distances from Allied bases and sources of supply. Eventually, resistance did give out, and the Americans were able to secure Wakde by May 20.

Sansapor situated on the Vogelkop Peninsula. The waters below Biak and Noemfoor islands are Geelvink Bay. The arrows indicate army troop movements after the Air Force had paved the way.[137]

BIAK ISLAND

An 1824 treaty between the Dutch and the British Empires divided the island of New Guinea at a line north and south at about Hollandia (modern day Jayapura). The oil-rich western section became a part of the Dutch East Indies. In 1941 supplies of oil from these very same fields were kept from Japan because of her incursions into French Indo-China. Oil, vital to the Japanese economy and war machine, was found in abundance on the Vogelkop Peninsula. Controlling this area was one of the first goals of the Japanese.

Biak is strategically located in the entrance to Geelvink Bay. From that island Japan intended to keep enemy ships and planes from entering the bay and disrupting the flow of oil. The point of taking Biak for the Americans was for the same reason, to have good, well-positioned airfields from which to cover and dominate Geelvink Bay and the Vogelkop Peninsula. The fighting distance that MacArthur intended to leap from Hollandia was comparable to the distance from San Francisco to Los Angeles, some 350 miles to the west. And yet in that same time period (spring of 1944), Allied bombers in Europe were not flying more than 300 miles *round trip* from England to make harassing strikes against German targets in Normandy (in advance of the secret D-Day invasion of June 6).

As at Wakde, A-20 bombing raids from Hollandia against Biak started on the same April 28. The attack was then suspended because the weather was so fiercely turbulent and foul. Not until after a full four weeks of bombing could an amphibious force of US Army troops land on Biak Island (May 27), made under air cover from the 5th Air Force. After some initial progress, Japanese defenders there fought back ferociously to retain the island. But unlike Wakde and more like Kokoda, humid, tangled jungles, intermeshed with ensnaring bushes covered vast areas of the island. Here at Biak that tropical forest hid some eleven thousand Japanese soldiers found to be fighting from concealed caves and fortified bunkers. And again, like Kokoda, the US greatly misunderstood the difficulty of the terrain and equally underestimated the strength of their adversary. For those reasons, fighting devolved once again into a grotesque, conventional ground war.

The Japanese made a determined effort to reinforce and hold Biak Island—like at no other point in the New Guinea war. Early in June they assembled a naval force with the intent of taking out the supply ships and troop carriers fighting under MacArthur's direction. From bases in the Caroline Islands and the Mariana Islands, located north of the Bismarck Sea (and south of the Philippines), Japan sent naval forces to positions within striking distance of the Americans on Biak. The Japanese war department would soon realize this to have been a colossal strategic mistake. Through the spring of 1944, American forces sailing under the command of Admiral Nimitz had advanced across the Pacific Ocean just north of the equator. They sailed in the general direction of the Philippines, capturing strategic stepping-stone islands and potential air bases in groupings called the Gilbert Islands, the Marshall Islands, and the Mariana Islands. Following the Quadrant strategy, Nimitz also bypassed many Japanese bases and staging areas, leaving them behind, to "wither on the vine," cut off from their supply lines. Only at about the time of this Japanese naval repositioning to Biak did the Japanese recognize the presence of Admiral Nimitz's forces in the Mariana Islands. At headquarters in Japan, not detecting Nimitz's progress was considered a fiasco. Biak was vital to its defense of the Vogelkop oil fields, but inadvertently withdrawing forces that could have confronted Nimitz in seas strategically closer to the Japanese homeland, and closer to their power base in the Philippines, was considered an enormous blunder. Japan had left these strategic positions vulnerable. The Japanese high command believed it would have served their purposes better to attack Nimitz first and then reinforce Biak. By then they knew the war was trending against them. But they could not imagine such ineptitude by their subordinate commanders, allowing Nimitz to advance so quickly, unchallenged, in a speculative attempt to keep MacArthur out of Biak.

REPRIEVE IN AUSTRALIA

During the weeks that Hollandia underwent redevelopment and reconstruction, Nadzab became the logistical hub for the move west. Nadzab Air Base served mainly as a supply center with five landing strips. It could also receive goods and men by sea from Lae, some fifteen miles distant via overland routes. In early 1944 it became the headquarters for General Kenney and the 5th Air Force. By early June men were being temporarily moved out of Gusap and stationed at Nadzab in anticipation of moving "permanently" to Hollandia. From about this time, pilots returning from missions out of Gusap were instructed to return to base via Nadzab as the only base at which they could now refuel.

Sydney Leave Area Pass

HAPP, L.W.   1ST LT   0-663723   Air Corps
Name   Rank   Serial No.
                              Grade

has permission to be present on leave in Sydney, N.S.W., from ___MARCH 19___, 194_,

report to A.R.C. Service Bureau, ___a.m.___MARCH 26___194_. A.P.O.:_713-2_

Manifest ___46 TC No. 15___

E.B.

Per _____

Sydney Leave Pass, 1944.

After the frantic activity to secure Hollandia, and with plans being laid for the 312th's redeployment to that base, Colonel Strauss granted leave to several of his pilots, recognizing the need to refresh his war-weary crews. On June 10 Len departed for fifteen days in Sydney. It was a time of luxury and relaxation, safely away from the front lines and the threat of violence. While on leave he calculated the time difference and placed enthusiastic calls to Julia, shouting down primitive phone lines strung together across the depths of the Pacific and linked through America's Rocky Mountains up to Chicago. He wrote long, leisurely letters home to his parents while eating heartily, pen in one hand, fork in the other. Certainly his family read in the magazines and newspapers of the horrors of the Pacific theatre wars, but for his part, Len learned to compartmentalize those horrors. He wrote to his parents of getting "all the breaks" in his ever upbeat way:

> The New Guinea war is fast drawing to a close. Business on the islands has been good and I do all mine with my A-20, *Little Joe*. These A-20s are the sweetest ships in the Army Air Force. Since my arrival in this theatre I have had all the breaks and my chance to fly

the A-20 in combat is one of the best. For a period of two or three months our squadron operated with P-40s, also a very worthy ship. No doubt you have heard of the Triple Play in the Guinea war and the landings along the northern coast. Our outfit is in on all these shows, and prepares the way for the Navy knockout. Of course the rest of the Fifth Air Force gives us a hand. As squadron Operations Officer I am kept quite busy and the time is passing rapidly. I have fifty-five combat missions and over two hundred hours of combat time. It takes a lot of prayers to bring a fellow home all those times. I love flying more every day and have about eleven hundred hours [total hours flying including noncombat flying, such as cargo transport]. My duties provide for a lot of flying besides combat flying. We are always getting replacements to train and there are ships to test. We also have a B-25 in the squadron that we use on milk runs to Australia and for cross country flights.

I live in a modest shack here with a ground officer from Green Bay and a fellow pilot from Grand Rapids. Together we keep the joint up to the latest New Guinea fashion. Our greatest pride is our kitchen which we manage to keep pretty well stocked. Squadron mess is plenty good, but it's those midnight snacks we go for. We have a small Aussie gas stove to cook with. From [Port] Moresby we brought a stock of canned soups and meats. On my last leave in Sydney I brought back 10 lbs of Kraft cheese and two lbs of fresh coffee. Grilled cheese sandwiches are now my specialty. From nearby native gardens we get cocoanut and such fruits as bananas, limes, pineapple and pan pan (like our musk melons). In a village farther distant the natives raise pretty fair coriander and the squadron has had one meal of corn on the cob from their fields. It was a real treat. Mail and fresh meat has been coming in rather slow, as the transports are pretty busy elsewhere.

There is a volume I could write on life over here and life on the continent of Australia. Since this letter is almost a book itself, I will save some for next time. It will be a happy day when we in service will free ourselves from the web which spider war has woven around our more wholesome endeavor.

Say hello to the gang for me.

Sincerely,

Len

Recognizing the need for secrecy, Len was remarkably glib about exactly from where and with whom he was operating.

At the end of his leave while in Australia, Len was ordered to pick up supplies for the move west. He enjoyed his time in Australia. In decades later correspondence Len recalled time spent in Brisbane and wrote, for example, of being granted, "honorary membership in the United Service Club of Brisbane...We were treated royally."[138] Such clubs and bars would have been celebrating the recent news from Europe of the liberation of Rome. Since landing on mainland Italy in September of 1943 the Allies there were initially bogged down by German and Italian forces. Battling 450 miles northward over nine months in traditional ground warfare, they overtook the capital on June 5—twenty months since Patton first arrived in French North Africa.

Records show that on June 28 Len was in Adelaide, 1,000 miles southwest of Brisbane, on orders to ferry aircraft from APO 925 (Adelaide, Australia) to APO 565 (Hollandia, New Guinea). He started out from Brisbane flying west over the tumble of interconnected mountain ranges known as the Great Dividing Range. It was an almost carefree, four-hour flight over the most geographically diverse corner of the planet he had ever traveled in his already full life. He crossed over pastel-colored mountains before reaching the central tablelands of New South Wales. Far from the threat of counter-attack, he traveled over the country in the way he loved to fly—blue sky above, or CAVU as he would write (Ceiling And Visibility Unlimited), with time to sort through his duties and his life. He crossed over randomly strewn mining towns, rain forests, swampy wild grasslands and eventually found the Torrens River leading into Adelaide, far to the south and west on the Gulf of St. Vincent.

On June 30 Len made a pickup in Melbourne, Area Command Two, Base Seven. It was just a short two-hour flight east from Adelaide. He then continued north and refueled in Brisbane, flying on again via distant Townsville, making his way further north to Nadzab and Hollandia. The further north he flew, the stronger the anxiety, stress, and actual threat.

NOEMFOOR ISLAND

By about July 1 a skeleton crew of the 312th was set up in wet and marshy Hollandia. In the weeks to follow, all aspects of the group, including Len's 389th squadron, would be reconsolidated there. While possessing an excellent harbor, the contours of the surrounding terrain and the erosion resulting from frequent heavy rainfalls made roads nearly impassable. Eventually water that did not flow back to the sea drained inland to nearby Lake Sentani. Scattered, grass-covered flatlands were made suitable for the pilots' quarters. Individual two- to three-man tents were set up about two miles from one of Hollandia's three airstrips, that being Cyclops Air Strip (as the seven-thousand-foot Cyclops Mountains run through Hollandia parallel to the coast). On his initial tour through the muggy area, the group flight surgeon "Doc" Walsh ordered dilapidated and vermin-infested latrines and former Japanese supply houses be burned to the ground. Surrounding jungles supplied abundant lumber for the rebuilding effort.

In sharp contrast to the idyllic ease of leave, the maelstrom around Len was deafening during those weeks he was away. While he was in Australia, Len's 312th Bomb Group struck Sorong Airfield on the far western tip of the Vogelkop Peninsula. Fifty enemy planes were destroyed. And by June 25 another 140 Japanese were killed, with 850 reported sick and wounded, at an airfield called Sarmi, located on the northwest coast of New Guinea near Wakde. And still there was fighting on Biak.

The massive distribution of Japanese forces defending Biak was unexpected, and the US Army's gruesome cave-to-cave battle to secure control of the airfields there continued. Ignorance of the terrain, as first experienced at Kokoda and repeated most recently by that unfortunate landing party at Hollandia, was again stymieing General MacArthur's already unreasonable expectations of quick success. At certain points along the Biak beaches, cliffs protruded to the sea from which the Japanese could take aim at platoons of Allied troops. American field commanders pushed their men to battle more vigorously and to seek the high ground. Reinforcements were sent in, Sherman tanks were deployed, but still progress was too slow for MacArthur. The clock was ticking. It was taking much longer than MacArthur anticipated, and becoming costlier. The delay was jeopardizing his overall war planning. Out of frustration he replaced field generals, demanding more progress.

With the urgency to secure a strategic, usable base faster, MacArthur ordered the Americans to attack further west of Biak and in fact capture a fifteen-mile wide by twelve-mile-long island called Noemfoor. It was located sixty miles west of Biak and sixty miles further into the enemy's resource zone—and almost 450 miles west of Hollandia. The plan there was to first take out as many enemy positions as possible by air, then deploy the necessary ground and naval forces for an invasion from the sea. Following that, they were to then reinforce the troops with paratroopers and finally to reconstruct the airfields. When repaired of battle scars, the island would be able to accommodate America's heaviest planes.

The 389th brought the devastating attack to Noemfoor on July 1. Their work immediately reduced enemy opposition to the American troops who landed there the following day. Forty-one C-47s dropped in units of paratroopers on day three of the attack. Unfortunately, in the scramble to advance rapidly, little-trained and poorly piloted, the first wave of planes dropped men from a life-threatening 175 feet off the ground, giving their parachutes tragic little time to open. Of the total 740 men dropped in, seventy died horrific deaths and thirty suffered severe bone fractures upon impact. The next wave got it better, dropping their paratroopers from the planned 400 feet.

Paratroopers landing on Noemfoor, July 1944.[139]

Facing the overwhelming Allied attacking force, many Japanese fled to the interior of the island. Reconnaissance photos taken by the 389th on the fourth day show landing strips to be evacuated and void of targets. On July 5 the Japanese mounted a counter-attack, but they were overcome by Allied forces. By August 31, after two full months of fighting, seventeen hundred Japanese had been killed in the battle. It took two months to ferret the enemy out of their bunkers and caves and to capture the tiny island. One can only imagine the horrors to come as the Allies approached the Japanese mainland.

THE DRINIUMOR RIVER

Back in March, as preparations to attack Hollandia began, MacArthur put on the Madang fake, causing the Japanese to redeploy troops back to the Madang area. In their haste and excitement, the Allies encountered, then lost track of multitudes of Japanese escaping from those Allied diversionary assaults. Those scattered Japanese, in fact, regrouped and traveled west to wretched safety up the Sepik River. Left behind the rapidly advancing battle line and east of the leapfrogging Allies, the enemy regrouped under their general, named Adachi. He ordered what grew to be fifteen thousand orphaned soldiers to move northwest from the Wewak area under the cover of jungle and clouds of mosquitoes, to where they expected to reach the Japanese base in Aitape. Sick and starving, with little or no provisions, these brave and loyal men made the unimaginable 350-mile trek through tangled brush and swamp, even managing to haul artillery.

Arriving in early July, they were in turn completely stunned to find Americans along the Driniumor River. Isolated behind the lines as he was, General Adachi had no way of knowing that by then the Americans had reached and overtaken Hollandia. Facing just the slimmest chance of victory, he urged his men to undertake a final attack to achieve what they could for their country. On July 10 the Japanese surprised US troops who were scouting randomly in the area to clear and maintain a buffer zone south of Aitape. The violent confrontation triggered a horrific battle. General Adachi advanced with five thousand troops, holding ten thousand back as reserves, waiting their turn to be called forward. The two opposing forces fought in thick jungle, in a manner that the Americans long hoped to avoid. With limited supplies and with starving soldiers, Adachi managed to force a ferocious back-and-forth battle. Allied reinforcements were called in. Ultimately, General Adachi struggled to get what men he could out of the Driniumor area and lead them back toward relative safety under the cover of jungle toward Wewak.

The Allies lost over 600 men with 175 wounded. Eighty-five men went grimly missing trying to find their way around the confusing tangle of swamps and jungle. By August 25 the battle of Driniumor River was considered over. It is estimated that General Adachi lost almost 8,000 valiant men in the fighting, but his troops were overwhelmed as well by disease and from starvation in this chance meeting.

PRIME MINISTER TOJO

The war was not going well for the Japanese. Even Len understood this, writing previously, "The New Guinea war is fast drawing to a close." And in fact, the Japanese sensed it too. As much as the Americans underestimated the severely constricting terrain on Biak Island, and how the Japanese successfully used it to their advantage, many in Japan believed that their naval forces blundered by not stopping US Admiral Nimitz in the open Pacific. That whole series of events leading up to the invasion of Biak, then threatening their oil flow, so seriously weakened Prime Minister Tojo that on July 18, 1944 he and his cabinet were forced to resign.

Prime Minister Tojo's personal rise personifies the rise of the modern Japanese nation. He had guided the country through critical times in the strengthening of the Empire. Through the attacks on Pearl Harbor, the flushing out of General MacArthur and the conquest of the Philippines, he celebrated the eviction of the British, Dutch, and French from their colonies and the securing of the Southern Resource Area. For a moment in time they ruled the Pacific. But by the summer of 1944 the Americans were upon them.

Len Happ decorated with the Air Medal. Len Happ photo.

Since Len's generation of pilots arrived, the 5th Air Force and MacArthur's frantic pace of action had not been stopped. As Prime Minister Tojo fell from power, on that same July 18, American pilots in New Guinea were awarded the Air Medal for combat missions flown during December 15, 1943 to May 15, 1944.

BOELA, THE SOUTHERN RESOURCE AREA

The key product of Japan's Southern Resource Area was oil. And General Kenney was now within striking distance—just barely—of the Japanese installations where they were exploiting and defending this valuable resource. In July, Len led one group among seventy-five A-20s to strike at an oil field and depot called Boela on Ceram Island west of the Vogelkop Peninsula. From the base at Hollandia, the target was some five hours distant (about the time it takes a modern day commercial jet to reach Seattle from Boston). In this unique mission, the squadrons actually overnighted part way to the target, nervously sleeping and refueling on still-contested Biak. Two planes from Len's 389th were shot down on this mission.

Liberating the oil fields of Boela, July 14, 1944. Note the A-20 emerging from the black smoke left, oil rigs in the bay right. Len Happ photo.

"EMPTY COTS AROUND"

Towards the end of June, Nadzab also developed a Combat Replacement Training Center. Such replacements would need to be trained in the unique aspects of fighting with the A-20 in the ominous weather and over the uncharted jungles of New Guinea. One such replacement pilot came to be assigned to Len's 389th Bomb Squadron, Joseph Rutter, who wrote a memoir about his time in the service. Through Rutter we get another very real sense of life on the ground and in the air during this time in Hollandia.

On July 27, 1944, after precombat training at Nadzab, Rutter was ordered to join his new combat group, the 389th Bomb Squadron, stationed at Hollandia. He immediately noted that "the 312th had lost five crews during its July operations and replacements were urgently needed."[140] When Rutter first arrived, he was told to find a bed in one of the shared tents. When directed to a tent with a couple of empty cots, he was informed that one belonged to Albert Eddy, then on leave in Sydney, and the other, he was told "is empty." Rutter wrote,

> Walter Van, we soon learned, had occupied the other cot until he failed to return from a mission to Babo in western New Guinea on July 9. The 389th Squadron had lost three planes on the Babo mission, hence the need for crew replacements…there were empty cots around.[141]

As MacArthur extended the battle lines so far forward, the air corps was undertaking low-level attack missions in lieu of traditional ground forces. Such assaults extended to locations where the Army could not reach, in areas supply lines could not support. Babo is located 450 miles from Hollandia on New Guinea's Vogelkop Peninsula. Len was one of twenty-three A-20s flying a low-level attack mission against Japanese supplies positioned there. Those supplies were protected by an estimated fifty anti-aircraft gun emplacements surrounding the base. During the bombing mission Colonel Strauss's plane was riddled with enemy gunfire but stayed aloft. Eight other aircraft were reported damaged by hellish flak explosions.

Sadly, another three A-20s were fatally hit by anti-aircraft fire; each crashed, killing their three pilots and two of their gunners. Miraculously, the third gunner was plucked out of the sea by American rescue operations.

COMBAT EVALUATION

Reflecting on the loss of comrades from the Babo and Boela missions, Len, as Operations Officer, repeated an admonition made in April when he wrote up a combat evaluation report urging primarily greater discipline, but now also urging tighter formations and closer coordination among pilots. But here, striving to improve squadron efficiency to avoid future losses, he more concretely appealed for a strategic change:

> Boela, was an entirely different type of target. First, starting from Biak shortened the flight and made the crews more alert. Second, open targets like the oil facilities are easier to hit. Having a clear view of the area gives the crews more time to line up on the targets of opportunity. The speed of the A-20 minimizes our casualties, but reduces the effectiveness of bombing unless the strikes are against open targets…8 to 15 second delay detonators require the aircraft to execute their runs at 20 to 30 second intervals, whereas, if a delay of 6- to 8- seconds were used, then the time over the target would be cut in half.[142]

To reiterate generally, if pilot one drops a delayed fuse bomb on the target, it explodes eight to fifteen seconds later. That means pilot two should not pass over the target until the sixteenth second. If pilot one drops a bomb with a delayed fuse of six to eight seconds, pilot two can pass over the target starting at the ninth second. Remember that the idea is to not get blasted with the debris from the previous explosion as happened to that poor pilot at the end of Middlebrook's duty. In Len's second example, pilot two is flying away seven seconds earlier as compared to the then current practice. Less time over the targets means less time in the sights of anti-aircraft gunners.

KOKAS

An amazing sequence of photos, which capture what the pilots of the 312th faced in New Guinea as clearly as anything, was found among Len's records. They are more descriptive than much of the written history on the Pacific War.

On July 22 Colonel Strauss led the 387th Bomb Squadron on a mission similar to the July 9 attack on Babo: a dangerous, lowlevel assignment, this time to bomb a Japanese seaplane base with supply transport barges in port at a town called Kokas. It is located in Sekar Bay, forming part of McClure Gulf, on the southwest coast of the Vogelkop Peninsula.

After the long inland flight toward the south and west, they bobbed low over a series of mountains in order to surprise their enemy and descended toward the harbor to drop their 250-pound bombs and to strafe anti-aircraft gun positions. As they departed the area with the job done, one plane, piloted by First Lieutenant James Knarr with Staff Sergeant Charles Reichley as gunner, was hit by flack, caught fire, and rolled to the right. Out of control, the A-20 plunged into the bay.

The descriptive images give an idea of how low the squadron was flying and at what speed, 280 miles per hour, by how quickly Knarr impacts the water and how quickly his plane crashes. One second separates each click of the camera, memorializing each dramatic frame of the action. It warrants emphasizing that his A-20 weighed fifteen thousand pounds when empty, was over seventeen feet in height and forty-seven feet in length. The wingspan measured just over sixty-one feet. Before our eyes we see this enormous machine shatter upon impact with the sea, disintegrating.

(Below left) The black clouds of smoke above and beneath the pilot indicates flak, which sent shrapnel bursting into Knarr's A-20. Smoke is already visible from under his plane. (Right) Catching fire, Knarr's A-20 tilts to the right. His right wingman (viewer's left) speeds away from the target area, his bomb doors still open.

Kokas one.

Kokas two.

Len Happ photos.

(Below left) Out of control, Knarr's A-20 plunged into the bay. The camera angle caught Knarr's left wingman then passing through the scene, speeding from the hostile target area, bomb doors still open. (Below right) The A-20 shattered on impact, killing him and his gunner, Charles Reichley. Knarr's left wingman speeds away from the target area.

Kokas three.

Kokas four.

Len Happ photos.

It was a five-hour round-trip mission from Hollandia. The three other planes landed back at Hollandia with damage from bullet holes and shrapnel. Shockingly and tellingly, none of the other pilots or crewmen saw Knarr's plane get hit or go down. As Middlebrook noted during his time in combat, these missions required all the concentration they could muster to calculate and navigate a course: fly for hours, often blind (on instruments) over hostile uncharted mountains and jungle, then dive down to twenty feet off the ground, drop bombs, shoot, kill, and get shot at, maneuver away from anti-aircraft fire and flak bursts, and then regroup into formation for another pass at the target before the flight back home.

This sequence of photos was taken automatically from another plane. Cameras were activated when that pilot's bombs were released as a way to later assess bombing success against the targets. In this instance, it was Knarr and Reichley's drama of death that was caught in the lens.

AGAIN, DISCIPLINE

Shortly after arriving in Hollandia as a "replacement" pilot, Second Lieutenant Rutter met Colonel Strauss. Strauss was already known to his new pilots as being extremely competent in leading his men on missions. He was considered more professional, more thorough, and safer to fly with than others. And Strauss got to know his airmen by having them fly "wing" with him once or twice. At the end of July, Colonel Strauss asked Len to train Rutter on flight procedures at Hollandia. Rutter recorded in his memoirs,

> The following morning, Lt. Happ, the Operations Officer, took…me [Rutter] on a familiarization formation flight around the Hollandia area. He also checked me out on the procedures the group followed related to joining up, formation flying, and peeling off for landing. [For example the] traffic pattern at Hollandia was uniformly clockwise from west to east…. We made a second formation flight on August 1, this one with the entire squadron, for further indoctrination.[143]

When Major Wells returned from leave several days later, Rutter was informed that he and another new arrival were to report to him without delay. They reported to the major's tent,

> …the tent he [Wells] shared with "Doc" Walsh, and Lieutenant Happ. We knocked on the screen door of the CO's tent and announced to Lieutenant Happ that we had come to report our presence in his squadron to Major Wells. It must have sounded by our tone that we

were paying a social call, for Leonard Happ wore a serious expression as he invited us to enter.[144]

In short, Rutter flubbed the introduction and was way too casual for Wells's comfort. Indeed, he attempted to shake Wells's hand rather than salute him. Rutter wrote,

> The look of distaste on Major Wells's face immediately told me I had made a serious mistake.... My only avenue of recovery was to slowly withdraw my hand, assume the position of attention, and hope somebody would say something—maybe about the weather.[145]

The major continued the meeting by asking detailed questions about his training and flight time in an A-20. The lieutenant continued,

> He lectured us on the necessity of sharp formation flying, the maintenance of discipline when hitting a target, and so forth—all without a smile. Lieutenant Happ seemed to save us from more of the Major's philosophy of command by saying he had already checked us out on formation flying and the procedures followed at Hollandia. When he finally dismissed us, we were happy to withdraw. I was careful to exhibit a more military manner in departing, including a crisp salute. Major Wells would be somewhat difficult for me to deal with in the months that followed.[146]

Wells had cause to be "difficult" with Rutter's casual attitude. This work took focus and concentration, otherwise you could die and take your poor gunner down with you. Wells very well may have still been brooding about the two planes of the 5th Air Force that were shot down on July 2. Even missions that destroyed forty new enemy planes were tainted when there were losses like this.

Dishearteningly, on August 11, Wells's longtime friend since their Savannah training days and counterpart in the 388th Bomb Squadron, Major William Pagh and another plane in his group were shot down by what was called a "terrific hail of flak." They failed to evade anti-aircraft positions over yet another staging/logistics airstrip called Utarom, on Kamrau Bay, south of Biak. Pagh, besides being the Commander of the 388th, was the flight leader on this mission. In disciplined military order, after he went down as the lead plane on that first pass, the remaining planes flew out over the bay, circled back to the airfield, and in single file, continued their mission to bomb and strafe the airfield.

Colonel Strauss, supported by Major Wells, put forth a recommendation and in Special Orders Memorandum Number 265 from General MacArthur in Brisbane, Len was promoted from first lieutenant to captain. Major Wells was, himself, just back from leave when Len's promotion came through and was still feeling grumpy toward Rutter. On September 7, 1944, the replacement pilot made a rough landing and broke a strut (part of the landing gear), whereupon Wells abruptly called out, "Rutter, you're grounded!" Len tried to patch up the situation. According to Rutter,

> After a couple of days, Leonard Happ, the squadron operations officer, suggested that I talk to the Major and ask to be put back on flying status.[147] Happ apparently took it upon himself to untangle the impasse created by my bullheadedness. At supper that evening he announced that he would check me out for flying the following morning. The three days of uncertainty I had endured seemed like three weeks and I welcomed Len's intercession on my behalf. On September 10 we went down to the strip and Happ made a circuit of the field with me lying on the deck behind him observing. Then we traded places and I took his plane around the pattern one time while he observed. In the smooth morning air I had no problem demonstrating that I did not always bounce my landings. Happ did notice that my 120 mile per hour approach speed was slower than he used and suggested that 130 might be better. The higher speed on the final [approach] did provide better control, a logical suggestion that I should have adopted on my own since the plane was somewhat heavier than those we had flown at Charlotte [North Carolina flight school training]. Although the incident was over, I suspected that Major Wells would not soon forget.[148]

THE GREATEST AIR FORCE VICTORY IN HISTORY

The Americans were now attacking and liberating the western part of New Guinea. This was one of many mineral-rich areas found throughout the former Dutch East Indies. Centuries-old Dutch place names abounded, staring with Hollandia and Noemfoor, for example. The Japanese had conquered and evicted the Dutch from here within the first weeks of 1942 following Pearl Harbor. Now in August of 1944, after weeks of intense bombing beforehand, and while still bogged down at Biak, Americans landed fresh fighting troops at beaches called Amsterdam and at Middleburg Island, all on the west coast of the Vogelkop (Dutch for "Bird's Head" because of the peninsula's shape). In this scattered burst of aggression, specifically on August 6, Australians reported that Japanese were fleeing various strongholds in Geelvink Bay and the Vogelkop Peninsula region. Japanese resistance on the peninsula regrouped at a port called Manokwari. The Allied forces chose to attack them there via undefended beaches near Sansapor, taking that location by the end of August and eventually isolating some twenty-five thousand Japanese on the Peninsula.

This was the most valued, most strongly defended area of Japan's conquests. Oil was found there in abundance. According to the historian Harry Gailey, "[Commanders in] Washington had looked at the region and projected production of as much as sixteen thousand barrels a day."[149] It was natural resources like this for which the Europeans originally came and colonized; it was why the Japanese had come to replace the Europeans as masters. With the isolation of those twenty-five thousand Japanese troops, it became the final enemy stronghold in all of New Guinea. Here, the arrival of the US Air Force marked the beginning of the end of the colonial economic system as called for by Roosevelt's Atlantic Charter.

Sukarno, the Indonesian Nationalist party leader, had strengthened his power base and unified the country under Japanese supervision. While there was still plenty of fighting ahead for the independence movement, Sukarno now watched the Allies approach. Japan was clearly losing the war, but still had the manpower to carry out their strategy of delaying the Allied advance.

The Japanese government, as well as its Imperial Army and Navy, showed no sign of capitulation or surrender. In a thinly veiled act to further co-opt the Indonesian leader, on September 7 the Japanese prime minister publicly promised to fulfill the country's long sought desire for independence (but without giving a framework or proposing a timetable). Seeing a Japanese capitulation in the making and finding that his goal may be within reach, Sukarno quietly organized and prepared local militias to repulse a Dutch attempt to reclaim power once the Japanese were gone.

Contemporaneously, the rest of Geelvink Bay was subdued by mid-August and MacArthur finally proclaimed the end of organized resistance on Biak Island. Battle operations there came to a halt by August 20, 1944. But the cost was high. Along with the 3,000 American soldiers lost were upwards of 7,200 sick from malaria, fever, typhoid, and rashes from the sweltering fight just below the equator.

Two operations early in the campaign showed that because of the impenetrable terrain, New Guinea was understood to be an air campaign: the spring of 1942 plan to parachute troops and supplies into the Kokoda Trail battle, aborted due to lack of planes; and the successful September 5, 1943 paratroop drops into Nadzab. Were it not for a robust air corps, those commanders of land-based forces, and America's noble infantrymen would have had to fight it out, as Japan hoped, in infinitely more difficult conventional combat. It was truly the first war of its kind and became the most successful demonstration of the use of air power in the history of the United States Air Force.

Limited to just 15 percent of America's wartime production, Kenney's pilots and crewmen gave birth to McArthur's brilliant strategy of leapfrogging past enemy strongholds to cut them off from their source of supply. Having established air superiority in this enormous theater, those forces now roamed in relative ease from the Coral Sea, through the Bismarck Sea and into the Halmahera Sea—the fifteen-hundred-mile length and four-hundred-mile breadth of New Guinea.

Since D-Day in Normandy the Allies were advancing and the US Air Force in Europe was, by August of 1944, weakening Nazi Germany. But, in applying the greater 85 percent portion of their industrial might and trained manpower, the Americans had not yet pushed Germany even out of tiny Belgium (achieved in February 1945). Almost concurrent with Biak, Paris was liberated on August 25, 1944. But the distance from air bases in the UK to Paris was not even 250 miles, when General Kenney's pilots were regularly flying twice that distance and more to their targets, under much worse weather conditions, with fewer planes and less equipment, facing menacing anti-aircraft rebuttals from deeply dug and hidden enemy fortifications.

PREPARING THE LIBERATION OF THE PHILIPPINES

The accomplishments of MacArthur's forces since early April brought him then to about nine hundred miles southeast of the Philippines. The General's humiliating retreat from the Philippines in 1942 hid his deep anxieties about this next phase of the planning, and motivated his desire to accelerate the hectic "further, faster" pace of the war. Confident in their control over this sector, MacArthur moved his base almost two thousand miles from Brisbane to Hollandia in September. The vast bay and her three runways were to become his grouping point and eventually his launching pad for his campaign to take back the Japanese-held Philippines.

Also in September of 1944, as a stepping-stone along that long route, Allied troops occupied Morotai Island, the northernmost island in the Halmahera Sea, northwest of New Guinea. This base put MacArthur only a few hundred miles from the Philippines. Located in the Molucca (Maluku) Islands group, northwest of the Vogelkop Peninsula, it was settled by the Portuguese in the 1600s, then claimed by the Dutch in the 1700s. Well within the Japanese Southern Resource Area, these islands are the original so-called "Spice Islands," as named by the Europeans colonizers who exploited them as a rich source of timber, wood resins, coconut, cocoa, cloves, nutmeg, and coffee.

Reflective of their great accomplishment, since about the time of Len's leave in mid-August, we start to see the reintroduction of the robust term FEAF which was the pre-Pearl Harbor name of the US Air Corps in this region: the Far East Air Force, with Kenney as its commanding general. Use of the term was discontinued when the Japanese overran the Philippines. But here, Len's leave orders of August 13 were granted "under the provisions of FEAF." It was a sign of the Air Force's growing strength and confidence.

With plans now being made for battle in the Philippines, MacArthur issued unusual terms of engagement dated September 18, 1944. The men were to sign this order, stating rank and date, confirming their understanding of the memo.

Subject: Restrictions on Aerial attack in Philippine Islands.

To: All Flying personnel [Hollandia]

IT MUST BE UNDERSTOOD BY ALL THAT THE LIBERATION OF THE FILIPINOS IS ONE OF THE PROPOSALS OF THE PHILIPPINES CAMPAIGN. LIBERATION WILL NOT BE UNDERSTOOD BY THE FILIPINOS IF THEIR POSSESSIONS, THEIR HOMES, THEIR CIVILIZATION AND THEIR LIVES ARE INDISCRIMINATELY DESTROYED TO ACCOMPLISH THIS. THROUGHOUT THE FAR EAST OUR MORAL STANDING AND HUMANITY DICTATES THAT DESTRUCTION OF PROPERTY AND LIVES IN THE PHILIPPINES BE HELD TO THE MINIMUM IN OUR MILITARY CAMPAIGNS COMPATIBLE WITH THE INSURANCE OF SUCCESS. [In other words, kill the enemy, not the Philipinos] OUR ATTACK OBJECTIVES ARE PRIMARILY SHIPPING AND AIR FIELDS IN THE LATTER AREAS, NOT BARRACKS, VILLAGES OR METROPOLITAN AREAS.[150]

ALL THOSE GUNNERS

The Air Corps was still operating officially under the Commanders' Choice policy for rotating men in and out of combat zones. Still, rotation out of combat remained ultimately contingent on war plans, available replacements and overall unit strength. At the time MacArthur was preparing to liberate the Philippines, many men were finishing their tours of duty and new replacements were continuing to pour into Hollandia. It was a time of ongoing regrouping of veterans with new men, and of resupplying stocks of war materials with fresh equipment.

On October 3 Len was ordered by Colonel Strauss to "proceed by military aircraft" with five other pilots to APO 922 (Townsville). They were to pick up new A-20s. The authority calling for the mission was referred to as General Kenney's "V Bomber Command." On October 16 similar orders were given to Len, First Lieutenant Donald Dyer and six other pilots, all sent to make similar pickups in Townsville. The orders sounded routine. But nothing in New Guinea, as Len had learned, was without danger. Every physical segment of the flight route was its own demon, resisting intrusion by the pilots, and consequently marked with red flags and warnings. The Japanese may have been cut apart, if not largely eliminated, but relentless threats from the hostile weather remained.

And such trips, arduous and stressful as they were, did not add to one's tally of combat missions. The flight may have carried men over contested battle zones, but it was not a combat mission if transport was the objective. And the crews flew upwards of three or four times as many transport missions as combat missions. Rutter tells more about these seemingly mundane transport missions in the following episode:

> The morning of October 11 was overcast at Hollandia and it threatened to be a day of steady rain. We were eating breakfast at the 389th mess when Len Happ, the Operations Officer, asked Lt. Albert Eddy if he was going to take the squadron's B-25 to Nadzab that morning. There were a number of gunners and pilots in the 312th Group who had completed their missions and were going to Nadzab to await transportation back to the States. Having looked at the lead-colored sky with low, smoky scud, and a gusty wind from the southwest portending changing weather, I was surprised when Eddy said, "Oh sure, we can get down there okay."

Perhaps because of the burden of combat experience or because of fatigue from threats endured, some pilots, nonchalantly, came to believe their jobs to be routine and that they had done this all before. Rutter continued,

> Happ also seemed a little surprised by Eddy's offhanded reply, but he looked around the table for a copilot to go with Eddy. Having judged by the weather that it was no morning to go anywhere, I concentrated on my dehydrated eggs and fried Spam. For reasons now lost in time, probably from flying his wing on a mission or two, I was not impressed by Eddy's style or his competence in a B-25. I hoped that Happ would not notice me and felt a wave of relief when he assigned Flight Officer Ralph Preston, a new man, to go along as copilot.

> A 388th Squadron B-25 was also taking some passengers to Nadzab that morning, and Captain Happ, with Don Dyer as copilot, was flying the group's C-47 to the same destination with some additional passengers and to pick up cargo.[151]

That B-25 of the 388th was piloted by Walt Hill. He carried ten pilots who had finished their tours and were destined to return to the States. Lieutenant Eddy carried ten gunners, men who had aspired to be pilots, but whose course in flight school training slotted them into gunnery. They, too, now after their months of training and surviving the worst of war, had notched their sixty missions, completed their tours, and were similarly headed out of combat. The weather front was moving in fast and soon after takeoff, all three of the pilots (the third being Len in his C-47) were fighting dangerous weather and flying on instruments. In fact, the weather was moving in so horrendously, conditions changed so fast, that shortly after the three planes departed, air traffic control closed the Hollandia runways. With that, engulfed as they were in a death grip of torrential rain, thunder, and wind, the pilots' first window of escape to safety closed behind them.

Rutter surmised that, "After first trying to get through the bad weather on instruments [the planes attempted to fly] beneath it on the deck [close to the ground or the surface of the sea]..."[152] In correspondence decades later, Len recalled the scene with sharp clarity, as though it had just happened,

> My co-pilot was Donald M. Dyer, Dos Palos, California. We were headed for Nadzab in lower New Guinea when I ran into this heavy storm. Lt. Eddy decided to go above it but must have underestimated the height of the thunderheads because he spun in [to the sea] as the story goes.

The B-25 in which Eddy was flying was literally a ten-ton monster, with a sixty-seven-foot wingspan. The beastly force necessary to destroy the plane must have been incalculable—grizzly paws of gushing wet wind twisting Eddy's 180-mile-per-hour flight path into the concrete of the ocean's engulfing surface, engines silenced and swallowed.

It was a hair-raising scene. It would be incorrect to say that Len knew the unpredictable weather along this coast, but he respected it. The experience would have been like Black Sunday, flying, tumbling as in an ocean wave, balancing a six-ton cross of steel and aluminum, in a desperate, controlled panic eastward within the eastward-moving storm.

With the calm temperament that guided his progress through flight school, Len continued,

> My decision to hit the deck [fly above the surface waves] turned out to be a good one. The C-47 was well equipped with good instrumentation and [was] almost brand new with green leather upholstery. We flew right on the deck, five to ten feet above the waves. I had flown out into the Bismarck Sea and still couldn't shake the storm. So I had decided that perhaps over the coast skies would be more clear. The scary part was flying on the deck in a torrential rainstorm and headed directly for the coast. Fortunately for us the weather did clear on the coastline and we made it to Nadzab O.K.[153]

Len said he went out to sea, north, to try to "shake" the storms that were harassing him. Unrelieved, he then looped back south, descending, overcoming instinct and aversion, to trust his altimeter, edging downward, again gently downward, five to ten feet above the restless, beckoning waves, heading directly into the granite of the Finisterre Mountain range which blocked his overland access to Nadzab. He survived, as did Walt Hill with his ten pilots on board. Neither Lieutenant Eddy, nor his copilot, Ralph Preston, nor the ten gunners was ever, ever found. Their loved ones never knew the joy of their safe return, nor the men the warmth of a homecoming embrace in gratitude for their service.

If not weather, there were always Japanese guns. A never-ending nightmare it could seem. Less than a week later, on October 17, the 389th lost another plane and its two crewmen. The A-20 was on a low-level mission to an enemy enclave called Sarmi, located along what should have been a familiar corridor running northwest from Hollandia along the coast, between Wakde and Biak. The plane crashed in the jungle, pathetically less than thirty miles from its base in Hollandia. The war was being pushed further, faster. Rutter wrote, "New Guinea's weather was an unpredictable factor and many planes were lost during the war because of it, either over the sea or over those parts of the map marked 'Unexplored.'"[154]

THE BATTLE OF LEYTE GULF

The rebuilding of Hollandia, the bringing in of new men and the transporting of equipment to and fro, was not simply to make the base operable. It was meant to make it a staging area for future offensive actions. During this time, the American aviation industry had been growing exponentially. In 1944 the US Air Force and Navy received as many as fifty-three thousand new planes, double the 1943 production, across six combat/attack categories of airplane types, plus some thirty-one thousand new training and transport planes. Soon, all of the personnel reshuffling and resupply activity began to suggest to the men of the 312th that they were to be part of an Allied buildup in Hollandia comparable to what Eisenhower put together in Britain for

D-Day back in June. In Rutter's words, "Day after day in early October naval vessels and transport ships gathered in Hollandia...until they filled most of the bay.... There were more carriers in evidence than I had imagined existed, plus numerous cruisers, destroyers and several battleships."[155]

A few news reports and several rumors had made their way to Hollandia regarding the massive D-Day assault on the beaches of France that June. Brothers, friends, and cousins were killed trying to take those beaches back from the Nazis. So the buildup at Hollandia impressed the men for both the vast accumulation of military hardware and for the implied scale of violence and hostility they would face. At that point in October, the men could not know that the heroic success at Normandy cost the lives of some 226,000 Allied men and women, not including those of some 25,000 civilians. General MacArthur had recently been named Supreme Commander of American sea, air, and land forces in the Pacific. In preparation for this new phase of the war, his September 18 memorandum asked his men to recall the principles underlying "OUR MORAL STANDING AND HUMANITY" in urging his men to avoid killing civilians or destroying their property. Having lived and worked with and among the people of the Philippines over a good portion of his career, MacArthur dearly wanted to reduce civilian casualties and property damage.

It was amazing how much had already been achieved. At the Quadrant Conference in August of 1943, when the US military was gathering strength, President Roosevelt and his Joint Chiefs of Staff ordered a two-pronged attack on Japanese bases throughout the Pacific: Nimitz was to neutralize strategic points in the Solomon Islands, on the northern edge of the Coral Sea, then move on to subdue the enemy at such island groupings as the Marianas and the Carolines; MacArthur was to take control of the southernmost Solomon Islands, mute Rabaul, control the Bismarck Sea, and pacify New Guinea, all on his way to the Philippines. Since then both men had executed the plan. They cut off and isolated Japanese forces on those far away bases and multiple dispersed islands.

The Philippines is a vague triangle of loosely woven-together islands northwest of New Guinea and north of the equator. They are separated from

New Guinea by a wide expanse of Pacific Ocean. The Mariana Islands lie to the east of the Philippines. The geography to be covered was vast. Leyte, one of the larger of the Philippine islands, located at the eastern edge and in the middle of the triangle, is over 1,450 miles from Hollandia. Further northwest is the main Philippine island called Luzon, on which the country's capital city Manila is located. Since their December of 1941 surprise attack, through October of 1944, the Japanese had insinuated themselves deeply into the country and built up a considerable and dangerous fighting force to hold and occupy their new colony. They supplied those soldiers largely through Formosa (Taiwan) to the north, located halfway back to Japan.

It would be a massive struggle to liberate the Philippines. The July of 1944 repositioning of Japanese forces in the Biak shift had unwittingly created even more space for Admiral Nimitz to advance from the east. Clearing the wide shipping lane of Japanese dominance between the Marianas and New Guinea facilitated the progress of MacArthur's forces from the south. The two prongs of attack would now come together into one mighty fighting force at Leyte Gulf, where the campaign to liberate the Philippines would begin.

In his tent Len sifted through combat plans for the upcoming battles. Outside, overlooking the port of Hollandia, the men of the 312th watched as an Allied amphibious force filled the bay with what official histories say were over 470 ships, ranging in size from thirty-six-man landing craft to 5,000-man troopships. Within days they set sail and were gone. Lying south of the equator, Hollandia, and all of New Guinea, is buffeted by the South Equatorial Current, which churns from east to west. Upon crossing the equator to the north, the fleet would be slammed by the Equatorial Counter Current driving from west to east. Meteorologists on board the ships had also forecast that a typhoon was headed toward the Leyte Gulf area. If it hit the expedition, it could cause a fatal, Spanish Armada-style catastrophe.[156] While a heavy storm did sweep the gulf area from October 14 through 17, by the early morning of the attack, skies were clear. Through the night of October 19–20, supported by an Allied naval bombardment on heavily armed Japanese positions, the US Army landed on three islands at the entrance to the gulf. The battle was engaged. For the time being, all the 312th could do was to wait in Hollandia; their turn would come later.

Back in April, the success of the leap to Hollandia on Black Sunday gave MacArthur and the 312th the capacity to strike deep into Japan's Southern Resource Area. When those forces bombed and overran the oil-rich Vogelkop Peninsula, it was the beginning of the end for the Japanese; and the beginning of the liberation for what would become the self-governing, independent nation of Indonesia. Deprived of that oil, and thus needing to establish priorities, one of the immediate effects on the Japanese air forces was that they could no longer fuel training planes for replacement pilots. The Japanese pilot training program, like those in the west, was necessarily months long, and physically and academically rigorous. And as in the west, the men selected for that duty were highly intelligent, well-rounded, and even tempered, the best representatives of Japanese society. Their system had produced the most respected pilots, flying the most advanced airplanes in the Pacific. By October of 1944, thirsting as they were for fuel, replacement pilots could no longer get the flying hours once required and move through their training in any significant numbers. Veteran pilots had to keep flying in spite of any combat fatigue or depression they may have been experiencing. And the new, now hastily trained replacement pilots were thrust into combat lacking the experience of those original pilots. The wheels were falling off the Japanese war machine.

In desperation, a horrendous new strategy was introduced by the Japanese high command at Leyte Gulf. Planes themselves would now be used as weapons, to be crashed deliberately into American aircraft carriers and navy destroyers. Besides being a terrorizing new "bomb," these suicide missions saved fuel as, hauntingly, the planes were filled with only enough for a one-way flight. Just as a conflicted Middlebrook contemplated insubordination when weighing orders to kill innocent Chinese (those forced to build Japanese roads and bridges in New Guinea), here on the Japanese side it is impossible to imagine what flyers were thinking when ordered by their commander to sacrifice their own lives by crashing their planes into the enemy. Dazed with fatigue, frustrated and forsaken by their own leaders, Japanese pilots complied.

The battle of Leyte Gulf presented the American forces with their first, spectacularly appalling experience with kamikaze fighters. Of course, the Japanese did not warn the Americans of this new form of attack. Thus, imagine the first sighting of a Japanese pilot attacking and dying in this shocking way. And then to see the episode occur again and again, only to slowly and suspiciously realize that you are seeing a deliberate pattern...that it is in fact a full-blown strategy. It must have shattered the hearts of even the most experienced fighter pilots or American Air Force commanders to witness suicide in this way. At the time, these attacks were thought by western pundits and later by historians to have been born of some mystical Samurai fanatical tradition. But, it has since been determined through diaries, written and left behind by these kamikaze pilots, that not one of them volunteered for this duty, not one of them felt the pull of any ancient Samurai code. They were coerced and shamed into it by desperate senior officers who had bungled the advantages their troops had thus far achieved in the war.

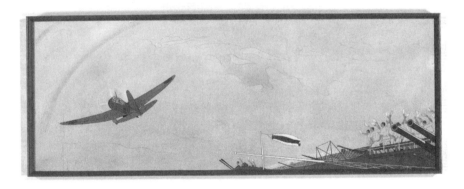

Carried out with grace, confidence, and self-assuredness, this approximately 8 feet by 5 feet painting by Shori Arai in 1943 is the third in a series entitled *Maintenance Work Aboard Aircraft Carrier*. Artists were sent with the troops to record heroic battle scenes in what Japan called her Greater East Asian War. It is inconceivable that one year later Japanese commanders could twist a pilot's pride and the romance of flight into horrific suicide missions in the name of duty or country. Shori Arai, "Maintenance Work Aboard Aircraft Carrier III" from the National Museum of Modern Art, Tokyo. (Reproduced here with the permission of the copyrite holder in Japan.)

Len read through the intelligence reports, anxiously following the progress of the battle. On October 20, 1944, General MacArthur's US Army, supported by Admiral Nimitz's naval bombardments, landed on the eastern shore of Leyte Island. A few hours later General MacArthur waded ashore, declaring via radio broadcast, "People of the Philippines, I have returned!" But the battle was far from won. While the US Army secured the beaches, protected from Japanese counter-attack by the US Navy, the battle raged for six more days through October 26. The sequence of land battles and naval engagements became known as the Battle of Leyte Gulf.

This battle brought a ghastly war of attrition much closer to the Japanese homeland. Their war plan was falling apart. Japan was losing strategic bases and colonies with which to trade and bargain for in a settlement negotiation. The Allies kept on coming. The island of Leyte itself would not be secured until the Americans established air superiority at the end of December, by which time MacArthur's forces were successfully cutting off Japanese resupply and reinforcements from the south. The Americans lost six warships and an estimated 2,800 soldiers in the battles. The Japanese sacrificed a gut-wrenching 12,500 men, including hundreds of kamikaze pilots and planes. The once massive Japanese Navy shrank by twenty-eight warships thanks to the overwhelming forces of MacArthur and Nimitz. And for the rest of the war Allied naval forces operated more freely throughout the Pacific. But on land, the Philippines were still honeycombed with the long dug-in forces of opposition.

Leyte Gulf is considered the largest naval battle in US history. In the course of researching this narrative, I asked an eighty-something veteran why vets do not talk about their service. He replied, "What is there to talk about?" Eventually he related that he served on two different aircraft carriers, including one in Leyte Gulf, as an aviation storekeeper. Even after decades, the many vivid memories of his service were raw and at his fingertips; memories he had been carrying like a cross since 1944. Still haunted, he counted off the exact number of three years, seven months, and twenty-seven days of his service. Then, overcome with melancholy, this veteran turned away, lowered his voice and gasped, "My brother came back from the Philippines in a straitjacket. They never could make him right."

CHAPTER 15

The Departure

The war in the Southwest Pacific Area was in transition: the Southern Resource Area was being liberated; New Guinea and Indonesia, the former Dutch East Indies, were for the most part cleared of major enemy emplacements; and General MacArthur had set his machinery in motion for the liberation of the Philippines. In mid-October 1944 there was a shuffle of commanding officers and Major Wells was promoted to lieutenant colonel and deputy group commander of the whole of the 312th under Colonel Strauss.[157] The trust Wells had in Len militarily and administratively made him an obvious choice to assume greater command as well. It was a strangely restless time. The men relaxed a bit after coming such a long way in battle, yet they were fearful of the next offensive, wondering if their luck would hold. Then suddenly and without a single shot fired, it was upon Len's father, Honorius, that an enemy struck. He collapsed at home in Park Ridge from what was termed a cerebral hemorrhage on Saturday, October 21.

The American Red Cross informed General Kenney's office of the death of Captain Happ's father. Just fifty-five years old, Honorius left his wife, Marie, and a young family, four daughters and four sons, all still dependent upon him. The memorandum noted that of the four boys, Len's brother Bob was in the Mediterranean, and that the next brother, Gerard, had signed on with the Marines.

In the command shuffle General Kenney abruptly canceled Colonel Strauss's request for Len's promotion, to replace Wells, and asked for another candidate. The colonel waited a day to gather his thoughts and to allow the paperwork to catch up with events. Confident that he had enough replacement pilots coming in, and had the troop strength to carry out battle plans far into the future, Strauss then ordered Len transferred out of combat and to a USA "redistribution center." And Rutter noted that, "Wells's place was taken by Captain Clifton Graber."[158]

There is no diary accounting nor surviving correspondence that describes how Len reacted to his subsequent departure from theatre. Colonel Strauss would have called Len into his tent, which by then had become commonplace for Len as the Operation Officer, however this time the Group Chaplin Clatus Snyder would have been present. When Len sat down, the men informed him of his father's sudden and unexpected passing. Strauss would then have directly followed up with the orders for Len's immediate transfer back to what the military still calls the Zone of the Interior (the mainland United States). Len was to be "redistributed" at Miami Beach, debriefed there, and reassigned. Documents show a priority clearance home was also granted with a twenty-two day leave of absence, officially referred to as "a delay en route." Strauss's personality suggests his message would have been, "Get yourself home, take a break, we'll finish things up here." An assistant operations officer gave Len his transfer documents and procedures to follow for departing the Southwest Pacific Theater. The growing Air Force bureaucracy took over from where Len's confused thoughts may have halted him. He had seen others go home before him, and with his number of missions he had long known that his tour was coming to an end. But he could not have expected departing in this way. Anxiety pervaded the whole of Hollandia as the battle to liberate the Philippines was moving forward. It was October 27, just a week into the desperate fighting raging at Leyte Gulf when Len was made staggeringly limp with this news of being "released from present assignment and further duty in SWPA" for processing to the U. S., "By command of Lieutenant General Kenney." As the fact of his father's death slowly sank in Len was abruptly transferred out of

New Guinea and away from his beloved 312th; he was not to be part of the Philippine campaign.

The previous year, when Garrett Middlebrook was grounded from flying combat missions, for example, he reflected on how he survived his year of combat and used the word "depression" in describing his mood at the time. He noted that others in his group felt the same way. When released from duty Middlebrook wrote that they did not react with joy—but rather with no emotions whatsoever. His line was, "My comrades were as emotionally spent as I was."[159]

Len's day had begun with a "battle ready" mindset preparing to move to the Philippines. Now the long period of nightmarish combat, the anarchy of engine noises and explosions, was at an end for Len; he was sorting through his gear and packing, anxious to get home. He had survived eleven months of air combat. There were thirty-three pilots in Len's original 312th Bomb Group when they left California. They had all mastered the new airplanes, learned to toss hand grenades, and climbed cargo netting together. Six of them had died in New Guinea: Doyle Dean, Anthony Hartley, Cyril Karsnia, George Nichols, William O'Connor and Walter Van.[160]

The "Priority 4 Clearance" was ordered for relatively immediate travel from Hollandia via Nadzab to Hamilton Field, California and further "processing." At Hollandia Len filled out, signed, and had approved by the Adjutant General an eight-point "Officers' Clearance Check List." The items on the checklist asked him to verify such things as his immunization records and his pay card, all necessary to formally release him from his current duties. He then signed to verify that all accounts had been paid and that there were no outstanding debts against him. He was officially checked out of Hollandia.

THERE, BUT FOR THE GRACE OF GOD

When Middlebrook was rotated out of combat eleven months earlier, there were so few Allied planes in New Guinea that he had to wait for an airplane seat to become available to ferry him back to Australia and then to the States.

While waiting, following policy, he was asked to train newly arriving pilots in the unique conditions of the New Guinea tropics for a month. Certainly a pilot of Len's character and experience would also have been used to help train new pilots entering this very challenging theater of battle. Given Len's reputation and service record, one could expect a similar transitional assignment for him. But Len was sent directly home.

As Len headed back to the States his colleagues encountered a surprise attack, during a routine air training mission, from some of those supposedly neutralized and isolated Japanese left behind and armed. The Australians were to starve them out and "mop them up." But as Rutter coldly observed,

> Grant Peterson, my tent mate, was still at Nadzab instructing at the Combat Replacement Training Center as we anticipated the move to Leyte. He was expected to return to the 389th by the end of November, but it did not work out that way. Pete was shot down... while leading a group of trainees over the airstrip at Wewak. Wewak had once been a very hot target and there were still thousands of Japanese Army troops in the area.[161]

Len always believed that he got "all the breaks" during his service. Had Honorius not died when he did, for instance, that may have been Len and not Peterson training those new pilots at Nadzab.

The Priority 4 Clearance appears to have been an extraordinary gesture on the Air Force's part. As with each of his sixty-four combat missions, a jeep took Len down the muddy, potholed road out to his waiting airplane. When he got there, his crew chief, Staff Sergeant Thomas Dobrowski, met him and this time expressed his regrets over the loss of his father. Then they wished each other the best of luck and promised they would write. Dobrowski threw Len's gear into the C-47 and stood back to salute as Len awkwardly climbed aboard, this time through the passenger hatch.

Per his "Certificate of Service," on October 29 Captain Happ, Leonard W., departed from the Asia Pacific for the USA. Clearing the jungle canopy, and upon reaching five thousand feet, the plane banked east down the hot, gusty coast. The pilot peered down at the "deck" to check the surface waves, then up into the cotton clouds above, looking for threats, habitually vigilant...out over the sea which had consumed Eddy's plane and all of those poor gunners. The plane skirted the Finisterres which tragically hid Hedges's men lost back in March, then veered inland along the temperamental Bismarck Mountains and over the billowing dark clouds which caused to the horrors of Black Sunday.

Like the waiting at Salinas, Len would have found it to be a long flight when he was not piloting. In his wallet was his picture of Julia, the one he'd carried every single day he'd been away. In correspondence he continually longed for her and must have become even more anxious to see her. There was a lot to think about, such as family, his father, the funeral, grave sites, household affairs, and his undetermined new posting. With brother Bob thought to be in the Mediterranean, neither Len nor Bob could serve as pallbearers. Hours passed, and soon he was over the Markham River valley, dropping down into Nadzab for fuel and exit paperwork. After Len's liaison officer checked him out, they took off from Nadzab. Climbing out of New Guinea for Len's final time, they could see in the distance the now abandoned Gusap Air Base. Peering into the godforsaken jungle one must have wondered what here was worth all that fighting?

Veering north, the pilot would pick up the familiar markings of Lae, Amelia Earhart's last known rendezvous point before being lost in 1937. From that point they headed southeast along the coast to pick up the Solomon Islands, to then tack northeast across the vast Pacific and the various stepping-stone islands heading for Hawaii and America. It was still very serious business, flying through the tropics, back across the equator and the International Date Line, made more stressful for Len being a passenger in someone else's plane.

Back at Hollandia, a replacement pilot took Len's empty cot; pilot Tom Jones took command of the *Little Joe*. It wasn't over. The 312th was on to the Philippines and Len was still in, as his enlistment papers noted, "for the duration of the war plus six months."

CHAPTER 16

Processing and Redistribution

HAMILTON, CALIFORNIA

On October 30, 1944, Len was formally received and processed by the "Debarcation—Port Control Section" at Hamilton Field in California. There had been a hopeful saying among the men, "The Golden Gate by '48"—meaning, as they departed via the Golden Gate (San Francisco) to join the war, they hoped their mission would, according to the whimsical rhyme, bring them safely home that way by 1948. Len made it back four years ahead of that. Out of range from Japanese bombs, but still in the service of the US military, he first cleared the military's "Medical Section" and was deemed, "physically examined...and found to be free of infectious and parasitic diseases and vermin infectation."[162]

Then he cleared the "Officers Section" and finally signed out. Len was officially back in the U.S.A. Having been granted "Class 4 Priority" air travel out of New Guinea, the Army honored that from Hamilton too, "within the Continental United States." In bafflingly brisk modern air force shorthand, the Air Transport Command, Pacific Division, West Coast Wing, Port of Aerial Embarkation, Hamilton Field, California, in Special Orders Number 91 on October 31 stated,

> Capt (2161) Leonard W. Happ, 0663723, AC HRPAE 31 Oct 44,
> ICW Per 10, SO #135, Hq FEAF, APO 925, dated 27 Oct 44, is asgd
> to AAFRS #2 Miami Beach, Fla. An emergency delay en route of 22

days is authorized to proper sta to which O will report 29 Nov 1944.
O will be reasgnd upon completion of processing at AAFRS #2...Lv
address: 314 S Cumberland, Park Ridge, Ill.

By Order of Colonel Keen:

(by) William C. Murray, Capt. Air Corps, Asst. Adjutant

The above memo roughly translates to: Len is here at Hamilton. He is
assigned to the Redistribution Station at Miami Beach. Once he is through
processing there, he will be reassigned. But, it was authorized that he could
take twenty-two days to get there; in fact, we only want him there by
November 29.

Len had five of what were called carbon copies of those rather innocuous service orders among the records in his Navigation Case. When
Middlebrook was sent home, his commander said to him, "Middlebrook, it's
time to go home." And more or less, off he went to teach navigation. Now
in late 1944, with the industrial quantities of men and equipment flowing
to the war fronts, the army bureaucracy was also generating paperwork in
industrial quantities.

With his twenty-two day "emergency delay" en route to his next assignment, Len went home to be with his family, to straighten out what he could
of Honorius's household affairs, and to mourn with his brothers and sisters.
While home he cautiously started to close one door and open another. No
doubt, the war was still ringing in his ears. There was still a chance he could
be reassigned to one of the many still contested battle fronts. In his preoccu-
pied state there were people he forgot to thank before departing, loose ends
that should have been tied up.

As he made his way back home, weary with anxiety and impatience,
and with twenty-two days to be a civilian again, he must have been giddy
with questions: "What will it be like with Julia? Has she changed? Have I
changed? Will it be awkward after so much time apart?" Every mile that he
traveled toward the Midwest he saw the country turn more colorful and
softer. He was flying away from the decay and gloom, the storm shrouded

mountains and the mud choked roads of New Guinea, toward the fertile prairies of Illinois and the majestic arching elm trees of Park Ridge, where autumn leaves blazed red and yellow.

Back stateside with his family and, importantly, with his girl, he found that his care in managing his long-distance relationship was paying off. She had waited for him. He made good use of his "22-day delay en route:" he got himself to a jewelry store, arranged an evening alone with Julia, got down on one knee and proposed. And while she excitedly agreed, her father put up a roadblock. Privately he spoke to Julia, avoiding a direct conflict with Len. He would not allow them to marry while Len remained an active duty pilot, in the middle of a very hot war. He reminded Julia, as Len himself feared, that Len could be reassigned to one of any number of war fronts. Julia's father reminded her that he also knew of what he spoke—he had once worn a uniform and been deployed to sail across a vast and dangerous ocean. As a World War I veteran, he knew firsthand the deadly destruction of war. It was understandable that he feared for her that Len could still be sent back into combat.

REDISTRIBUTION: MIAMI BEACH

When Len enlisted in Chicago, he and his gang were sent the next day to cadet training school—the first of many training bases those prospective airmen would attend. By the time Joseph Rutter enlisted, it took upwards of eight months until space was found for him in a cadet program where he could actually enter basic training. Ramping up for war, the government could not build facilities fast enough. There were so many men flowing through the ranks while fighting raged across two oceans that the War Department came to lease hotels and apartment buildings to bunk troops.

In Miami Beach alone, starting in 1942 some half a million men were processed through three hundred hotels and apartment buildings that were used for housing, training, and rehabilitation. Hotels were converted into either military administration offices or barracks, hotel dining rooms became mess halls. At various times hotel pools or the nearby ocean were used to teach lifesaving techniques, while areas of beach were closed off for rifle ranges and physical training. By 1944 these hotels and other available buildings were grouped into an army redistribution station for men returning from combat. The base was to provide for rest and relaxation, and as importantly, to facilitate the evaluation and processing of the returnees for future assignments.

We saw above that Len's Navigation Case held five copies of orders assigning him to Miami Beach. The army was now processing, training, and deploying so many soldiers that there came the need for that many more administrative personnel to keep track of them all, to coordinate their movements, document their expenses, and to make sure they got to where they were supposed to be going. All of these men needed seats on transport airplanes, boats, or trains, plus housing and food. The demand for administrative personnel became so great that men, and sometimes women, aged thirty to forty-five were recruited out of business or teaching positions into any variety of administrative military duties.

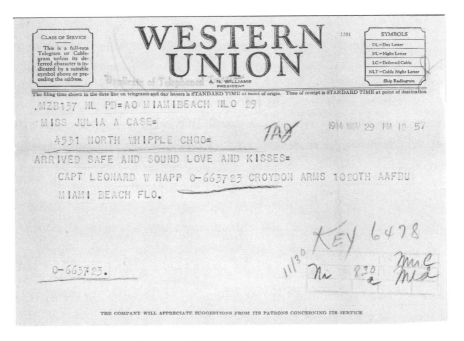

1944-style telegram.

Before the age of texting or Twitter, Len sent Julia a fabulous old-style telegram. His message clicked along cable wires to an office in Chicago. The decoded message was printed out on ticker-tape and pasted onto the body of a Western Union form. A messenger then carried the message to the address and the person to whom it was intended. It was marked with colored pencil clearly confirming to whom it was ultimately hand delivered. It took all that in those days to assure Julia that her fiancé had arrived on base safe and sound, exactly on the date required of him.

He was officially stationed at Army Air Force HQ, Redistribution Station Number 2, Miami Beach, Florida; his assigned quarters were at the Croydon Arms Hotel, on Collins Street in Miami Beach. Later that night his November 29 letter mentioned that out of Chicago, "We were slowed down by weather and by stops at Indianapolis, Evansville, Nashville, Atlanta, Jacksonville, and Orlando.... The last three places looked very familiar to me as I've spent time at these three airports before...[although] much has happened since I've been there." His room was a half block from the wide, white sand beaches where he wrote romantically of a full moon on the water. He said he was looking forward to getting a lot of rest and he was, "halfway through that book, 'The Green Years' [By A. J. Cronin]...it is so very good." Then he wrote with great discretion of military matters, adding, that it would be several days at least before he knew anything about his next assignment.

Seeing through the boredom of army life, there is a recurring theme which manifests itself again here: Len's appreciation of nature. Like squeezing the mud through his fingers at Grider Field, marveling at the Southern Cross over the south Pacific, or his joy in the wonders of flight, Len takes consolation in the natural beauty of his world. It is a tonic to him, marveling at the constellations and breathing the fresh sea air of Miami's Biscayne Bay. He saw God's creation as a validation of his faith and a source of his optimism. It invigorated him and gave him the strength to push through his frustration. It felt life-affirming to walk among the palm trees on the beaches, seeing so much of the world around him unfazed by war, going on almost as usual. On one occasion he wrote to Julia, "this afternoon [I] walked through Biscayne Park in Miami. It is beautiful there...sort of a tropical garden. There are various launches docked along the piers, many of which are hired out for daily deep-sea fishing tours."

As in training, the men were tested at this redistribution center and evaluated psychologically as well. They were asked about the conditions they experienced on the ground, in combat, and about living conditions like food, bunks and supplies. They were then given various competency and literacy tests. As Len was decompressing, he was also required to take various skills tests, which he thought were meant to evaluate him as a candidate for either an instructor's job or for another pilot assignment. As it was with much about army service, there was a heavy dose of boredom while waiting.

The debriefing would necessarily bring up detailed memories of his comrades and living conditions in New Guinea. Humor, horror, and great friendship would mix in the telling of his experiences to the officer taking notes. He remarked how odd it felt to simply stand up and not worry about being shot at, or to sleep through the night without being awoken by air raid signals. There would be details he would hide, or perhaps bury; certain inexplicable, private details that were not necessary to share with these curious officials. Some things would stay just between Len and his comrades, some things too difficult for others to understand.

As part of his processing for "redistribution", an Assignment Recommendations memo dated December 1 was generated. It prefaces the subject of his reassignment with Len's service record as, "64 combat missions, totaling 202 combat hours, total flying time [including transport hours] of 1150 hours...as Operations Officer, Squad and Flight Commander in A-20s and P-40s from 1 November 1943 to 31 October 1944." The final line of the memo noted Captain Happ's request for future assignment desiring to be a Base Operations Officer.

In actual fact, Len wasn't sure if that heavy dose of combat experience excluded him or not for future combat duty. He wished the summary highlighted his work as operations officer more, it was a role in New Guinea he really cherished and it was something for which he received commendation from his superiors. He sought to work closely with the senior base officers to interpret Air Force orders and missions, then direct the activities of base personnel in carrying out those orders. He was, above all, formally seeking to be closer to his family and Julia. Feeling anxious by the uncertainty and delay, on November 30 Len despaired, uncharacteristically lamenting, "[the] Army routine is so very much different from that which I knew in the old squadron." Then clearly sorting out his moods, pulling out of melancholy, the former accountant and bookkeeper soberly wrote with surprise, "I was introduced to the fact that I have 1943 income taxes to pay!"

"THE PSYCHOLOGICAL SECTION"

Len explained some of the actual processing and testing that took place in a nearby movie theater. He wrote Julia,

> From 1 until 4:30 this afternoon we spent with the psychological section.... Here we took about a half a dozen or more aptitude tests. Many silly questions had to be answered. There was a mathematics test. We had a mechanical aptitude test about wheels, cogs, levers etc.! The exams included an English test. There was not much grammar.... The whole thing seemed to be given to determine a pilot's qualifications for instructing.

The men were evaluated for general health and intelligence. Depending on their previous service, they were tested for motor skills, memory, attention, alertness, hearing and seeing. But there seemed to be no interview or test to evaluate fatigue or depression. The rest and relaxation was expected to help fix that.

WAR HOLLANDIA

Meanwhile, Len's comrades back in Asia fought on mechanically without him. Rutter wrote unenthusiastically how the 312th carried on:

> My sixteenth and seventeenth missions were to Sarmi Peninsula near Wakde Island on November 5 and 6. The Japanese were still

resisting as they had been since my first mission on August 4. Our ground forces had only one objective: to prevent interference with the airstrip on Wakde by keeping the enemy away from the shore opposite the island...bombing and strafing runs on the Japanese lines served as support for the troops holding the perimeter line.[163]

And then,

Both the rainy season and the determined Japanese resistance slowed the conquest of Leyte.... The 312th's ground echelon, which included most of our equipment and men...was scheduled to depart for Leyte on November 12...planes and crews could be moved north when an airfield became available.[164]

Len's trusted plane and his close friends of the past three years were all behind him now. Joined in the initial thrill of serving their country, he wrestled with nebulous regret and struggled with feelings of guilt for having safely exited the front, where the continual threat of calamity and violence had gripped all of them daily. The sad divide of safety and yes, even ease, over the long distance now separating him from those friends grew. Then he recalled, he had promised Dobrowski he would write.

THE CROYDON ARMS

Separated from his unit, separated again from Julia, their engagement unsettled and in discomforting limbo waiting for his next assignment, Len was tortured by anxiety. As always, he turned to pen and paper to work through it. Over the next weeks he wrote volumes to Julia, every day, four pages at a crack, amounting to some sixty-five pages.[165] The correspondence reflects how those Len encountered were also adjusting to whatever was meant to be next—driven not by fate, but carried along more by the flow of the war, as in an inner tube on a river. His particular war experiences remained in the background. Of some of the consequences, at one point Len says, "none of this is serious." But clearly, as he wrote about the combat vets he was meeting in Miami, all were treading water, spinning in their inner tubes to face forward, hoping that the calm water of their prewar lives was just around the next bend. At this point, as Americans prepared for the close of 1944, the currents of life were pulling people in swirling trajectories through rock-strewn waters.

First there was Julia. In spite of their commitment to one another, and the ring on her finger, she was still, in an official and legal way, single. At age twenty-three when Len proposed, she was living with her parents and teaching math and physics full time at Chicago's Roosevelt High School. Len was aware that anything could happen. She might tire of waiting; she might meet someone else. He could be sent back to a war zone at great risk to his life once again. Over the course of the next few weeks, Len continually agitated his superiors to be reassigned closer to Chicago, nearer to Julia and to his widowed mother and siblings. From the Croydon Arms on December 1, he wrote longingly, "While you gaze at your ring...I'm considering our marriage from all angles." To pass the time he went to movies, the beach and to college football games with other officers. He also went to Catholic mass and took communion. And every day he heard about guys being reassigned, "redistributed" here or there, for better or worse, but not him.

One of Len's strategies in seeking a Chicago-area base assignment was to have a family friend and attorney, Henry Blum, make an appeal to the Air Force on his behalf. He first tried to argue a hardship case as he wrote Julia, "When I told them [Air Force administrators] here why I was needed home, they asked for a Red Cross verification of the setup at home, and also a request by an attorney for my presence. I won't say too much about it because you know the Army."

This appeal to their family friend and attorney sets the tone for his time in Miami Beach. It was Len's first formal initiative to persuade the Air Force administration that his next assignment must be closer to home. It may have been a long shot, but worth pushing for, given some of the unappealing options laid out for other pilots, as he wrote to Julia:

Some A-20 pilots are going to Del Rio, Texas! That's under a cactus plant alongside the Rio Grande on the Mexican border—just above Laredo, Texas. Would you like that, honey? I don't think you would, but there are parts of Texas I'm sure you would love.

Laughlin Army Air Force Base in Del Rio, Texas was, at the time, the largest pilot and air crew training base in the States. It made sense that experienced combat pilots were wanted there as potential instructors.

Before going out to the movies one night, while in the midst of writing Julia, Len's phone rang. His St. Paul grammar school mate and Park Ridge buddy Willis "Bill" Connor was in Miami Beach being "redistributed" too. He had been in New Guinea for the better part of three years. Bill was part of that frantic, initial phase of America's effort to slow the Japanese advance on Port Moresby. He was deployed to the gruesome 1942 Battle of the Kokoda Trail, and later was in on the ground effort to secure the Huon Peninsula. He landed at Saidor as part of the January 2, 1944, offensive when Len was just weeks in theater, and was still at Saidor on Black Sunday, April 16, 1944. Miraculously, Bill slipped past death to make it home. Surviving what they did, it should be easy to understand why both men would have such strong faith. Len and Bill attended mass every day during this time period.

Through Henry Blum, Len was introduced to the Masseys. Mr. Massey was a retired construction engineer. He and his wife of thirty-four years lived on one of five islands in Biscayne Bay between Miami and Miami Beach. Len wrote Julia that,

He apparently had something to do with construction of docks at Manila, because he lived there for some years and spoke of 'Doug' and 'John' MacArthur. At the dinner table Mr. Massey showed me two silver match boxes which were remaining favors from a birthday dinner which [they hosted] for Douglas MacArthur on his 42nd birthday!

Mrs. Massey told me that she had six children but all are dead. I don't know how all that happened. They have everything that money can buy. But they are so alone now. I was filled with melancholy when I left.

That evening gave Len more to think about. The Masseys' deep losses compounded his drive to work for a better life. As he reflected on his father's premature passing, he became more determined to have Julia with him. He wanted to be upbeat in his letter, but sadness overcame him. In their way, the Masseys reinforced Len's commitment to faith and his down home, family values.

Then one day, in a wonderful surprise, Len literally bumped into his good pal Lieutenant Lee Anderson from his very own 312th Bomb Group. He said it was a "dream" running into "Andy." While marking time, awaiting reassignment, the chance meeting gave him the backwards-looking, partially buried joy of the shared world from which he was just torn away. On the evening of December 4, telephone lines were tied up for three or four hours inhibiting his call to Julia. He took up his pen again, writing her that,

...Upon leaving the post office today and after mailing "Green Years" to you, I met a squadron buddy of mine, Lt. Anderson, or "Andy" as we knew him. We practically fell into each other's arms. He was one of the first fellows to leave for the States, and was certainly surprised to see me. Andy has had malaria since he's been home and that's why he's still down here. You have no idea how happy we were to see each other. Andy is a fine fellow, and it was almost a dream to see him again. He's from a farm in North Dakota. I met him here at about 4:30 this afternoon and I just left him. We had a few beers as you may have seen from this scratching! [deteriorated penmanship] Darling, I have had a happy time with him. Andy and I had been thru a lot together. He was certainly surprised to hear how I got home so soon.

In a few days I'll be able to tell you something definite about my next station. Gosh I'm sweating that out! Andy told me that a few of the other A-20 pilots who have been through here are already in Del Rio, Texas. What a spot to be sent! It is not too far from San Antonio, tho. I really think I can get out of going there.

Len continued to learn from Andy of even more A-20 pilots being reassigned to Del Rio, Texas. He in turn wrote of it to Julia, in a way to prepare her for that unhappy eventuality. His situational anxiety aside, Len was a naturally optimistic and well-traveled fellow. If he thought Del Rio was an unattractive option, it must not have been a very good place at all.

Then again on December 5, still waiting for word, Len told Julia of the latest misfortune to befall Andy. Having been hospitalized and released, following the malaria issue, he was now "back in bed with the 7-year itch! He never came down with a thing over in Guinea!" In other words, Andy had contracted scabies, a contagious skin infection caused by mites or skin parasites. According to the World Health Organization, the six countries with the highest rates of scabies are: Cameroon, Ghana, Indonesia, New Guinea, the Solomon Islands, and Vanuatu. It seems the most intense concentrations of cases are found in the South Pacific and North Australia. Years later the army determined that for servicemen in New Guinea,

> Heat combined with oppressive humidity generally was an overriding condition. This reduced the degree to which men could perform their assigned tasks effectively. Clothing and skin surfaces, continually damp, provided splendid pasture for growth of all kinds of fungi, native to tropical areas. Rare was the individual who did not suffer from some sort of skin fungus. The principal areas affected were the feet, groin, armpits and hands. Flight surgeon's daily records attest to the never-ending struggle to control the invader. As a long-range factor, men who meet at reunions of the 312th still discuss[ed] their current bouts with treating fungus which was incurred over thirty years earlier.[166]

Dwelling heavily on his future, Len sensed his letters and conversations had been weighing on Julia. He wanted to project his enduring sense of optimism. In order to be upbeat he reassured Julia: "None of this is serious tho and we expect to go deep sea fishing in a day or so. I'm also getting football tickets for the Miami U. vs. Texas A. & M. game on Friday nite. It is so much a dream for us to be here together."

But most curiously, this man of well-chosen words, of obvious depth of character and education, twice used the term "dream" when referring to his meeting and being reunited with Lee Anderson. Len tells Julia, "It was almost a dream to see him again." and then the next day, "It is so much a dream for us to be here together."

Lee Anderson, left, Len on the right, in Miami Beach, December 1944. Len Happ photo.

One can not overstate the strong emotional bonds of brotherhood that united these men in their time at war. In his chronicles, Russell Sturzebecker, tells us that the 312th felt themselves to be an unusual group because they trained together for eighteen months before they entered combat and stayed together as a unit throughout their various successes and moves. And certainly their most urgent missions were those in which they searched the jungles and mountains for missing crews, such as those three planes lost when travelling with Ken Hedges's group near Alexishaven last March.

Middlebrook shows us an exceptionally special example of this brotherhood. Well into his twelfth month of combat in New Guinea, Middlebrook's squadron leader asked him a favor regarding the recent death of their commanding officer (CO), a man by the name of Cox.

> [My squadron leader] asked me to go to Cox's tent and screen his belongings and pack them to be sent to his grieving parents...I was aware that [he] was trusting me to examine and scrutinize my CO's personal belongings and correspondence, both official and private, and to maintain discreet confidence of my findings. When one of our comrades was killed or designated missing in action, we carefully screened his belongings, discarding any objectionable items so that his distraught wife or parents would not find photos, books, letters, or other items which might offend them.[167]

Among Middlebrook and his peers, men actively censored the contents of their fallen comrade's belongings before they were sent home to their families, as they were convinced that if you weren't "there" you could not possibly understand what they had to do—the little escapes, objects, eccentricities, treats, motivators, and good luck charms—to survive mentally and physically in that godforsaken land.

Then there is this point found in a study called, The Medical Service of the AAF:

> No one who has studied successful flyers will deny that their psychic constitutions are unique and that there is a fairly consistent configuration of their personality structure. The act of flying yields a distinct gratification, particularly to the pilot, and it appears that this libidinal devotion serves the airman as a powerful shield against the threat of failure and death. The existence of strong emotional currents in flyers, and the inadequate perception of their meaning by non-flyers...intensifies a mystical unity of the flyers against all others.[168]

A "mystical unity" binds these men. We will never understand all they endured, nor the courage needed to do what they did. Reuniting with Andy brought those profound feelings to the surface, feelings forged over almost three years of living in close contact, training, fighting, and dying, with the victorious men of the 312th.

TREADING WATER, SPINNING

Over time some resignation crept into in Len's tone. Henry Blum's intervention failed and the battle to secure a reassignment close to home was wearing on him. He updated Julia on December 6:

> Darling, I'm fighting hard to get stationed close to home. Today I lost a little ground in that regard. I can't say how. This Army is bigger than you or I, dearest. I'm quite unhappy tonight because my hopes of being stationed close to home were shattered a bit today...

Len was told by the Air Force administration that they saw no emergency in Park Ridge. The family seemed well enough provided for. Discouraged, Len put an optimistic smile on the news and resolved to carry on, with the closing comment, "This may be a blessing and I don't realize it."

Next Len learned that a high school friend, a Captain Allen Perraud and his wife Bernadine LaBeau, were living at Miami Beach. Perraud had, coincidentally, also served his year or more in the Southwest Pacific Theatre and was awaiting reassignment. But it had been a fragile time for Bernadine. Newly wed, she was left behind at home after her honeymoon and now here she woke every day in Miami Beach with no friends and uncertain what and how her life on a military base would be. Len admitted to Julia:

> Allen and Bern got married when he got out of flying school. He went overseas soon after, and in my theatre. The couple say they never regretted getting married in the face of what they did. Bern admits she leads a lonely life, and now she does not meet the peo-

ple with whom she can really become friendly. Never-the-less they have their home wherever they go, and seem happy with their lot.

Len realized in fact, that such a life would be an unacceptable hardship on Julia, so used as she was to the stimulation of a rich home and social life. To be handcuffed to an enlisted, active duty pilot would crush her spirits. Still, Len wanted to make Bernadine's situation seem conventional by suggesting, "That's the way it is these days." As he wrote they "seem happy with their lot."

All the while, Len was going to Air Force administration offices to restate his request, every morning in fact, to push for a posting that would eventually make a better "home" for himself and Julia. It was a laborious and tedious time for him. Len's correspondence became lame with trivia and with his longings and loneliness. He nonetheless continued to incorporate scraps of news concerning his continuous fight with the brass. "This weekend I should be able to tell you something definite—if not, surely by Tues. we should know. All the fellows who reported here when I did are already out. My papers are being held up because I'm being stubborn!"

Len and Andy continued to break the tedium with movies. But then one evening Andy brushed Len off early because he had a date, another example of the rhythm of an ordinary life. And yet, even while comrades, even "brothers," Len and Andy were different men. Len held to his core values of prudence and temperance while Andy embraced his new environment and enjoyed his time with women, "wolfing" as Len called it. Len's clergy friends would have marveled at the symbolism: Len was cleared back into the States, "found to be free of infectious and parasitic diseases and vermin infectation," while Andy was in and out of the hospital fighting scabies.

The next several days, scattered as they are with references to being out with "the guys," found Len consumed with the uncertainty of his next assignment. On December 10 he confessed to Julia, "This waiting is hard on me" and that "red tape still keeps us from knowing anything definite….The days seem so long now that I am just waiting to hear." Continuing,

I arose in time to spend an hour at headquarters before going to dinner! [lunch] Awful, isn't it? My business for the day just now consists of checking with headquarters to see if my assignment has come thru. After a strenuous hour there I decided to hit the beach for the rest of the afternoon.

Every soldier's case but Len's seemed to be sorting itself out. Even Bill Connor was on his way out to Camp McCoy in Wisconsin, an infantry training center.

But on December 14 the mood changed as Len finally had good news:

I'm ever so happy tonite because I've a victory to tell you about. Yep, I won, honey, and if things work out half way decent I shall see you before you receive this letter! My assignment is with the Troop Carrier Command at Stout Field, Indianapolis, IND!

The new assignment even had some prestige associated with it. Len was jubilant.

I'll know more about the set-up when I get to Stout Field.... The Troop Carrier Command is a hard outfit to break into. I won't get into technicalities but here's the deal: I leave here on or about the 16th of Dec. I've wired Stout Field for a ten-day delay en route. If this is granted I'll have until the 28th of Dec to report to Stout Field. If this delay en route is not granted, I'll still be but four hours from Chicago by the slowest method of transportation!

Len's reassignment had been determined. He was euphoric that he was not reassigned to a combat role overseas—his worst fear. He was not going to be stuck in Del Rio, Texas, either. He was excited. His battle with the brass, with the Air Force bureaucracy, was worth it. He was given a day to get his quarters cleaned out and get to his next post.

His last night, December 14, turned into a farewell party—a celebration for all his buddies, not like his hasty departure from New Guinea where most of his comrades remained. He also wrote that other friends and officers had learned their fates as well. Enthusiastically, probably tipsy, he took the time to tell Julia who was going where:

> This afternoon I was in my room here alone when Lt. Schatzman came in all smiles. He had been assigned to a basic school in his home town, Macon, GA. How happy he is! A few minutes later, Andy came in, smiles but a little disappointed. He is bound for Del Rio, Texas and received his orders today. How did we miss this, Julie my dearest? To top this off, Lt. Hogan found out that he is assigned to Brooks Field, Texas, not far from his home town of Houston. Honey, we really celebrated tonight I'm telling you. Andy, of course, wasn't too happy. He'll be OK tho, I know. Bill Connor leaves tomorrow a.m. for Camp McCoy, Wis. If he gets a delay en route I should see him again in Park Ridge. Gosh I'll tremble with Joy to be with you around Christmas and also see my brother Bob.

The emotion, the gratitude, was building inside him. That last line encapsulates everything he had been working toward—simply put, getting back to normal; a normal home, social, professional, and eventually married life.

AIR FORCE TROOP CARRIER COMMAND

Special Orders, Number 345, assigned Len to Stout Field, Indianapolis, Indiana, and the 800th Army Air Force Base Unit, I, TCC (Troop Carrier Command). Originally Stout Field was built in 1926 as a stopover and refueling station, along a transcontinental air route from New York City to Los Angeles. At one point during the war this base gave specialized training for air assault and air resupply missions. It is an alluring 180-mile drive from Chicago.

Anxious to confirm his good fortune after posting his letter, and buoyant with the expectation of the good things ahead, as soon as he rose the next morning Len sent off an extravagant Western Union telegram. The ticker-taped message to Julia read, "ASSIGNED TO INDIANAPOLIS SEE YOU LATE SUNDAY NITE."

Over the course of that hectic day, his new assignment orders transferring him to Stout were confirmed in writing. Len packed, settled his accounts at the base facilities, signed out of his quarters, and made holiday plans in Park Ridge. Another telegram, which originated with a Brigadier General Old at Stout, graciously granted Len's request for an eight-day delay en route to this next post. Len was therefore not required to report for duty until the new year, as he had wildly hoped.

In between receiving and complying with the fine points of the reassignment orders, Len also made arrangements to have his mail forwarded. While at the base post office he picked up a Christmas card from Hollandia and the members of his Roarin' 20's squadron. Len read it feeling a mixed sense of pride and a sobering sense of responsibility to the unit and his beloved comrades. The men were still fighting out there, carrying on without him. His back stiffened as if called to attention; his heart raced as dreams and memories reverted back to the sticky mud and oppressive heat, rain leaking through the canvas curtains and the humid stench of New Guinea. The card described the 312th's sojourn so far: Savannah, DeRidder, Rice, Salinas, Australia, New Guinea, and now an arrow pointing to Tokyo.

CHAPTER 17

MAET

Crudely put, industrial quantities of fresh men and armaments were going one way toward the battle fronts and tragically, plane loads of injured and wounded men were coming back. The Allies were succeeding and the war was intensifying, both in Europe and Asia. Further expanding on the broad theme of the US having been unprepared for war, as more planes became available, Medical Air Evacuation Transport (MAET) squadrons were activated. They began with flights from the battle fields of Europe, transporting high priority cases of wounded men to medical facilities in Great Britain. By January 1945 approximately 10,000 aircraft were specially designated for this purpose—compared to those lonely 260 broken down aircraft available to General Kenney for combat in 1942 Australia.

While the smug and testosterone-filled strategies of violent armed conflicts normally claim the majority of space and ink in war books, there are these other facets to war. Neglected are the stories of caring for the sick and wounded; unexplored are the stories of the stress and struggle inside each soldier. Most combatants confronted these raw and disturbing sides to war during their time, especially on the front lines. But normally, only the glory stories of using powerful machines and defeating a cunning enemy make it into the history books.

Injured soldiers were normally moved away from the battle fronts by ambulances and boats to infirmaries in theatre. With this new service, special cases were airlifted from the UK across the Atlantic to hospitals in the US where care could be administered closer to the homes and families of these wounded men. It was an extraordinary service and one of the most honorable commitments to the men in uniform that could be made. On the one hand, by squadrons and platoons men were waging war across the globe, causing untold death and destruction. On the other hand, the Air Force took on the added role of fighting to save the individual lives of our wounded men, precious and irreplaceable lives. One by one they fought to restore the singular bodies of what enemy steel and explosives had wrecked.

In Europe the casualty toll from the gruesome December to January Battle of the Bulge in Belgium's Ardennes Forest mounted. The new air evacuation commanders faced logistical issues similar in scope to managing the original point-to-point series of supply bases from America to Australia. This time, from Europe back to individual American hometowns. Medical facilities had to be established at myriad locations and pilots, planes, ground crews, and ground transport all had to be newly trained and organized into an efficient service branch.

PILOTS TO THE WOUNDED

In order to move these patients, the twin-engine C-47 aircraft was rigged with racks to hold eighteen to twenty litters of patients. Sometimes referred to as a Skytrain, it was one of the very few commercial/civilian aircraft capable of this purpose at the time. When converted for military use, two much more powerful Pratt and Whitney engines were installed, replacing the original civilian-use engines. This aircraft type, with which Len was by now so familiar, was an enormous sixty-four feet long with a wingspan of ninety-five feet. It sat on the runway at seventeen feet tall. Empty it weighed over 18,000 pounds. As a troop carrier it could transport twenty-eight men or 8,000 pounds in men and equipment. With these military grade engines the plane could climb to 10,000 feet in ten seconds and cruise at speeds of 160 to 230 miles per hour over a 1,350-mile range—similar to flying half-way across America on a single tank of gas. Planes were staffed by specially trained Medical Air Evacuation Transport personnel. Crews consisted of medical technicians, flight nurses, and flight surgeons. The planes carried medical supplies like blood plasma, oxygen, morphine, portable heaters, elaborate first aid kits, and blankets. At the time this service was launched, planes were used exclusively for what was considered "emergency" evacuation only. Eventually, more than one million battle-scarred patients were transported to hospitals near their native homes all around the forty-eight United States.

As seen at Miami Beach, the Air Force took those combat veterans who had rotated out of battlefields and redistributed them to work, among other places, at training bases such as Del Rio, Texas, as instructors. By late 1944 the Allies had made good progress against the enemy on several fronts of the war. Casualty rates were declining and larger numbers of replacement crews were available for rotation. The Crew Rotation report shows most commanders in the field were still largely operating under the Commanders' Choice policy, using the number of missions flown as the determining factor for sending a pilot home: forty missions for heavy bombers, sixty missions for medium bombers, for example. One can see that the policy was applied arbitrarily by Middlebrook being grounded after an incredible sixty-four missions in his five-man B-25, while Len was rotated out after sixty-four missions in his two-man A-20 and the single-seat P-40. Nonetheless, the Air Force and the War Department policy stated:

> When, in the opinion of an Air Force commander, a combat crew (or member thereof), as a result of prolonged combat duty, is so reduced in operational efficiency as to affect the efficiency of the unit, that crew (or individual thereof) will be relieved from operations either for:
>
> a. Assignment to non-operational duty within the theatre.
>
> b. Assignment to the Zone of Interior (continental United States).
>
> c. Detached service for 30 days in the United States for rest and rehabilitation (but not discharged). [And then reassigned per point a. or b. above].[169]

STOUT FIELD, JANUARY 2, 1945

Len arrived wearily at Stout Field after spending the holidays at home and took up the anonymous quarters assigned to him in building number T-129, room number one in section B. It was a kind of no-man's-land. War was grinding forward on two fronts and the Air Force was busy allocating supplies and housing troops as required by battle plans. Lending a degree of uncertainty about exactly why Len was reassigned to Stout, he was promptly shuffled over to the 814th AAF Base Unit, Squadron "A" as a pilot, "By command of Brigadier General Old."[170]

While adjusting to his new surroundings, he was saddened by the realization that the world he had known for the last three years was fading away. As fierce fighting continued, Len learned that his old 389th Squadron was the first of the 312th's bomb squadrons to relocate to a forward base on Leyte in the Philippines. Led out by Colonel Strauss through hot battle zones and cruising at 10,000 feet, their January 3, 1945 journey took them from Hollandia to Biak for fuel. The weather had been dangerously clear, which therefore favored any stray Japanese still actively hunting American planes along the route. From Biak they flew to Morotai, just two degrees north of the equator, where they stayed overnight. They departed there in good weather and arrived in gray rain and mud in Leyte on the fourth, as Len was learning his new routine at Stout. Once the new base was secure, the other three squadrons of the group followed the same course from Hollandia the next day.

Len's 312th began fighting across Leyte and onto the Philippine island called Samar, just north of Leyte, without him. Covered by the 5th Air Force, US Army units made another amphibious landing, this time at a place called Ormoc Bay. After a major ground and air battle, the landing force cut off all Japanese ability to reinforce or resupply their troops on the island of Leyte.

It was bittersweet for Len to learn of this. He felt envy mixed with pride for his old unit. Then, a guilty sense of relief crept in, knowing that at Stout he was far beyond the range of Japanese flak. He hated the killing but loved the men with whom he served. Throughout his time in the Pacific, Len endured agony and fear, loneliness and boredom, violence and privation, and the deaths of many friends and colleagues. He held Colonel Strauss in high esteem as a pilot and a leader. He had the respect of Major Wells and the combat record of a job well done. But now, those men, his friends and comrades, including his crew chief Tom Dobrowski, were still in hot action on the front lines.

As he did what he could to get integrated into life at Stout, Len was again filling out forms.[171] His "Form 5" asked for a "copy of personal orders placing individual on flying status; orders announcing individuals' aerial ratings; [and] certificates showing completion of transition flying training." It was as though he was an anonymous pawn to the Air Force bureaucracy. He probably thought, "after twelve months of conquering a geographic area the size of England and France, dodging bullets and flak, staying aloft in nightmarish weather, flying P-40s, C-47s, and A-20s—really? You are asking me to verify this crock?" He also filled out a "Familiarization with Flying Equipment" certificate, naming no less than eleven different types of aircraft in which he had competency as a pilot or copilot, many from his intense training days. In documents signed that same day, and upon examination by a Captain Fissel of the station hospital, Len was deemed, "qualified for flying duty."

On that same January 3, when Colonel Strauss was leading Len's old squadron into the next phase of the war in the Pacific, Len himself was ordered to fly from Stout down to Randolph Field in San Antonio, Texas, the first flight in this next phase of his service, as copilot of a C-47. In preparing his flight plan, Len considered the one-way trip to be about as far as the risky round trip from Gusap to Wewak, almost twelve hundred miles distant, and it brought back sobering memories of the impossibly turbulent mountain torrents mixed with apprehensions of enemy attack. He imagined Dobrowski preparing *Little Joe* for her next combat mission in the Philippines. But his mission, he knew in reality, was simply a bit of repositioning of people and aircraft, transporting two staff sergeants to that station and delivering an aircraft to Bergstrom Field, in Austin, Texas.

LUZON ISLAND

Dobrowski was indeed getting the *Little Joe* ready for her next combat mission. Starting in early January the four bomb groups of the 312th kept pace with MacArthur's effort to push the war further and faster, from Leyte north to Luzon. Colonel Strauss announced in combat briefings of January 6, that they were to attack Japanese-held Clark Field, only about forty miles northwest of Manila. It was, at the time, the largest air base in the Philippines. Each bomb group flew an aggressive number of combat missions—about twenty per month—throughout the Philippines. Joseph Rutter was a lead pilot that January morning. Of his first Philippine mission for the 312th he wrote, "Tom Jones, flying *Little Joe*, a plane originally assigned to Len Happ, was on my right wing."[172]

Throughout February the job of the Air Force was to clear the way in advance of marine and army troops fighting throughout Luzon. Japanese forces on the peninsula west of Manila, called Bataan, became cut off from their supplies and a strategic island at the entrance to Manila Bay, called Corregidor, was captured by the Americans.

Toward the end of May 1945, organized Japanese resistance on Luzon was overcome. But as in New Guinea, exceptionally strong Japanese forces hidden in the ridges of north-central Luzon held out and were still fighting, far behind the front lines.

FROM JAPAN'S POINT OF VIEW

In January of 1945 Japan's military leaders anticipated the Americans' next leapfrogging moves and began to plan for them; parliament considered moving the Imperial residences from Tokyo further inland to Nagano. Reminiscent of the Illinois War Council, Japan began to train civilians to fight. The Army was expecting to confront the US in what they called the "Decisive Battle" at home, on Japanese soil. The term carries historic and symbolic reference to the strategy of using overwhelming force to destroy an enemy, as employed by the Japanese to defeat the Imperial Russian Navy in 1905.

Japanese leaders feared that loss to the Americans would mean colonization and foreign subjugation. Their strategic thinking remained constant: while they may not win, they expected not to surrender, and thus negotiate a favorable truce. By negotiating with the Americans they believed they could retain some of their colonial possessions. Their primary motivation for not losing was to maintain their independence and pride: they had been as successful as any European country at playing the Euro-style colonial game and the Imperial Army had not lost a single war since its inception in 1871.

FURTHER, FASTER! TO MANILA

As the Americans increased their hold over the Philippine countryside throughout Luzon, the time came to push the Japanese from positions in the capital they had held since early 1942. The Battle of Manila, February 3 to March 3, 1945 was recorded as the bloodiest urban battle of the Pacific War. In spite of General MacArthur's written admonition to avoid it, or perhaps because he foresaw it, the battle brought about the deaths of approximately one hundred thousand civilians and the hideous devastation of historic and cultural landmarks throughout the city. American victory in this battle ended almost three years of comprehensive Japanese occupation.

And while the exclamation, "People of the Philippines, I have returned!" was made upon MacArthur's arrival on Philippines territory at Leyte a few months back, in actuality the victory at Manila was the true realization of this dream: his return to the seat of power in a liberated Manila. Tragically, however, the Americans came to learn that only one-third of the tens of thousands of Philippine and American servicemen MacArthur left behind when he was chased out in March 1942 survived to see his return.

IWO JIMA

The town-by-town or, in this case island-by-island, traditional battles that the Joint Chiefs sought to avoid seemed to be required in this phase of the war. Once again, America was engaged in traditional battles of attrition to occupy strategic islands close to the Japanese mainland. The first American landing on Japanese territory was at an obscure, eight-square-mile volcanic island north of the Philippines (and still 750 miles south of Tokyo) called Iwo Jima. For the Americans it was a stepping-stone to mainland Japan.

The US Marines invaded in February 1945 after weeks of relentless aerial bombardment. As at Biak, the Japanese carved themselves into a honeycomb of tunnels and underground bunkers throughout the small island. The battle over essentially two airfields quickly devolved, becoming endless and ugly. Combat was marked by brutal bloodshed and marauding disease during the intense months that followed. While the US lost over six thousand men, some twenty thousand Japanese soldiers were estimated to have perished trying to hold on to the island.

FAR EAST FORCES

What is now known as the Bismarck Archipelago Campaign culminated with the seizure of the island of Los Negros and then Hollandia following what the 312th posthumously called Black Sunday, in April 1944. The campaign was considered formally wrapped up and won for the United States at the end of November 1944. Len and his comrades received a Bronze Battle Star for their part in it.[173]

A bronze battle star for the Bismarck Archipelago Campaign, awarded as a follow-up to the Asiatic Pacific Theatre service ribbon (background).

And then, what was anticipated to be a period of relative ease and stability so near to Chicago, collapsed into murky, inexplicable malaise—and worse.

"MISERABLE"

January 8, 1945 Stout Field:

Len struggled to establish a sense of order and normalcy in his new assignment. His first transport mission to and from Bergstrom was a twenty-four-hundred-mile round trip that took twelve to fourteen hours, by far longer than any New Guinea mission. Normally buoyant and seemingly never rash, here at Stout, barely over a week into this posting, after arguing, petitioning, and lobbying for a month to be assigned up north, Len was back lobbying for yet another, different assignment. In December he had been not only relieved but upbeat and proud of this assignment to Stout. Now, he was, as he had been in Miami Beach, again searching for something else, some other posting. It was puzzling and wholly uncharacteristic of him. Len knew that Julia's family would not let her marry an active duty pilot. Yet, he wrote her with this disjointed idea:

> I have a good chance to get an assignment at Bergstrom Field in Austin as an instructor. I have no doubt that you would enjoy living in Austin. I've been there before and it is a beautiful town. But tomorrow I'll have to start trying to get stationed there.

Then, came a shock. He wrote Julia of being mysteriously grounded.

> On this trip to Texas I was miserable. I've never felt quite that discontented about anything…. I'm completely fed up on the life I see around me…leading a lonely life…. When I returned today, I saw our flight surgeon and he grounded me for this month to work something out.

Personnel Order Number 8, "By order of Colonel Johnson," formalized the order. It confirmed "grounding Capt. Leonard W. Happ…from duty requiring regular and frequent aerial flights, effective 8 January 1945," and had its source in the "Office of the Flight Surgeon, Station Hospital, Stout." No further explanation was given. He was to stay put for a month to rest and get his strength up. All the more perplexing, this incident came about after Len's first flight behind the wheel since all those hair-raising missions in New Guinea. Now, the medic saw something in his demeanor that worried him. The evaluation revealed enough justification to ground Len as a way of safeguarding the pilot himself, his crew and the aircraft. Something was indeed off. For just after optimistically raising the odd idea of moving to Bergstrom, Len had switched moods using highly charged phrases in that letter to Julia, "miserable...discontented...fed-up...lonely..." before he glibly ended with "to work something out."

Being grounded is humiliating for a pilot. The term generally has derogatory connotations as when Major Wells used it, calling out to Rutter, "You're grounded!" And yet Len did not push back on the order. Nor does treatment seem to have accompanied the grounding order. The flight surgeon simply admonished him to eat properly and to exercise more, as though time and a stronger constitution would fix him up in a jiffy. For all the threats to his very existence that he had come through—the lost comrades, the flak-shattered windshield, the horrendous heat, humidity, and rain—it seems unusual that this would be the first time Len lashed out about his unhappiness in writing. Luckily, he talked to a flight surgeon, rather than taking to the air in that mood...or was it a condition?

As in cadet training Len was obligated to read and apply new materials on wide-ranging military and aviation subjects. This second set of documents at Stout required him to read current regulations and fill out forms confirming his compliance, for example a "Pilots' Information File." Len signed off on another ninety-two pages of documents, procedures, and instructions, confirming his understanding of them. These were meant to prepare pilots, flight surgeons, aviation medical examiners, and flight engineers for their upcoming missions. They gave direction in such subjects as, "Safeguarding Classified Materials," "Air Space Reservation and Flight Hazards," "Winter Flying," and a section titled, "To Bail or Not to Bail."

At the end of his day, January 9, Len called Julia from a common-area telephone. When he returned to his room, he pounded out another four pages to her. These letters have the feel of a continuation of those conversations. It was as though, following their talk, Len felt compelled to respond to Julia's apprehension, or maybe premonition, that he wrote beseeching her, "Please don't worry about my not flying just now—it means nothing."

His grounding could not have boosted the Case's confidence that marriage while Len was still in service was wise. The young couple was deeply disappointed that they could not marry right away. On January 11, Len started his letter to Julia by writing that he was just back from having seen a movie with a couple of other pilots.

> I have been getting over my "ailment." [Per doctor's orders] I've been hitting the gym. You should see me at the punching bag! Inside the gym we play basketball, volley ball, or badminton...In the game room here we have two pool tables, and I'm getting plenty of practice.

Throughout these several days Len waxed on, trying to puzzle together his future with Julia, trying to fight boredom and regain his American dream. His correspondence from Miami Beach was full of enthusiasm. He would gush to Julia, "You have to meet this guy," or, "I can't wait to tell you more about that guy." But lately none of the new people he was hanging out with at Stout merited mention by name. They were just passing figures to him. Len felt out of place and out of sorts at Stout. While medically grounded, boredom was taking its toll. The pace of his writing dragged with innocuous updates: "I spoke to you tonight about a pilot's lazy life. When one doesn't fly there is no other duty unless you have a job such as operations officer, etc. Teachers have to work for a living, huh?"

And then, with crushing awareness he confided:

> I was glad to read [from you] that I sound more cheerful over the phone. Had no idea that I had such an adjustment to make upon returning to work in the States.

FATIGUE OR LAZINESS, A CHANGED MAN

Commanders at Stout evidently did not get the memo on the Air Force Crew Rotation policy. As Len was new to his unit, Colonel Johnson could not have been conscious of Len's "prolonged combat duty" nor could he recognize, as the medic must have, Len's "reduced operational efficiency." Captain Happ was at the base as a transport pilot, an officer after all. Seven days later, January 16, Johnson issued an order called a Revocation of Grounding, putting Len back in the cockpit.

Throughout the war the US War Department continued to fine tune the Crew Rotation policy. They communicated on the subject with field commanders dealing with pilots under the now vast and various geographic and meteorological conditions in which men flew and fought. Men were flying all types of aircraft—heavy, lightweight, fast and super fast, high flying and super high flying—originally starting from the European and the Southwest Pacific Theatres. But by 1944 there were Northwest African Air Forces and Middle East Air Forces, planes flying along the boiling equator, over snow-capped mountains, and above sandy, dry deserts. Yet in all of the studies, and within all the commentary from the commanders and generals, there is precious little reference to the impact on pilots flying in this new service of medical evacuation—they were flying in home territory, the official term is the Zone of the Interior. The entire Crew Rotation report deals only with in-theatre combat crews. And in theater, Colonel Strauss, Major Wells, and "Doc" Walsh saw Len, saw all their pilots, on a regular basis. Based on what they saw, they could recommend "leave" or rehabilitation to help their pilots.

While the Air Force was initiating the new medical evacuation service, nobody was paying attention to the pilots flying those missions. Whoever the commanding officer was at Stout knew Len barely for a week. He may have known Len for the one mission he flew that previous week, but not much more. He could not see a before and after picture of Len in service; no one at Stout could see if he was indeed a changed man. Len's doctor at Stout knew the difference between fatigue and laziness, and evidently saw signs of trouble. He read Len's respectable combat record, his total flying hours in theater, and urged caution, only to be overruled. Similar personnel conflicts described in journals and histories followed this same pattern: a flight surgeon grounded a pilot for medical reasons and the commanding officer overrode that diagnosis. The generals had a war to fight, and in this case, they had to move men—badly wounded, honorable servicemen. They would not be bothered by excuses to prevent fully trained pilots from flying. The science and the prognoses, whatever the statistics and their implications suggested, were all new and dubious.

From Stout Field, again following up a phone conversation with Julia, Len took to his pen that same January 16 and sorted out his situation now with clear news about his future.

Tonite I forgot to tell you to address mail to me to:

829 M.A.E.T. Sq.
Randolph Field, Texas

Medical Air Evacuation Transport is what MAET stands for, and we operate out of there to the West Coast. Confusing isn't it? [Len was to be based at Bergstrom in Austin, Texas but mail was to be sent to an office at nearby Randolph Field in San Antonio, some 75 miles away]. I'm on TD (Temp Duty) orders which means per diem @ 7 bucks a day. Of course in some towns we stay at the best hotels, and this will cut the per diem to shreds! The single men here get most of these Air Evac trips. I'll have a better set-up soon tho, I feel sure. With a little more time in the ship I can get an instructor's job with a more permanent assignment. Something better will come up for us soon honey, just wait and see.

His hope for moving to Bergstrom and becoming a flight instructor did not materialize. Instead, he was assigned there temporarily.

And with combat speed that same day, Len settled accounts with eighteen different offices on base, signing out of Stout. An Officer's Final Clearance form states, "I will depart from this Station 16 January 1945 for 807ᵗʰ AAF Base Unit, Bergstrom Field, Austin, Texas (temp duty) pursuant to authority contained in paragraph 4, Special Orders No. 16 Headquarters Army Air Base, Stout Field..." His temporary commanding officer became Lieutenant Colonel Lawrence C. McMurtry, Troop Carrier Liaison Officer. The Special Orders specify that "temporary duty" in this case meant "sixty days for the purpose of participating in Air Evacuation activities at School of Air Evacuation, Randolph Field." As if reacting to an enemy air raid these new orders sent the men into action. It was to be a sixty-day burst of energy to clean up the backlog of waiting patients.

While having been frustratingly close to Chicago, just a half a day's drive away, Len again felt far away from Julia. Like a ball player traded and abruptly uprooted, he moved to a new town. He was again alone. While he and Julia talked on the phone some of those evenings, his follow-up letters told her more of his daily life. They have the feel of personal conversations, intended to draw Julia near—to bridge the distance. They focused on the anecdotes of army life, social, medical, and technical issues related to Len's day-to-day existence at this time. Julia's life at home felt to be moving ahead in many ways while his was, again, moving away in another direction. The couple's major ambition was to get married, yet he was on very active duty and his future was uncertain. Ominously, the letters also revealed signs of stress and fatigue, if not outright signs of danger.

That night, January 16, Len's anticipation and nervous energy were directed to preparing a flight plan, to plot a course and calculate fuel needs. He remembered the flight briefings from Colonel Strauss and the delegation of attack responsibilities among his squadron mates. Dobrowski had learned to anticipate Len's needs and those of the *Little Joe*. But now Len had to review all the prep work himself and inform an anonymous crew chief. With his affairs in order and his plane fueled, Len took off from Indianapolis bound for San Antonio in a wild campaign to catch up with the mounting number of wounded... and another roll of the dice.

CHAPTER 18

The Final Flight

HYPOXIA

Len had started on these MAET missions flying more frequently, in fact, than he had in New Guinea. His correspondence reads well and in these letters he appears to be normal. In hindsight, there were many red flags warning that something could be going seriously wrong. He lamented his "gypsy" schedule, complained of toothache, of weight loss, and of uncharacteristic incompatibility with the other pilots. While he was accepting of Lee Anderson's wolfing, for example, here in MAET, in his correspondence with Julia he was a bit judgmental. He lamented that many pilots with whom he then flew liked to carouse, when he himself did not.

Today we know that athletes, needing plenty of oxygen to perform at their best, had to make adjustments when competing in the 1968 Olympics in Mexico City, for example, or as athletes today do when playing at Denver's "Mile High" Stadium. We say the air in those cities is "thinner." In Mexico City, sitting seventy-four hundred feet above sea level, we have learned that oxygen is only 77 percent of what we are used to at normal ground level.

Over time, scientists made a breakthrough by discovering that the concentration of oxygen becomes less dense, and the air temperature cooler, at higher altitudes. Flying at higher altitudes was also found to be more efficient in that the plane required less fuel—allowing them to carry more bombs or cargo. While innovative oxygen masks were developed and sometimes used by pilots and crewmen for experimental high altitude flying, they were found to be awkward and bulky, making it difficult for the men to move about in the plane.

Eventually airplanes with entirely sealed and pressurized cabins, to match ground levels, were tested. They were fed with oxygen and vented with something called an "outflow valve" at the rear of the plane. Such planes required new design features and structure, then different metals and materials, for these planes to endure the higher heights. After the failed test flights of the XB-29, Boeing renewed their efforts and the first few military planes with pressurized and oxygenated cabins entered military service in late 1944.

An article written in 1999 by Linda D. Pendleton called "When Humans Fly High"[174] shows that those who studied this field identified clear physical stresses associated with flying higher. While the human body varies in its individual reactions to the circumstances of flight, the retina itself is very sensitive. Researchers found generally that the retina of the eye demands more oxygen than any other organ of the body, even the brain itself.

Five thousand feet is considered by most pilots today to be a low altitude. But even at this "low" altitude, without sufficient oxygen the brain will begin to suffer degradation in functions. The first symptoms are pleasant, like mild intoxication, because your faculties are dulled. You may feel a false sense of security. The condition is caused by hypoxia, a deficiency of oxygen reaching the brain and other organs. Pendleton called it an

> insidious and progressive condition and is almost undetectable by the pilot...without supplemental oxygen in the cockpit the pilot will gradually and progressively lapse into incompetence while maintaining an absolutely euphoric faith in [his/her] own ability.[175]

Neither Middlebrook's B-25 nor Len's A-20 nor the C-47 MAET transport ship had pressurized, oxygen-rich cabins as we have today. Their cabins were enclosed to protect against the wind and weather, that's all.

At eight thousand feet there is 25 percent less oxygen than at sea level. At an altitude of about ten thousand feet night vision is now degraded by 15–25 percent. The blood [oxygen] saturation has dropped…and your brain is receiving the absolute minimum supply of oxygen. This is the absolute highest altitude at which you should have any trust at all in your own performance although your judgment is already severely compromised. Euphoria will prevent true self-assessment of your abilities. Physical hypoxic symptoms such as tingling and headache may not become apparent for four hours or more at this altitude, although judgment has long gone by the wayside. Above 10,000 feet blood oxygen saturation and performance degrade steeply.[176]

Len was by nature optimistic and upbeat. Today doctors tell us that early signs of hypoxia are anxiety, confusion, and restlessness. Len was clearly grumpy and uncharacteristically negative, again seeking different base assignment. A medic grounded him for a month on January 8. But the grounding was voided and he was flying again by January 16. As he started flying again, his correspondence read normally. Following Pendelton, hypoxia may have been fueling a euphoric mind set.

In the 1940s, the science about hypoxia and its consequences on different organs and tissues were certainly unknown by the commanders scheduling these flights. The generals had a war to fight and field hospitals were overflowing with wounded. Len and his C-47 Skytrain flew onward. He wrote from hypoxic heights,

I left…this A.M. and came down past or over some more scenic country. We were above an overcast sky until entering the San Joaquin Valley. These Mts. are from 12,000 to 14,500 ft. high and the top of the overcast was about 7,000 ft. [Most bad weather occurs at lower altitudes, closer to the ground, so a pilot naturally flies above it.]

In this sixty-day burst of activity his odometer spun the miles higher and higher. Steel engines groaned, propeller blades whirled invisibly round and round, the C-47 Skytrain spewing clouds of smoke, racing forward into a dark tunnel, further, faster, well into February. Len flew on, from

Bakersfield, California, to Albuquerque, New Mexico, to Pampa, Texas, then Austin, Texas, a distance of 1,650 miles. Then, Austin to San Antonio to Indianapolis, 1,200 miles; Indianapolis to Camp Edwards on Cape Cod, 1,000 miles; down to Washington, DC, and Charleston, more miles; to Atlanta, dashing back to Charleston and to New Orleans, more miles; streaking back to San Antonio—all at oxygen-deficient heights.

ASH WEDNESDAY

February 14, 1945, was foreboding in that it was both Valentine's Day and Ash Wednesday. The romance of Valentine's Day mixed with Ash Wednesday, the start of the Catholic season of Lent, a period of self-examination, repentance, and fasting. It is a time to focus on one's relationship with God. Practicing Catholics like Len and Julia would have attended a service that day to have a cross marked on their foreheads in ashes by a priest with the blessing, "Remember you are dust and to dust you shall return." The season lasts forty days through Holy Week (the week before Easter) until the celebration of Easter itself, recalling the forty days that Jesus spent in the desert. Len wrote, "I went to mass and communion, and got my ashes. I went to services at noon at Bergstrom Field, Austin. As I said on the phone, we were there a day for inspection of our airplane."

On that Ash Wednesday, with his plane inspected and certified air worthy, Len was again ordered onward. The heavy pace continued, flying emergency medical missions from Randolph Field in Texas, to Coral Gables, Florida. Len wrote to Julia,

> I'm sure that this duty will not continue much longer. I'm so tired of this life, as you know...It certainly is not a life for a married man, but there are so many others in the same boat or worse than I just now. Tomorrow A.M. we take off for Coral Gables, Florida. This is the latest, anyhoo. The life sounds interesting, doesn't it? It is in a way, and there are thousands, perhaps, who would trade jobs with me. I must be satisfied and hope for better circumstances.

After the fourteen hundred miles back east to Coral Gables, Florida, Len spent the night at the Biltmore Hotel. The once-fashionable hotel was converted during the war into a sixteen-hundred-bed hospital with officers quarters. In his February 15 letter to Julia he spoke about the fatigue caused by both the grueling pace and his lack of oxygen:

> Our trip today from Randolph was made nonstop around the Gulf via New Orleans, Biloxi, and Tallahassee. We averaged very good speed as we always do from West to East. Total flying time was six hrs and ten min. We flew at eleven thousand feet and both of us [pilot and copilot] are quite tired due to lack of oxygen.

That line was immediately followed by Len writing what the Air Corps thought to be true as cadets made their way through flight school, "It [oxygen] really isn't needed until one reaches twelve thousand for any length of time." It demonstrates how the General Kenney generation of commanders, or the aptly named Brigadier General Old commanding at Stout, could have no appreciation for men feeling fatigued. With their World War I experience, or their solitary and lofty reconnaissance flight experience at a few thousand feet up, bobbing and gliding in search of Pancho Villa from the blue skies over 1920s Mexico, they would naturally have trouble understanding unseen forces affecting the pilots. World War II aviation medics were bravely facing the clear fact that

> the military attitude is essentially a no-nonsense one.... [But] some doctors challenged this [attitude] before the war was over. [Because] in the case of the highly trained, almost irreplaceable aircrew, a somewhat more flexible, less arbitrary [i.e. science-based] form of treatment was obviously in order.[177]

Len had been up and down all over New England and the central Atlantic seaboard, then roller-coasted throughout Tennessee, Georgia, and Missouri to the snow-capped Rockies to California and even as far as Walla Walla, Washington. In continuation he vaulted with gurney upon gurney from Coral Gables back up to Camp Edwards on Cape Cod, 1,450 miles; to Memphis, Tennessee, 1,150 miles; to Daytona Beach, Florida, to Staunton, Virginia, then Trenton, New Jersey, for another 1,200 more miles; back to Indianapolis, 600 miles; forced to abort due to weather near Shreveport, Louisiana, to take refuge in Stuttgart, Arkansas, another 560 miles away. Ever onward, Len returned to Austin and then Indianapolis, 1,100 more miles; then, from Indianapolis to Malden, Missouri, to Sedalia, Missouri, and back again to Indianapolis. The Sedalia mission was flown on March 13.

Len had been intent on writing Julia daily to keep her close, but it had been a strain for him to keep up. There was absolutely no energy evident in his recent letters. For Len, the previous day had been such a full one, he could not write. This round trip alone was seven hundred miles, but there was more to the mission.

> Got in late last nite from a flight to MO. darling, and I was too tired to write. We flew from here to Malden, MO., a troop carrier base recently closed. At the field they have some gliders that have to be transferred to other bases. Yesterday we pulled one from Malden there to Sedalia, MO. More fun. [Sedalia Army Airfield, was a training base for glider pilots.] Did you know we did glider work here too? This was my first experience towing a glider. After ferrying the gliders from Malden to Sedalia we came back to Stout here. Didn't take off with the glider pilots until after supper. We flew 8 hours and 40 min yesterday [or close to 2,000 miles].

To that Len added a disheartening comment about another missed opportunity. It followed, at first, a joyous chance encounter with a man by the name of Ray Kiley then living in Indianapolis. When Len was assigned to Stout, Chicago had seemed so easily accessible and close. But fate would not bring him and Julia together. The time between his reassignment north, to his subsequent temporary duty south at Bergstrom, afforded not one free getaway (leave of absence) to Chicago as they hoped. Len grew up knowing the Kiley family in Park Ridge. Meeting up with Ray, a Loyola grad and fraternity brother, was a delight for him. In all his vagabond months in and out of Stout, Ray was one of only two happy social connections Len ever did make in the Indianapolis area. He confided to Julia,

> Ray's mother was going to call you. Maybe you have heard from her by this time. We are all sorry down here that you can not make it on St. Pat's Day [Saturday, March 17, 1945].... Lu, Ray's wife, was going to write to ask you to come down anytime.

After eight hours and forty minutes flying that previous day Len was writing in a deeply melancholy tone, betraying yet another failed reunion with Julia. Those words led to perhaps the most painful line written throughout Len's whole ordeal since enlistment. In response to Julia's beseeching him longingly on the phone to find a way home he wrote: "Darling, I do want to get to Chicago to see you. It just seems that I can't get away [from] here long enough."

It had been barely two months since the doctor's orders grounding Len were revoked. Self-pity did not come easily to Len. He preferred to recognize the suffering and sacrifices the patients he flew had made, while enduring those of his own. Curiously, between these latest missions, records show that Len had just recently read and certified his compliance with Form 24-A and its subsequent updates, twenty pages of instructions and regulations directed to "all AAF pilots, flight surgeons, aviation medical engineers and flight engineers" in order to keep him current. He was scheduled to go up again but then, suddenly, there was nothing. Emptiness. No more phone calls, no letters, no orders, or entries in this MAET travel diary. There were no more verses of despair or longing. Nothing.

TRAGEDY

The losses of men and planes in noncombat situations increasingly moved doctors to search for answers too. They had been noting anecdotally that pilots, flying high and fast in their unpressurized cockpits, simply "wore out" sooner than enlisted men. It was for that reason Len was (and most other pilots of his generation were) rotated out of New Guinea long before his friend and former crew chief, Tom Dobrowski. In fact, Dobrowski was still at it. As a testimony to his undiminished mental endurance and the quality of his work, he and the *Little Joe* were still on the front lines, in the Philippines, well into March 1945, for example, long after Len had gone.

The medical science related to flying was struggling to keep up with the impact of the new flight technologies on pilots. The long ramping up of American production lines for planes and guns, and the training of men to fight, simply overshadowed the medical needs within the armed forces. As time passed, medics discovered that too many pilots were dying either in training or in non-combat-related incidents. It took doctors and the top brass a precious long while before they learned that modern flying without oxygen in unpressurized cabins (including noncombat transport) produced both physical and mental strain that compounded the normal fatigue that came with stress. But the terms "pilot fatigue" and "depression" remained ill-defined throughout the war, causing ongoing conflict between medics and "the brass." The mere existence of the Boeing XB-29 prototypes tell us that some in the Air Force knew that flight without pressurized cabins infused with oxygen at or above that plane's proposed flying altitude of between 18,000 and 32,000 feet would be impossible for pilots and crew. But for years after the war, both pilots and their commanders remained cavalier about those altitudes between 10,000 and 18,000 feet. A few passages here briefly examine elements of aviation medicine as it evolved with the technology of human flight itself:

> At the start of World War II, military airplanes were flying much faster and higher than ever before, creating new medical problems for aircrews. This technological revolution in aviation was yet another argument [in spite of the resistance from the older generation generals] for a medical service specialized in aeromedical support.[178]

Originally founded as a medical research laboratory at Brooks Field, the School of Aviation Medicine moved to Randolph Field in 1931—that same

Randolph Field in and out of which Len had been flying since his days as a cadet. Their studies were beginning to show that by 1944:

> Pacific Theatre airmen survived far more time in combat than did their counterparts in Europe, only to be grounded by psychological problems, particularly low morale and fatigue. More than 30 percent of noncombat casualties were psychological.[179]

Recalling that upwards of 85 percent of all military war matériel was going to Europe to stop the Nazis, the numbers of individual cases of "fatigue," "exhaustion," or "depression" in the Pacific Theater would appear to be small. Pacific Theater pilots represented only 15 percent of all air force pilots. But in percentages among all pilots, these statistics for Pacific Theater pilots must have jumped off the page because of the proportions. The group historian of Len's 312th, Russell Sturzebecker, having lived through it, tells us of how the weather in New Guinea affected the men:

> Continuous rain generally occurring between midnight and dawn with corresponding high humidity not only has a physiological effect on men but a psychological one as well. Aberrant behavior patterns [unspecified by the soldier/author] developed as the rainy seasoned continued.[180]

And in fact, according to military historians, statistical reporting only tells part of the story. Conditions on the ground were often miserable.

> Fought out against nature in the jungle wilds, men on both sides collapsed, exhausted from the debilitating tropical heat and humidity; soldiers shook violently from malarial chills or from a drenching in tropical downpours. Others simply went mad. The neuropsychiatric rate for American soldiers was the highest in the Southwest Pacific theatre (43.94 per 1,000 men). The same monotonous field ration-bully beef and biscuits for the Australians, C-rations for the Americans, left soldiers undernourished and susceptible to the

uncountable tropical diseases that flourished in the warm, moist jungle.[181]

The pilots certainly experienced all of the above. But from The Medical Service of the AAF[182] we learn of certain additional physiological issues with which this new generation of pilots also had to contend. In the early days, all it took to be a pilot was the nerve to do it. We remember that the previous generation of wartime aviators flew in slow (seventy miles per hour) and lumbering British or French biplanes a few thousand feet off the ground. Their white scarves fluttered romantically from their sheepskin-lined jacket collars, nothing but goggles between them and the weather. By the 1940s aviation medics were only just discovering that speed and gravitational forces were creating noteworthy changes in the ways this pioneering, dive-bombing generation of pilots functioned. Air Force historians W. L. Craven and J. L. Cate wrote in 1983,

> The stresses that the combat flyer encounters daily exist nowhere else.[183] Gravitational issues were discovered and studied as G forces for the first time. The typical maneuvers of flight (and particularly dive-bombing combat flight), such as acceleration, turns, dives, and the pull outs from dives, generated centrifugal forces on the blood and tissues of the pilot, the magnitude of which is measured in G's, or multiples of the force of gravity.[184]

These physiological changes included changes in brain functions. And furthermore, the evolution of instrument flying, flying blind, night flying, challenged a pilot's abilities to

> orient himself in flight when all spatial reference points are absent… depth perception, reaction time, and ability to tolerate rotary and confused motion, has a bearing on the capacity to fly safely.[185]

As such, it would have been troubling for Len's doctor at Stout to read how disorienting the night of January 17, 1945, was for him to land in Boston, in the dark, on runways banked high with snow.

It was eventually found conclusively that one of the problems facing Southwest Pacific Area Air Forces was that of "morale" and "fatigue." In September of 1943 Middlebrook recorded that he was getting tired after twelve months in theater and questioned his own "emotional stamina." He was twenty-four years old at that time. He wrote, "A depression enveloped me and I felt awful knowing I no longer had the sharpness of mind nor keen-ness of wit to survive [any more missions]...I began to realize I was spent." Then later, "My comrades were as emotionally spent as I was."[186] Len, how-ever, seems not to have felt anything unusual was coming on that he could articulate. Studies tell us that army doctors initially used the term "morale" to describe various states of fatigue. They went on to officially replace that term with the word "fatigue" itself, categorizing their findings with terms such as pilot fatigue, flying fatigue, combat fatigue, and aeroneurosis or fear of flying. As written in 1955, for most doctors, however, the question of a diagnosis was a moving target:

> Since every individual will "break" at some point after a certain amount of emotional insult, depending on the adequacy of his basic personality make-up, there will be a gradation from one extreme to the other. The attempt to draw a definite line of demarcation there-fore appears to be impractical.[187]

War and front-line battle conditions were understood to fuel fatigue, depression, or mental breakdown. The following excerpt from a paper out of the Office of the Surgeon General in 1955 describes it all; the impact on the airmen not only in New Guinea, but perhaps at Stout in many respects as well:

> Complete isolation from civilization and the remoteness of home life affected the individual. Normal human relationships with mem-bers of the opposite sex and general family life were completely lacking. Substituted in their place were the lonely jungles, the prim-itive natives, and the close association with a small group of men for long periods of time with resultant bickering and personality

clashes. Primitive living conditions were also a vital factor in a theater where heat, mud, rain, dust, insects, and jungle predominated. [And...] diet was monotonous and unappetizing in the majority of cases, with only rare issues of fresh meats and vegetables being available. Over a long period of time these factors sapped the will of men whose bodies were already weakened by the monotony of their existence.[188]

Instances occurred of failure to regain the weight normally lost by personnel entering the tropics. "This weight loss was often excessive, frequently as great as fifty pounds and could have been counteracted by an adequate dietary intake."[189]

Finally, on the other hand, successful flyers were known to have psychic constitutions and personality structures that were unique to the group. As the authors, Mae Mills Link and Hubert A. Coleman, observed, "The act of flying yields a distinct gratification, particularly to the pilot, and it appears that this...serves the airman as a powerful shield against the threat of failure and death."[190] This temperament, they noted, could actually further cloud the diagnosis of medical problems.

In many cases a pilot's understanding of his current position in flight was glossed over by a kind of intoxicated state of exuberance. The impairments to good judgment came, in other words, from some things besides a naturally occurring upbeat and confident personality. That upbeat personality and a pilot's confidence in his abilities were stoked by "lack" of oxygen, which only much later came to be recognized.

On his February 15 MAET flight ending in Coral Gables, Len flew for six hours and ten minutes, most of it at eleven thousand feet. Out west his January 28 mission to Walla Walla, Washington, took him over Mts. Rainier, Hood, and Shasta—with peaks all reaching approximately fourteen thousand feet. So it is concerning to read that in flights in New Guinea or over tropical fronts, "Altitudes exceeding 12,000 feet were frequently reached...[and] no accurate record was kept of anoxia deaths or serious mishaps due to lack of oxygen."[191]

Flight group medics in war zones were trained as best they could be to notice clues to a pilot's overall "deterioration." Evidence of even simple nasal congestion caused pilots to be grounded until all symptoms were gone. But the primitive nature of their understanding of the severity of the medical condition pilots faced is revealed by the fact that the War Department authorized the air forces in the Southwest Pacific to dispense medicinal whiskey to air crews upon their return from combat missions as an antidote to combat stress.[192]

Unfortunately, when the Air Force initiated the medical transport service for the wounded, nobody seemed to be paying attention to the pilots flying those missions. Over the course of those months neither flight logs nor service records were maintained; we don't even really know the name of Len's commanding officer. The far majority of his flights were only recorded in his letters to Julia. As innocent as it sounds, Len's biggest problem was one of neglect. Neither Sherrad nor Johnson nor McMurtry, who were issuing these various flight orders, had any real responsibility for their pilots. They seemed to act more as flight schedulers than as commanders or supervisors. In New Guinea, Len's hours, of both combat and transport missions, were meticulously recorded by the Air Force. He interacted with Strauss, Wells, Walsh and Dobrowski daily. Not here, not in the MAET Squadron. There was no keeping track of how long or how high, nor under what conditions, these MAET pilots were flying. At each stop in this travel period, time and distance estimates have been recreated, based only on Len's records and correspondence, to represent what Len was doing. After some missions, what he had done—how long he had flown—was remarkable enough for him to express so himself in that evening's correspondence. But there is no supervisor, no adjutant taking notes, nor recording the hours nor accumulating a case history. He was following orders, flying against the odds.

To Julia, to any reader, his correspondence during his MAET days read like an adventure tour through the forty-eight United States. But the pace and extent of duty pushed him beyond the very limits of his capacity. It was murderous duty. A lawyer may have referred to the lack of oversight as criminal neglect. Len went missing after those months of intense flying, having just flown his 30th MAET mission. The pace of those missions exceeded the frequency of his New Guinea missions, yet Len performed at the same high altitudes, thus multiplying whatever stresses he had built up in New Guinea. Len averaged five and one-third combat missions per month in New Guinea. While no one would claim that MAET missions were the same as combat missions, he averaged at least fifteen MAET missions per month and certainly logged twice the air hours per mission.

All the way back in January a doctor tried to put a stop to Len's dangerous and deteriorating condition and was overruled. Now, sixty days later, he fell missing and silent, and Julia was in a cloud of confusion searching for answers. There was no record of what happened, nothing in the Indianapolis newspapers and nothing in the *Park Ridge Herald*, which had diligently recorded so much of the comings and goings of their home town boys. There were no hospital records at Billings nor a police blotter. After Julia called in desperation, Len's mother sat silently among her daughters and two at-home sons, and prayed for her eldest son.

Len had survived in a wild, untamed, and unknown land, witnessing and carrying out unspeakable violence against an enemy he barely understood, to the upper limits of his physical and mental capacity. On American soil but continuing to serve, he had written just a few weeks earlier (February 20), of his simple aspiration for the war's end:

> How I dream of the day when I will be back leading a more worthwhile and purposeful life. To be more exact, I mean I want to work and feel like I am accomplishing something.

And now his fiancé and his family feared for his life.

PALM SUNDAY

Anyone in a time of personal pain is prone to doubting their faith and/or their god. Like most Catholics Julia was found at mass on Palm Sunday. Len frequently claimed to have gotten all the breaks in his army life. But the odds had rolled against him. Outwardly it was Julia's personality to show no vulnerability, no weakness while secretly longing for deliverance. She would have been tired of the war imposing hardships on her life, like the rationing schemes and the recycling schemes, resentful about having to postpone her dreams for the future. She was helplessly searching her memory for a clue, some reason why he had simply abandoned her. With no letters, no calls, no record of his disappearance, part of her felt embarrassed that he had left her, twenty-three years old, a single woman and a school teacher, living at home with her parents.

Palm Sunday initiates a solemn "Holy" week for Catholics, culminating in the tragic story of Jesus's death, which all added to Julia's war-induced sense of foreboding. In an uncanny way, there are similarities between Len's time of suffering through his MAET duty and the Catholic cycle of Lent and Holy Week. Len's correspondence throughout Lent was replete with abstinence, self-examination, and a focus on his relationship with God. Holy Week recorded Jesus's betrayal, suffering and death. It is reminiscent in a secular sense of the commanders who abandoned their responsibility for Len's well-being, leading in turn to Len's hypoxia-impaired flights and his tragic disappearance. Julia had reason to be concerned. Len's habits had been constant. There had been uncharacteristic gaps in his correspondence, such as from January 18 to 23 and then January 26 to 29, when presumably he was just too busy or too tired to write. Even then, about the time of his flights to "our western territory," the "gap year" feel had completely faded from his writing. Now Holy Week was passing, marking another week for which Len's whereabouts were unaccounted.

EASTER SEASON

Upon returning home late in the afternoon the following Saturday, the day before Easter, Julia was met at the door by her mother holding a sealed envelope from Indianapolis. Once inside, Julia unfolded the letter and blinked her eyes clear to focus first on the handwritten date. Then with the words, "I beg you not to worry if this does not all make sense," he began. "It is shameful of me to have kept you without mail, darling. I never knew I possibly could have failed in this way. Please bear with me a while longer." She raced through the words left to right, turning the pages over and back, looking for clues to what happened. Then she started a second, more deliberate read-through. He was alive.

Billings General Hospital was located at Fort Benjamin Harrison, Indiana. Built in 1941, the facility, just east of Indianapolis, was designed specifically to care for war wounded. We do not know what brought Len there, nor what kind of care was extended to him during those weeks. Veterans do not talk about their war service, and they certainly would be reticent to talk about any malaise, "depression," or "fatigue" leading to hospitalization. Unlike the earlier January 8 event, we know nothing of what triggered this. His ordeal is a mystery. There are still weeks unaccounted for. To him the end of his military flying career was a nightmare and an embarrassment of which he barely wrote and never spoke. Besides alluding to his own "thinking" which put him in the hospital, Len used another troubling word either figuratively or literally: "operation"

> I can imagine what you are going thru—wondering just what is going on at this end. Darling, let's just call it a major operation, one that will be a means of accomplishing what has been my chief thought—my being worthy of you.

Even medical historians say that while the field of mental health has been studied since time immemorial, there exists little evidence of how individuals were cared for until the nineteenth century. And even that evidence is scarce. What appears to have been "treatment" during the war years, as Len discovered in Miami Beach, consisted of warm baths, healthy eating, exercise, and fresh air in a calm environment to restore a sense of regeneration and equilibrium. It should also have been reasonable to assure that active duty pilots were made to exercise and maintain good physical health. In addition to that, down time between missions and periodic rest leaves should also have been recommended and provided. During Len's training and in-theatre service, Colonel Strauss was good about sending Len on periodic leaves to San Francisco or Australia, but we see no breaks during his time in MAET. The commander's mentality at Stout toward Len—and likely dozens of others like him—was reminiscent of the desperate General Kenney in October of 1943, when he said basically of the few pilots that he had, "fly 'em until they break." Len was so pressed in his duties that he could barely get off base to see his old friend Ray Kiley in Indianapolis. And in fact, he never could sneak off to Chicago to see Julia as he long anticipated by the move to Stout.

The Sedalia mission turned out to be Len's final flight as an Air Force pilot. In retrospect it is no wonder he was found in a hospital. It was certainly preferable to being lost, submerged in the breathless depths of the Gulf of Mexico, or splattered to pieces on the floor of the Grand Canyon. He could easily have become a statistic, missing in action in his own country, lost forever like those who strayed MIA from Ken Hedges back in March of 1944, or like Albert Eddy and all those gunners who went down in the Bismarck Sea just that past October. From delivering death and destruction to a fierce enemy, to delivering hope and healing to hundreds of patients and their families, flying had been his whole life for more than three years. After these rigorous, high-altitude missions throughout the States, at a frequency and duration that far exceeded his New Guinea missions, Len's flying was abruptly "amputated." Under Special Orders Number 103 of April 13, 1945 from Colonel Sherrard, Len's long aviation service came to an abrupt end. Captain Leonard W. Happ, Air Corps, was removed from "duty requiring regular and frequent aerial flights." The order cites a letter from the Office of the Flight Surgeon, Station Hospital, Stout Field, with the subject heading, "Grounding of Officer Flying Personnel."[193] Unlike January 8, the grounding order stuck.

CHAPTER 19

Full Circle

W ithout appreciating the fine points of their draft registration papers, men originally thought that combat was, or would be, the completion of their obligation to the military. But while the Air Force recognized it needed to limit pilots' combat missions, they also needed experienced pilots as teachers and trainers in their flight schools and frequently reassigned them there. A study of the physiology of WWII pilots written in 1968, yes 1968, concluded:

> Many of the men returning to the United States for leave [or redistribution] after a tour of combat duty...were medically or psychologically unfit for further combat....Intelligence Officers who interviewed these men [as Len at Miami Beach], reported that the majority objected to the leave plan as being both unfair and unnecessary and that nearly all of them wanted a program which would give them three to six months [leave] in the United States between tours of (combat) duty. The commanders overseas found that leave in the United States only whetted the crewman's desire for permanent relief from combat.... A flight surgeon found that approximately one-third of these veterans were in worse emotional condition after 30 days leave than before.[194]

Len's documents show he was a patient at Billings from March 24 to April 7. But they do not say why. As a good Catholic, Len was seemingly raised from the dead. A week after Easter he was released from the hospital, resurrected to a new life, to begin a new duty assignment. After lying in bed and thinking through his past battles, on Saturday, April 7 he was released "from observation and treatment at this [Billings General] hospital."[195] He signed out of the hospital officers club. He verified that "all private debts incurred while at this station [hospital] have been paid." And since "the military attitude is essentially a no nonsense one," upon release from the hospital, he was immediately required to report to his commanding officer for a new duty assignment that same day.

Recalling needs defined at the Miami Beach Redistribution Center, the modern Air Force needed administrative personnel in industrial quantities, too. He was reassigned as a technical supply officer. Len's resume from his accounting days at Bermingham and Prosser, and his record as an operations officer in New Guinea, made him a prime candidate to undertake back-of-fice duties. With his grounding, Len's time was filled with new accounting and bookkeeping tasks. This latest appointment was one among many signs that he had been through the worst. The riskiest and most dangerous experience of his military career was over.

COLONEL STRAUSS

At about the time Len was coming up to speed with the business side of running an air transport base, brushing up on his bookkeeping and accounting skills, he learned that Colonel Strauss had recently been rotated stateside too, out of combat, after serving his tour in the Southwest Pacific. He had been commander of the 312th from its inception in Savannah in 1943, and had shaped it into the cohesive fighting force that it was. He was thirty-three years old and had been overseas in this war for seventeen months. He flew approximately 126 combat missions himself, in formation leading his men. West Point-trained, Strauss would continue to serve in various Air Force capacities for several decades, commanding, teaching, and eventually retiring as a brigadier general.

Joseph Rutter tells us of the March 10, 1945, ceremony to honor Colonel Strauss at their then-current Mangaldan Air Base in the Philippines (well north of Manila in Luzon Province). Len would have loved to have been there to salute his leader and comrade. A commemorative afternoon review of the troops was undertaken with a ceremonial flyover by the four squadrons comprising the 312th Bomb Group. Rutter noted that the flyover included Len's former plane, the *Little Joe*.[196]

RUTTER

On April 7, 1945, the same day Len was released from Billings, Joseph Rutter was grounded by "Doc" Walsh. After completing sixty-three combat missions over ten months in theater he was sent home. He was clearly disturbed by the change to his status. Rutter emphatically wanted to hang around a bit longer with "the gang." Searching for a reason, Rutter noted that Doc Walsh "did not mention there being any evidence in my demeanor that indicated fatigue." Rutter beseeched the physician, hoping that he could stay and eventually make Captain. But the Doctor replied, "Take the opportunity Joe, go home while the going is good."[197] And so he begrudgingly did, sailing with several thousand men on a troop ship out of Leyte via Biak to pick up more returning soldiers, including many wounded. Uncertain now of his future, in a bittersweet, quiet moment Rutter reflected, "Operating an A-20 alone, except for the gunner in the rear, down on the deck dealing out mayhem to the enemy, had been the most challenging and at times exciting life, and could not be repeated."[198]

After weeks crossing the Pacific, Rutter transited across the States to the east coast and home. When he stood before his girl in a newly pressed uniform, proudly and expectantly preparing to propose, she took the quiet moment alone to say she had since become engaged to another.

During the war Rutter kept notes on his experiences and took photos which later became the basis for his 2004 memoir. At no time throughout his narrative does he make reference to writing a letter home, so focused was Rutter on his time in the service. After the war, he sorted out his thoughts, stewing for fifty years about that harrowing, turbulent time and what happened to him. Only from the distance of a half century could he write out these memories for his family and for posterity.

HOP

From Stout Field, Indianapolis, Len wrote Julia on April 9: "Just finished a chapter of *Try and Stop Me* [A compilation of jokes and humorous anecdotes by Bennett Cerf]... Thank you so much for the book." Yet the realities of war continued to encroach,

> Today I received a letter from Carolyn Hopperstad. She is in Springfield, MO., where Hop is at O'Reilly General Hospital. She said Hop has a fractured skull and a broken nose. [It is unknown how or from what.] Carolyn is with Hop almost all day long. She says he'll be in the hospital 6 to 8 months. A brain specialist said Hop's injuries aren't as bad as the first examinations showed. It certainly is a tough break for Carolyn and Hop. I answered her letter today.

But in a letter dated April 24 Len confided a hollow and haunting update: "I heard from Carolyn 'Hop' [Hopperstad] the other day. Hop is getting fixed up pretty well." Hopperstad had been a close friend and roommate since their days together as young cadets at Brooks in 1942. He was one of Len's witnesses to the signing of his last will and testament in July of '42. But contrary to this optimism of "getting fixed up pretty well," they never did make Hop "right." Sadly, Hop struggled with neurological disorders for decades after the war.

LIEUTENANT COLONEL WELLS

With Colonel Strauss's departure from the theatre, command of the 312th passed to Len's former tentmate, now Lieutenant Colonel Selmon Wells.

Wells was a poster boy for the 312th. He shot down a Japanese bomber and was later shot down himself and rescued at sea with his gunner. Now, as group commander, Wells's impact on the progress toward Japan was fierce and immediate. From their base in the northern Philippines, the 312th was sent to strike butanol production plants in Formosa. Butanol is a vital component in the production of aviation fuel. The long-distance missions flown were at the "upper limits," as Len would say, of the A-20s' flying range.

PRESIDENT FRANKLIN D. ROOSEVELT

Since the massive landings at Normandy back in June of 1944, the Allied effort to retake Europe from the Nazis had progressed inexorably. By August, Paris was liberated; the Soviet Union was driving the Germans out of Central Europe; in the Pacific, Americans had liberated several countries and were at Japan's doorstep. President Roosevelt knew we were winning the war.

Ever true to the policy of defeating Germany first, and sensing her imminent collapse, President Roosevelt, Winston Churchill, and Joseph Stalin met at a Soviet resort on the Crimean Peninsula called Yalta in January of 1945. There they planned out the division and postwar occupation of Nazi Germany and the reestablishment of national borders (Austria, Czechoslovakia, and the rest). Envisioning further the eventual achievement of the ideals of the Atlantic Charter, President Roosevelt led the negotiations at Yalta on the agreement creating the United Nations. With the expected decolonization of so many occupied lands, the United Nations would give voice and influence to the new nations in world affairs.

With the world seemingly coming into balance, and as if recognizing his work to be ending, with the United States bringing about the end of imperialism and the European colonial economic system, the exhausted and secretly ailing president traveled to his retreat at Warm Springs, Georgia in early April. There, sadly, on April 12, 1945, he suffered a massive stroke and died. A grieving nation mourned for weeks. Vice President Harry S. Truman was quietly sworn in as America's next president.

THE GRAVEL AGITATOR

Len grew stronger and healthier in the iridescent springtime. In this third role, now as an administrative officer, he came full circle from where he started before the war. He brought his organizational and financial management skills to the logistical needs of the emergent Air Force of the United States of America. It was, in its way, a natural preparation for his reentry back into postwar civilian life.

First processed off the battle front, now eased out of the cockpit, it does not sound like victory, but it was. This highly trained, expensively paid for Air Force asset served his time well and honorably. As a tech supply officer, with feet firmly planted on the ground, his life in hand, he was coming back to a normal existence as snow gives way to bloom. The Air Force machine was kept humming with constantly evolving training and fitness programs, special air transport divisions, specialized fighting units, medical evacuation divisions, and other increasingly sophisticated "developmental" divisions. It may no longer have been the intimate Army Air Corps that Len once knew; it may have been virtually unrecognizable to Middlebrook. It was now a powerful world force, with first-rate men and machinery, overseen by a world-class administration, lovingly referred to as a "bureaucracy."

In his new capacity Len reformatted many of the base worksheets and instituted new accounting procedures to be more compatible with the standard bookkeeping practices he'd been taught at Loyola. In writing to Julia, Len's tone was again casual and relaxed, even poking fun at himself and his new position.

> When I'm completely healed from this "depression" I'm certainly going to be less serious and more joking about everything. Sounds funny, huh? …Flying caught up with me at the most inopportune time that's all I'll have to say. It will just take a while to get used to being a 'gravel agitator' as we call a ground officer.

> My job down here is nothing to write home about. However I'm beginning to forget more and more about the importance of my

Army life, trying to place our happiness as the important thing now and always.

After participating in the incredible and historic battles in the Pacific. He wrote, "News on the home front down here is not at all exciting, dear. I remember the days when I could write 'thrillers.' My job now is less exciting—almost as dull as teaching mathematics!"

His natural habits and the normal rhythms of his life were being restored. And for the first time since arriving at Stout, Len could actually look forward to seeing Julia, as he envisioned when he first received word of this transfer back in December. They had been talking on the phone trying to organize a glorious weekend together. With building strength he wrote,

> Again, it was wonderful to hear your voice. I'm much happier now with the thought of you coming down here for a few days. I think too that you would feel more comfortable staying in town, rather than at the Kiley's. Any-hoo, I'll work on it this week. We will have a wonderful time while you are down here. I've been thinking of the Sapphire Room at the Washington Hotel[199] as a good place for dinner and dancing.

Six weeks since the forlorn St. Patrick's Day weekend and Len's disappearance, Julia made her way down to Indianapolis for Saturday and Sunday, April 28 and 29. It was a "dream" for them to be together again, giving them energy to battle through the intolerable distance, the forced correspondence and inadequate phone time. On Monday, April 30, Len wrote, "It was certainly hard to get going this week after such a wonderful weekend. I really felt lost when you left. Those hours spent with you were really hours of life once more."

JULY 1945

With Len's grounding, a wedding date had been set, implying Julia's parents approved their marriage as long as Len was no longer flying. In spite of everything, in spite of the continuing rationing and recycling, all of the contrasting emotions, the lost friends, his father gone, the broken hearts along with the absurdities brought on by the war, Len wrote, "We will make it a happy day." In short order invitations were issued, a wedding dress was selected, bridesmaids were suited up, decorations were planned for a banquette hall, and the priest engaged to perform the ceremony. Len buoyantly wrote,

> I really am looking forward to our planning more for July 7th [the wedding date]. Gosh, there seems a lot to be done, or am I telling you!...Darling I hope you are feeling as happy as I toward the 7th.

His well-forged value set kept the mystery and unpredictability that threatened him throughout his wartime experience from overwhelming him. The world he was reentering was a world of clarity, a world he understood. Len felt fulfilled. Things came right again. After the anguish of their long separation and after streaming gallons of ink across forests of writing paper in correspondence, Len and Julia indeed married on July 7. The priest blessed their marriage and sent the new couple out into the world.

Len and Julia exiting the church to a crowd of well-wishers. Len Happ photo.

Then, reminiscent of Hollandia, Len received an Officer's Final Clearance form discharging him from Stout. His handwritten signature appears on no less than twenty positions, indicating base offices, libraries, mess halls, base post offices, sales commissaries, and others, confirming that "the above named officer has either cleared his accounts or made satisfactory arrangements for such clearance." The form goes on to certify,

> I will depart this station at 17:00, 12 July, 1945 for SEPARATION CENTER, FORT SHERIDAN, ILLINOIS. RESTRICTED SPECIAL ORDERS NUMBER 192 OF 11 July, [Len was]...released from assignment and duty with 814th AAF Base Unit [and was to] proceed home to 314 Cumberland Avenue, Park Ridge, Ill.

His supreme ordeal was over. His service was at an end. The army came to realize that they did not need a battle-tested combat pilot running technical supply operations for a sleepy transport base in Indianapolis. They decided they had gotten everything out of him that they could; he had given his all to the service. It had been three and a half years since he enlisted at the Aviation Cadet recruiting center in Chicago. The week following his wedding Len rolled his father's Ford Roadster out of the garage with Julia in the passenger seat. To the south was Lockport and his CPTP flight school. Well into the 1960s when Len would drive with his children in the car he would make airplane noises, dipping his shoulders from side to side. This time would have been no different: As he started the engine he would have told Julia to "prepare for take-off." This time, his plan took him to the north. Into the clouds they soared, north up Route 41, him growling engine noises with a big grin and over-dramatically mimicking the banks and turns of flight in the drive up to Highland Park. There, he signed his formal discharge papers, closing out his air force career at Fort Sheridan. He returned to civilian life, rejoining a world that was about to experience the most physically devastating and politically far-reaching changes man has ever known. A month later, Japan would unconditionally surrender.

CHAPTER 20

End of the New Guinea War

The surrender of Japan officially ended the Battle of New Guinea,; and for which the men of the 312th received a second bronze battle star. Were it not for a robust air corps, America's noble infantrymen would have long been fighting it out, as Japan had hoped, in much prolonged jungle fighting. Americans at home would have become frustrated by the lack of progress, and the death. Surely Japan could then have achieved her goal of a negotiated settlement. It was truly the first war of its kind. It was the most successful campaign in the history of the US Air Force, with the first demonstration of the corps achieving air superiority over an enemy.

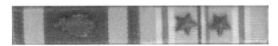

The Asia Pacific ribbon with a second bronze battle star for New Guinea, and with the Oak Leaf Cluster.

Still and all, in vast New Guinea it actually took years for word to reach all of the individual Japanese soldiers. Cut off from home, initially pursued as they had been by Australian forces, they lay hidden in the interior, long after the battle had moved on. Incredibly they survived and did not surrender personally until they could be convinced by Japanese military officers that the war was indeed over. In 1949, for example,[200] eight Japanese soldiers were discovered and found to have survived in the jungle thanks to the help of a village chief. The soldiers were among those who had withdrawn across the Finisterres from Finschhaven six years previously, and were found living one hundred kilometers inland from Madang. They arrived back in Japan in February 1950. And there are many more pages of such stories.

New Guinea was lost in time when it was "discovered" in 1511, it was a mysterious outpost when Japan attempted to colonize it in 1942, and has certainly not advanced in our consciousness since. Yet that was the battle ground. That was General MacArthur's line in the sand, Australia's buffer zone between security at home and certain subjugation by Imperial Japan. And New Guinea happened to be truly and literally the starting point for that vast change in the makeup of the new political and social order of the post-World War II era that we enjoy today.

THE DEMISE OF THE EURO-COLONIAL SYSTEM

Since our founding America has espoused the ideal of self-government "of the people," and power exercised through the rule of law "by the people" and "for the people." Because of the dramatic political changes brought about by victory, this work could have evolved into a book titled *The Liberation of Asia*. Immediately after the war, nationalist protests in virtually all Euro-colonial lands showed the now badly weakened colonial rulers just how costly their continued presence could be. The so-called nonviolent movement initiated by Mahatma Gandhi and the Indian National Congress, in a series of well-orchestrated civil disobedience actions over decades, for example, finally succeeded in making its point with the British. Throughout Asia, German conquests on continental Europe weakened the ties to those respective European colonies. Japan, while able for a time to sweep in and appropriate a trove of resources for herself, could not hold on in the face of overwhelming American power. Colonial ties were thus severed for good.

In the aftermath of the German, Italian, and Japanese surrenders, the following nations took their inspiration from the Atlantic Charter and threw out their old masters, establishing their own governments:

Albania returned to independence in 1947 (from Italy),

Algeria became an independent country in 1962 (from France),

Angola in 1975 (from Portugal),

Austria in 1955 (from Germany),

Botswana in 1966 (from the UK),

Cambodia in 1953 (from France),

Ethiopia in 1947 (from Italy),

India in 1947 (From the UK),

Indonesia in 1945 (from the Dutch/Holland),

Jordan in 1946 (from the UK),

Kuwait in 1961 (from the UK),

Korea in 1945 (from Japan),

Laos in 1953 (from France),

Lebanon 1943 (from France),

Libya in 1951 (from Italy),

Malaysia in 1957 (from the UK),

Morocco in 1955 (from France, parts from Spain in 1956),

New Guinea in 1975 (from Australia),

Niger in 1960 (from France),

Nigeria in 1960 (from the UK),

Pakistan in 1947 (from the UK),

Philippines in 1946 (from Japan),

Rhodesia in 1965 (from the UK),

Senegal in 1960 (from France),

South Africa in 1994 (the end of apartheid),

Syria in 1946 (from France),

Tunisia in 1956 (from France),

Vietnam in 1945 (from France),

Zambia in 1964 (from the UK).

Once in control of their own destinies, those nations, as imperfect as they may be, grew freely as independent countries.

MAKING HISTORY

While the political, social, and economic results were revolutionary, the costs and destruction of the war must be considered unfathomable.[201] In the broadest sense, the casualties (below) include all losses of military personnel, whether from death or wounds in combat, surrender, illness, accidents, or desertion. In the Pacific, in the early days of the war, the Allied armies experienced about one hundred casualties from heat or disease for every single combat death. Across the globe, America spent over 419,000 lives, following the initial aspirations of Roosevelt's Atlantic Charter, to rid the world of the oppressive European colonial economic system.

Killed or missing in Asia Pacific, 1941 to 1945:

USA	Japan	Australia
111,606	1,740,000	9,470

Wounded

USA	Japan	Australia
253,142	94,000	13,997

Taken prisoner

USA	Japan	Australia
21,580v	41,400	21,726

Additionally, the War of Resistance against Japanese Aggression, 1937 through 1945, cost China an estimated four million soldiers, with three million wounded and upwards of fifteen to twenty million innocent civilians tragically killed in the fighting.

AIRMEN EDUCATION CLASSES

In the Civilian Pilot Training Program the plane most pilots started flying, including Len, was the lightweight Cub model made by the Piper Aircraft company. It had seats for instructor and student, a single engine, and an overhead wing. It was simple and affordable, making it popular with many of the CPTP programs across the country. It stood six feet eight inches tall and twenty-two feet long on the runway with a wingspan of about thirty-five feet. It weighed 765 pounds empty. The lightweight forty horsepower engine made it somewhat similar in strength to the sixty horsepower Ford Roadster in which Len drove down to the Lockport airfield from his parents' home in Park Ridge. Once in the air, it cruised at about seventy-five miles per hour, and on a full tank it could get Len about as far as Milwaukee and back with a flying range of 190 miles.

Joliet "Muni"
Spring, 1940

The Piper Cub airplane. Len, left, with his Lewis Holy Name flight instructor, Harry Berg at Joliet, IL Municipal Airport, 1940. The sum total of the technology behind those early planes was the engine spinning a wooden propeller and the mysterious "lift" created by the contour of the wing. Len Happ photo.

From the 1930s skepticism about the future of flight, America came to dominate the airways. Founded in 1929 Curtiss-Wright, makers of the O-52

Owl and the P-40, among many other models, ended the war as the largest aircraft manufacturer in the nation, producing both civilian and military aircraft. Their work engaged and stimulated suppliers from a broad spectrum of new industries and sciences. By 1945 aviation became America's largest contributor to GDP. From retractable landing gear to sophisticated cockpit and control tower technologies, to developments in physics, radio communications, metallurgy and jet propulsion, aeronautics lead the American economy into a new era.

Fortunately, whatever caused Len's hospitalization, he was restored to good health, and after the war led a full and complete life, including a return to carefree hobby flying. Studies in the nature of oxygen continue to fascinate. We have come to learn that in extreme cases of oxygen deprivation, brain cells die, and in four minutes a stroke may be induced, causing weakness, loss of sensations, or loss of motor skills. Research done in the 1990s, referring particularly to hypoxia-inducing factors, found the underlying molecular process of cell transformation when responding to oxygen in the body. So significant were their findings that researchers William Kaelin, Peter Ratcliffe, and Gregg Semenza received the 2019 Nobel Prize in physiology for their work.

Pioneering studies like this led to myriad technical advances that make it not uncommon to see today, for example, a person breathing with a portable "oxygen concentrator," a device for people requiring supplemental oxygen. While pressurized airplane cabins supplied with oxygen are commonplace to the point where the flying public need not even think about it, the Federal Aviation Administration (FAA), established in 1958, now encourages "civil aviation pilots, FAA crews and FAA aviation medical examiners..." to take classes[202] on the "physiological and psychological stresses of flight." These courses are administered through the Civil Aerospace Medical Institute (CAMI) in Oklahoma City, which evolved from the Air Corps medical center at Randolph Field. The classes deal with "Physics of the Atmosphere, Respiration and Circulation," stress, hypoxia, and rapid decompression. Students may even participate in a "safe, practical demonstration of 'pilot's vertigo' using a Spatial Disorientation Demonstrator." CAMI, whose mission is to study "factors that influence human performance in the aerospace environment," counts on the services of approximately thirty-five hundred authorized medical examiners (physicians) around the world today.

TIME HEALS

Some fifty years after his combat service, Garrett Middlebrook spoke for many veterans when he wrote,

> It has not been particularly easy for me to reveal my personal emotions and weaknesses because a combat soldier considers his emotions to be very private, but to relate courageous acts without also revealing my doubts and fears would be pure fiction and not historical facts.[203]

The pilots of New Guinea flew missions to bomb not just, euphemistically, "Japanese targets," but to shoot, kill, and destroy Japanese combatants, Japanese men. And the airmen suffered with the fact that in many cases innocent civilians were unintentionally killed. More than a few of them wrestled with the moral conflicts and the contradictions between their patriotic duty to carry out "orders from above" and their own ethical or religious systems. It took Joseph Rutter, as well, some fifty years to sort out his feelings, his experiences, and maybe his relationship with his commanding officer.

Len's service from cadet to gravel agitator spanned three and one half years, almost the entirety of World War II. From pilot training to MAET, Len tested and flew eleven different types[204] of aircraft as the US Army Air Corps evolved into the United States Air Force. His service has been cited, his acts recorded, and his words quoted in no less than four books. Through the care of Crew Chief Thomas Dobrowski, and the skill of her pilots, the *Little Joe* hung in there and also survived the war. In fact, "Len Happ's plane" was chosen to represent the New Guinea campaign at the United States Air Force Museum in Dayton, Ohio, where it is replicated in full detail. The museum rightly honors Lieutenant Tom Jones, *Little Joe*'s final pilot in the

Philippines, and Thomas Dobrowski, her crew chief throughout her service, with their names authentically painted on the side of the ship.

Len himself never spoke much about his time in the war. As time passed, after it was over, he meticulously organized his papers and photographs; he uncreased their edges, ordered and bound all his papers, letters, and souvenirs. He even marched in Fourth of July parades with other veterans. Over the course of decades an apologia, an explanation, was building inside of him. It must have been difficult to have unspoken, unspeakable memories, while the country saluted and praised you for your service—so he packed them away in his Navigation Case. Len's Air Force reunions brought him great joy and helped him reflect on and validate what he did in New Guinea more than the parades ever could. Ever the optimist, Len always walked with a broad smile, his bearing proud and erect. He wore his Brooks Field class ring until the day he died, at age sixty-nine, on February 21, 1988.

Len Happ believed he got all the "breaks" in New Guinea. Len Happ photo.

APPENDIX

Summary Cadet Pilot Training

US ARMY AIR CORPS 1942-1943

JANUARY 1942

Kelley Field, San Antonio, TX—5 weeks: Basic drills and basic soldiering. Classroom courses and testing. Introduced to the model PT-19 aircraft.

Grider Field, Pine Bluff, AK—10 weeks: Ground School. Aerobatics, Navigation in the PT-19 and AT-6 aircraft.

Perrin Field, Sherman, TX—8 weeks: The Link Trainer flight simulator, flying on instruments. Night flying the BT-13 aircraft. Radio and code work. Aerobatics.

Brooks Field, San Antonio, TX—9 weeks: The O-52, Aerial Observation aircraft. Classroom courses, cross-country navigation, and code work.

Brooks Field, San Antonio, TX—September 6, 1942 Cadets graduated and made officers as second lieutenants in the US Army Air Corps.

SEPTEMBER 1942

Hunter Army Air Base, Savannah, GA—21 weeks: V-72, A-31, A-24 and P-51 aircraft. Group exercises, dive-bombing dropping sacks of flour, close air support. War games on Carrabelle Beach, FL in the 312th Bomb Group.

DeRidder Army Air Base, DeRidder, LA—8 Weeks: A-24 dive-bombing, strafing, close air support of tank movement. War games on Quantico, SC.

Rice Army Airfield, the Mohave Desert near Blythe, CA—12 weeks: A-24 and P-40 dive-bombing dropping sacks of flour, and practice against land targets and air-to-air targets. Desert conditions training.

Salinas Army Air Base, Salinas, CA—9 weeks: Flying the A-24 and P-40, basic soldiering, climbing cargo nets, waiting.

Camp Stoneman, Pittsburg, CA—1 week: Basic soldiering, climbing cargo nets, waiting. Total 83 weeks (almost 21 months), 7 training bases, 9 aircraft types.

On October 31, 1943 men and equipment were shipped via San Francisco to Australia, attached to 5th Air Force and deployed into Port Moresby, New Guinea.

BIBLIOGRAPHY

Aerospace Studies Institute, *Combat Crew Rotation*, Maxwell Air Force Base, Alabama: The Historical Studies Branch of the USAF 1968. https://www. afhra.af.mil/Portals/16/documents/Timelines/USAF%20Rotation%20 Policies/AFD-080424-048.pdf?ver=2016-08-30-151431-133.

Anderson, Charles R. *Papua: the U S Army Campaigns of World War II.* Washington, DC: US Army Center of Military History, 2015.

Anderson, Charles R. Map Southwest Pacific Area 1942, Papua, the U S Army Campaigns of World War II, Washington, DC: US Army Center of Military History, University of Texas Libraries, Perry-Castaneda Library Map Collection, 2015.

Arana, Marie. *Bolivar.* New York, NY: Simon and Schuster, 2013.

The Atlantic Conference & Charter, 1941. Washington, DC, United States Department of State, Office of the Historian, 2015. https://history.state.gov/ milestones/1937-1945/atlantic-conf.

Blount, James H. *The American Occupation of the Philippines, 1898–1912.*

New York, NY: G.P. Putnam's Sons, Knickerbocker Press, 1913.

Breunig, Charles. *The Age of Revolution and Reaction, 1789–1850.* New York, NY: W. W. Norton & Company, 1970.

Brinkley, Alan. *Franklin Delano Roosevelt.* New York, NY: Oxford University Press, 2010.

Browne, Courtney. *Tojo: The Last Banzai.* New York, NY: Holt Rinehart & Winston, 1967.

Budge, Kent G. *Antimalarial Drugs. The Pacific War Online Encyclopedia*, 2016, http://pwencycl.kgbudge.com/Q/u/Quinine.htm.

Budge, Kent G. *Hollandia. The Pacific War Online Encyclopedia, 2013.* http://pwencycl.kgbudge.com/H/o/Hollandia.htm.

Chaboud, Rene. *How Weather Works.* London, UK: New Horizons, Thames and Hudson Ltd., 1996.

Claringbould, Michael John. *Black Sunday.* Australia: Aerosian Publications, 1997.

Claringbould, Michael John, 1985 to 1987 Correspondence with Len Happ, from Australia

Columbia University. *Japan's Modern History: An Outline of the Period.* 1991. http://afe.easia.columbia.edu/timelines/japan_modern_timeline.htm.

Conrad, Sebastian. *German Colonialism: A Short History.* Cambridge, UK: Cambridge University Press, 2011.

Craig, Teruko. *The Autobiography of Shibusawa Eiichi: From Peasant to Entrepreneur.* Tokyo, Japan: University of Tokyo Press, 1994.

Craven, W. L and J. L. Cate, Eds. *The Army Air Forces in World War II*, chapter 13 called The Medical Service of the AAF. Washington, DC: Office of Air Force History, 1983. https://www.ibiblio.org/hyperwar/AAF/VII/AAF-VII-13.html.

Dower, John W. *Blacks Ships & Samurai.* Cambridge, MA: Massachusetts Institute of Technology, 2008.

Drea, Edward J. (Brochure) "New Guinea, The US Army Campaign of World War II." Washington, DC: The US Army Center of Military History, 1993. http://www.history.army.mil/brochures/new-guinea/ng.htm.

Eisenhower, Dwight D. *Crusade in Europe.* Garden City, NY: Doubleday & Company, 1948.

Elliott, J. H. *Imperial Spain, 1469–1716.* London, U. K.: Penguin Books, Ltd., 1990.

Esposito, Vincent J. *The West Point Atlas of War: World War II: The Pacific.* New York, NY: Black Dog and Leventhal Publishers, Inc., 1959.

Esterer, Arnulf K. and Louise A. *Sun Yat-Sen: China's Great Champion.* New York, NY: Julian Messner Division of Simon & Schuster, Inc., 1970.

Ethell, Jeffrey L. *Jane's Aircraft of World War II.* Glasgow, U. K.: Harper Collins Publishers, 1995.

Freese, Barbara. *Coal.* Cambridge, MA: Perseus Publishing, 2003.

Frei, Henry. *Why the Japanese Were in New Guinea.* Tokyo, Japan: Tsukuba Women's University, 1991. http://ajrp.awm.gov.au/AJRP/remember.nsf.

Gailey, Harry A. *MacArthur's Victory,* The War in New Guinea 1943-1944. New York, NY: Presidio Press, The Random House Publishing Group, 2004.

Gastgeb, Ken. *The Transcript* (newspaper) Norman, Oklahoma, 1988.

Gatzke, Hans W. *The Present in Perspective.* Chicago, IL: Rand McNally & Company, 1965.

Gauguin, Paul. *Paul Gauguin's Intimate Journals.* Translated by Van Wyck Brooks, Bloomington, IN: Indiana University Press, 1958.

Gier, Ann. *This Fire Ever Burning.* Techny, IL: Holy Spirit Mission Sisters, Divine Word Missionaries, 1986.

Grey, Ian. *Ivan, The Terrible.* Exeter, UK: A. Wheaton & Co., 1963.

Grim, Norman J. *To Fly the Gentle Giants: The Training of the U S WW II Glider Pilots.* Bloomington, IN: Author House, 2009.

Han Suyin, *A Mortal Flower,* St. Albans, UK: Granada Publishing Limited, 1975.

Han Suyin, *Birdless Summer,* London, UK: Jonathan Cape Ltd., 1968.

Hambleton, Edgar. Correspondence to Len Happ, 1978–1979.

Happ, Joseph, biographical essay of Marie K. Happ, 2015. www.hap-pfamily.org.

Happ, Leonard W. Personal correspondence from Len Happ to Julia Case, 1942 to 1945.

Happ Leonard W. Correspondence to Michael Claringbould. 1987.

Happ, Leonard W. Personal 201 File, military records Leonard W. Happ collection, 1942 to 1945.

Harada, Masato, Director. *Emperor in August* (historical dramatic movie), Japan, 2015.

Harrison, Mark, *The Economics of World War II*, Cambridge, UK: Cambridge University Press, 1998. citeseerx.ist.psu.edu.

Hedges, Ken. Correspondence to Len Happ, 1979.

Hickey, Lawrence J. et al., *Rampage of the Roarin' 20's*. Boulder, CO: International Historical Research Associates, 2009.

Higa, Tomiko. *The Girl with the White Flag*. Translated by Dorothy Britton. Tokyo, Japan: Kodansha International Ltd., 1991.

Hiney, Tom. *On the Missionary Trail, A Journey Through Polynesia, Asia, and Africa With the London Missionary Society*. New York, NY: Atlantic Monthly Press, 2000.

Hirrel, Leo. *Bismarck Archipelago: The U S Army Campaigns of WW II*. Washington, DC: US Army Center of Military History, 2003.

Illinois War Council, *Final Report of the Executive Director*. Springfield, IL: State of Illinois, 1945. Reference copy courtesy of University of Michigan Libraries, Ann Arbor, MI.

Karasaki, Taro. *Putting a Face on Emperor Showa in "Emperor in August"*. Asahi Weekly, August 20, 2015. Tokyo, Japan: Asahi Shimbun.

Ladenburg, Thomas. *The French in Indochina*. Houston, TX: University of Houston, Digital History, 2007. Digitalhistory.uh.edu.

Lahmeyer, Jan. Populstat Populations ©1999 / 2006. Rounded numbers based on www.populstat.info, 2016.

LeRoy, George V. *The Medical Service of the AAF*. Washington, DC: Office of Air Force History. Craven, W. F. and J. L.Cate, Eds. 1955. www.ibiblio.org/hyperwar/AAF/VII/index.html.

Long, Gavin. *MacArthur*. London, UK: B. T. Batsford, Ltd., 1969.

Manchester, William. *A World Lit Only by Fire*. New York, NY: Back Bay Books / Little, Brown and Co, Hachette Books Group, 1993.

Mandela, Nelson, *Long Walk to Freedom*, Randburg, South Africa: Macdonald Purnell (PTY) Ltd., 1994.

Map, New Guinea Area 1942-1944. Washington, DC: The US Army Center of Military History. United States Army center of Military History, 1989. University of Texas Libraries, Perry-Casteneda Library map Collection.

Map, New Guinea Operations, 22 April—27 May 1944. Drea, Edward J. New Guinea Campaign Brochure. Washington, DC: The US Army Center of Military History, 1993. University of Texas Libraries, Perry-Casteneda Library map Collection.

Map, The Pacific Areas, 1 August 1942. Washington, DC: United States Army Center for Military History, 1989. University of Texas Libraries, Perry-Casteneda Library map Collection.

Map, Southwest Pacific Area, 1942. Charles R. Anderson. Papua, the U S Army Campaigns of World War II. Washington, DC: US Army Center of Military History, 2015. University of Texas Libraries, Perry-Casteneda Library map Collection.

Mark, Jason. *The Story Behind the California Desert's New National Monument.* Oakland, CA: Sierra, The official Magazine of the Sierra Club, February 12, 2016. www.sierraclub.org.

Mel Tierney American Legion Post 247 Park Ridge, Illinois: Servicemen's File documentation 1941–1946. Archived by "Illinois Digital Archives" which is a service of the Illinois State Library and the Office of the Secretary of State, Springfield, IL.

Middlebrook, Garrett. *Air Combat at 20 Feet: Selected Missions from a Strafer Pilot's Diary.* Bloomington, IN: Author House, 2004.

Mills Link, Mae and Hubert A. Coleman. *Medical Support: Army Air Forces in World War II.* Washington, DC: The Office of the Surgeon General, 1955. http://www.afhso.af.mil/shared/media/document/AFD-101203-018.pdf.

Moresby, Isabelle. *New Guinea: The Sentinel.* Melbourne, Australia: Whitcomb and Tombs Pty. Ltd., 1943.

Morison, Samuel Eliot. *Admiral of the Ocean Sea: A Life of Christopher Columbus.* Boston, MA: Little, Brown and Company, 1942.

Nanney, James S. *Army Air Forces Medical Services in World War II.* Chicago, IL: The University of Chicago Press, 1998. http://www.afhso.af.mil/shared/media/document/AFD-100923-014.pdf.

New Guinea and the Approach to the Philippines, Introduction to. (The website states, "The primary source for this text is the US Army Center for Military History".), 2015. http://www.worldwar2history.info/New-Guinea/.

Nitobe, Inazo. *Japan: Some phases of Her Problems and Development.* London, UK: Ernest Bend Limited, 1931.

Orwell, George. *Homage to Catalonia.* London, UK: Penguin Classics, 1989.

Pendleton, Linda D. *When Humans Fly High: What Pilots Should Know About High-Altitude Physiology, Hypoxia and Rapid Decompression.* Aviation News Magazine, November 7, 1999. AVWeb.com, Aviation Publishing Group. http://www.avweb.com/news/aeromed/181893-1.html.

Phillips, Kevin. *William McKinley.* New York, NY: Time Books, Henry Holt and Company LLC, 2003.

Pierce, Marlyn R., *Earning Their Wings: Accidents and Fatalities in the United States Army Air Forces During Flight Training in World War Two,* An Abstract of a Dissertation. Manhattan Kansas: Kansas State University, 2013.

Porter, Michael E. *The Competitive Advantage of Nations.* New York, NY: The Free Press, a Division of Macmillan Press, Inc., 1990.

Reida, Immolata. *Selfless.* Techny, IL: Holy Spirit Mission Sisters, Divine Word Missionaries, 2013.

Roosevelt, Franklin Delano. *Fireside Chat* (radio broadcast), February 23, 1942. New Paltz, NY: Mid-Hudson Information Center, 2016. mhric.org/fdr/fdr.html.

Rugoff, Milton. *The Travels of Marco Polo.* New York, NY: The New American Library of World Literature, Inc., 1961.

Rutter, Joseph W. Correspondence to Len Happ, 1979.

Rutter, Joseph W. *Wreaking Havoc: A Year in an A-20.* College Station, TX: Texas A & M University, 2004.

Selig, Nicholas C. *Forgotten Chicago Airfields.* Charleston, SC: Arcadia Publishing, 2014.

Shibusawa, Masahide. *Honorary Commercial Commissioners of Japan to the United States of America.* Tokyo, Japan: Shibusawa Eiichi Memorial Foundation, 2009.

Shibusawa, Masahide. *Iwasaki Yataro and Shibusawa Eiichi.*

Tokyo, Japan: Shibusawa Eiichi Memorial Foundation, 2010.

Schilling, Mark. *A More Complex Portrayal of Emperor Hirohito.* Tokyo, Japan: Japan Times, August 5, 2015.

Stevenson, Fanny and Robert Louis. *Our Samoan Adventure.* New York, NY: Harper & Brothers, 1955.

Stone, Octavius C. *A Few Months in New Guinea.* New York, NY: Harper and Brothers, 1879.

Strauss, Robert. Correspondence to Len Happ, 1979.

Sturzebecker, Russell L. *The Roarin' 20's: A History of the 312th Bombardment Group.* Kennett Square, PA: KNA Press, 1976.

Todd, Lewis Paul and Merle Curti. *The Rise of the American Nation.* New York, NY: Harcourt Brace & World, 1968.

Townsend, Susan. *Japan's Quest for Empire 1931–1945*, 2011. http://www.bbc.co.uk/history/worldwars/wwtwo/japan_quest_empire_01.shtml.

Woods, Michael. *Conquistadors.* London, UK: Ebury Publishing, Random House, 2010.

Yafa, Stephen. *Cotton.* New York, NY: Penguin Books, 2005.

Yenne, Bill. *Hap Arnold: The General Who Invented the US Air Force;* Washington, DC: Renery History, 2013.

SELECTED INDEX

NOTES TO TEXT

1   Michael J. Claringbould, *Black Sunday*, Aerosian Publications, Australia, 1997.

2   Bill Yenne, *Hap Arnold: The General Who Invented the US Air Force*, (Washington, DC: Regnery History, 2013), 161.

3   W. L. Craven and J. L. Cate, Editors, *The Army Air Forces in World War II*, (chapter 13 called *The Medical Service of the AAF*), (Washington, DC: Office of Air Force History, 1983), 391, 392, https://www.ibiblio.org/hyperwar/AAF/VII/AAF-VII-13.html.

4   Ibid., 393.

5   Ibid., 417.

6   Dwight D. Eisenhower, *Crusade in Europe*, (Garden City, NY: Doubleday & Company, 1948), 26.

7   Illinois War Council, Final Report of the Executive Director (Springfield, IL, Printed by authority of State of Illinois 1945), 6.

8   Thomas Ladenburg, *The French in Indochina*, (Houston, TX: University of Houston Digital History, Digitalhistory.uh.edu, 2007), 2.

9   Franklin Delano Roosevelt, *Fireside Chat*, February 23, 1942, (New Phalz, NY: Mid-Hudson Information Center, 2016). mhric.org/fdr/fdr.html.

10   *Pacific Areas* map, United States Army Center for Military History 1989, 1 August 1942, (University of Texas Libraries, Perry-Casteneda Library map collection, 2016).

11   Gavin Long, *MacArthur*, (London, UK: B. T. Batsford, Ltd., 1969), 85.

12   *Southwest Pacific Area 1942*, map, Anderson, Charles R. (2015), Map Southwest Pacific Area 1942, Papua, the U S Army Campaigns of World War II, US Army Center of Military History, Washington, DC (University of Texas Libraries, Perry-Casteneda Library map collection).

13   Dwight D. Eisenhower, *Crusade in Europe*, (Garden City, NY: Doubleday & Company, 1948), 21, 22.

14   Ibid., 2.

15   Gavin Long, *MacArthur*, (London, UK: B. T. Batsford, Ltd., 1969), 84.

16   Ibid., 85.

17   Marlyn R. Pierce, *Earning Their Wings: Accidents and Fatalities in the United States Army Air Forces During Flight Training in World War Two*. Manhattan Kansas: Kansas State University, 2013, 77.

18   Ibid., Pierce, p. xv.

19   Ibid., Pierce, 70.

20   Gavin Long, *MacArthur*, (London, UK: B. T. Batsford, Ltd., 1969), 88.

21   Isabelle Moresby, *New Guinea, The Sentinel*, (Melbourne, Australia: Whitcomb and Tombs Pty. Ltd., 1943).

22   Dr. Henry Frei, *Australia-Japan Research Project*, 1991, http://ajrp.awm.gov.au.

23   Octavius C. Stone, *A Few Months in New Guinea*, (New York, NY: Harper and Brothers, 1879), 2.

24   Ibid., 2.

25   Ibid., 2.

26   Ibid., 2.

27   Australia-Japan Research Project, June 1, 2004, http://ajrp.awm.gov.au.

28   Detail, *The New Guinea Area* map, from the *New Guinea Campaign* Brochure, Edward J. Drea, University of Texas Libraries, Perry-Casteneda Library map collection.

29   Published in the Park Ridge *Herald*, September 17, 1942. Recorded by members of the Mel Tierney American Legion Post 247 in Park Ridge, Illinois, and archived by "Illinois Digital Archives" which is a service of the Illinois State Library and the Office of the Secretary of State.

30   Marlyn R. Pierce, *Earning Their Wings: Accidents and Fatalities in the United States Army Air Forces During Flight Training in World War Two*. Manhattan Kansas: Kansas State University, 2013, 116.

31   Ibid., 119.

32   Ibid., 53, 54.

33   At a desperate point in 1942 President Roosevelt needed some success to maintain popular support for the war effort. American men were dying while industry was still gearing up for the war. To demonstrate we could "reach" Tokyo and "fight back", Doolittle was sent to lead a small group of B-25s which took off from a secret aircraft carrier in the Pacific. James Doolittle flew to Japan,

entered their airspace almost un-noticed and bombed Tokyo and other targets in Japan. Unable to return to their base after the 12-hour mission, Doolittle and crew continued flying west away from Japan. Once out of gas, they abandoned their planes and parachuted to safety in a secret area of Ally-friendly China. News of the successful mission was wildly celebrated in the US.

34   Marlyn R. Pierce, *Earning Their Wings: Accidents and Fatalities in the United States Army Air Forces During Flight Training in World War Two, An Abstract of a Dissertation.* (Manhattan Kansas: Kansas State University, 2013), 231.

35   See southeast corner of map Chapter 14, page 99.

36   Gavin Long, *MacArthur,* (London, UK: B. T. Batsford, Ltd., 1969), 107.

37   Garrett Middlebrook, *Air Combat at 20 Feet: Selected Missions from a Strafer Pilot's Diary,* (Bloomington, IN: Author House, 2004).

38   Ibid., 9.

39   Ibid., 11.

40   Ibid., 12.

41   Ibid., 13.

42   Ibid., 13.

43   Ibid., 21.

44   Ibid., 25.

45   Ibid., 27.

46   Ibid., 29.

47   Gavin Long, *MacArthur,* (London, UK: B. T. Batsford, Ltd., 1969), 108.

48   Ibid., 106.

49   Ibid., 85.

50   Ibid., 85.

51   Ibid., 111.

52   Rounded figures from Wikipedia.org/wiki/United_States_aircraft_production_during_World_War_II.

53   *Skyscraper,* the Mundelein College school newspaper, October 23, 1942.

54   Garrett Middlebrook, *Air Combat at 20 Feet: Selected Missions from a Strafer Pilot's Diary,* (Bloomington, IN: Author House, 2004), 51.

55   Ibid., 62.

56   Ibid., 63.

57   Edward J. Drea, Brochure, *New Guinea, The US Army Campaign of World War II*, (Washington, DC, The US Army Center of Military History, 1993). http://www.history.army.mil/brochures/new-guinea/ng.htm.

58   Garrett Middlebrook, Air *Combat at 20 Feet: Selected Missions from a Strafer Pilot's Diary*, (Bloomington, IN: Author House, 2004), 152.

59   Ibid., 154.

60   Ibid., 150, 151.

61   Ibid., 154.

62   Ibid., 155.

63   Ibid., 156, 157.

64   Ibid., 159.

65   Ibid., 159, 160.

66   Ibid., 159.

67   Harry A. Gailey, *MacArthur's Victory*, The War in New Guinea 1943-1944, (New York, NY: Presidio Press, The Random House Publishing Group, 2004), 43.

68   Garrett Middlebrook, *Air Combat at 20 Feet: Selected Missions from a Strafer Pilot's Diary*, (Bloomington, IN: Author House, 2004), 162.

69   Ibid., 172.

70   Ibid., 173.

71   Leonard W. Happ, *Statement of Aircraft Accident*, Personal 201 File.

72   Leonard W. Happ, Personal 201 File.

73   Lawrence J. Hickey, et al. *Rampage of the Roarin' 20's*, (Boulder, CO: International Historical Research Associates, 2009), 13.

74   Len Happ correspondence to the Australian Foreign Service Officer and author, Mike Claringbould dated 14 April 1986.

75   Leonard W. Happ, Personal 201 File.

76   Leonard W. Happ, Personal 201 File.

77   Leonard W. Happ, Personal 201 File.

78   Russell L. Sturzebecker, *The Roarin' 20's, A History of the 312th Bombardment Group*, (Kennett Square, PA: KNA Press, 1976), 12.

79   Printed Notice (Chicago) August 1942. Courtesy Chicago Public Library.

80   *West Side News* (Chicago), April 22, 1943. Courtesy Chicago Public Library.

81   Printed Notice (Chicago) August 1942. Courtesy Chicago Public Library.

82   *West Side News* (Chicago), April 22, 1943. Courtesy Chicago Public Library.

83   Lawrence J. Hickey, et al. *Rampage of the Roarin' 20's*, (Boulder, CO: International Historical Research Associates, 2009), 27.

84   Kappa Gamma Pi was founded June 30, 1926. The society was organized to be an association of distinguished women graduates whose purpose would be to exert a positive influence upon their communities.

85   Bill Yenne, *Hap Arnold: The General Who Invented the US Air Force*, (Washington, DC Regnery History), 161.

86   Marlyn R. Pierce, *Earning Their Wings: Accidents and Fatalities in the United States Army Air Forces During Flight Training In World War Two, An Abstract of a Dissertation.* (Manhattan Kansas: Kansas State University, 2013), 231.

87   Garrett Middlebrook, *Air Combat at 20 Feet, Selected Missions from a Strafer Pilot's Diary*, (Bloomington, IN: Author House, 2004), 249.

88   Nimitz had been made Commander in Chief of what was left of the United States Fleet by President Roosevelt, ten days after Pearl Harbor.

89   *New Guinea Area* map, 1942-1944, American Military History, (Washington, DC: United States Army center of Military History, 1989). (University of Texas Libraries, Perry-Casteneda Library map collection).

90   Garrett Middlebrook, *Air Combat at 20 Feet, Selected Missions from a Strafer Pilot's Diary*, (Bloomington, IN: Author House, 2004), 421.

91   Ibid., 121.

92   Ibid., 424, 425.

93   Edward J Drea, Brochure: *New Guinea, The US Army Campaign of World War II*, (Washington, DC, The US Army Center of Military History, 1993) 10. www.history.army.mil/brochures/new-guinea/ng.htm.

94   Garrett Middlebrook, *Air Combat at 20 Feet, Selected Missions from a Strafer Pilot's Diary*, (Bloomington, IN: Author House, 2004), 491.

95   Ibid., 529.

96   Vincent J. Esposito, *The West Point Atlas of War*, (New York, NY: Black Dog and Leventhal Publishers, Inc., 1959), 68.

97   Garrett Middlebrook, *Air Combat at 20 Feet, Selected Missions from a Strafer Pilot's Diary*, (Bloomington, IN: Author House, 2004), 597.

98   Edward J Drea, Brochure: *New Guinea, The US Army Campaign of World War II*, (Washington, DC, The US Army Center of Military History, 1993), 11. http://www.history.army.mil/brochures/new-guinea/ng.htm.

99   The Historical Studies Branch of the USAF, (Maxwell Air Force Base, Alabama: Aerospace Studies Institute), *Combat Crew Rotation*, 1968.

100   Gavin Long, *MacArthur*, (London, UK: B. T. Batsford, Ltd., 1969), 85.

101   The Historical Studies Branch of the USAF, (Maxwell Air Force Base, Alabama: Aerospace Studies Institute), *Combat Crew Rotation*, 1968.

102   Russell L. Sturzebecker, *The Roarin' 20's, A History of the 312th Bombardment Group*, (Kennett Square, PA: KNA Press, 1976), 17.

103   Public Domain image from the US National Archives, (Washington, DC, Archival Research Catalog (ARC)). Image sourced from ibiblio.org (2015).

104   Octavius C. Stone, *A Few Months in New Guinea*, (New York, NY: Harper and Brothers, 1879), 4.

105   Ibid., 4.

106   Ibid., 5.

107   Ibid., 6.

108   Ibid., 6.

109   Paul Gaugin, *Paul Gauguin's Intimate Journals*, translated by Van Wyck Brooks. (Bloomington, IN: Indiana University Press, 1958), 207.

110   Ibid., 207.

111   Ibid., 207.

112   Civil Defense brochure. Courtesy Chicago Public Library.

113   Russell L. Sturzebecker, *The Roarin' 20's, A History of the 312th Bombardment Group*, (Kennett Square, PA: KNA Press, 1976), 29.

114   Garrett Middlebrook, *Air Combat at 20 Feet, Selected Missions from a Strafer Pilot's Diary*, (Bloomington, IN: Author House, 2004), 163.

115   Detail, *New Guinea Operations*, map, from the *New Guinea Campaign* Brochure, Edward J. Drea, University of Texas Libraries, Perry-Casteneda Library map collection.

116   Lawrence J. Hickey et al. *Rampage of the Roarin' 20's*. (Boulder, CO: International Historical Research Associates, 2009), 74.

117   The "extract" (copy) was enclosed in a 2 April 1986 letter to Len, from the Australian Foreign Service Officer and *Black Sunday* author Michael Claringbould.

118 The document copy is found in 2 April 86 correspondence between Len and the Australian Foreign Service Officer and *Black Sunday* author Michael Claringbould.

119 Octavius C. Stone, *A Few Months in New Guinea*, (New York, NY: Harper and Brothers, 1879), 5.

120 Nathan Adler logbook, per Brian Onish (Adler's grandson) correspondence, December 9, 2020.

121 Garrett Middlebrook, *Air Combat at 20 Feet: Selected Missions from a Strafer Pilot's Diary*, (Bloomington, IN: Author House, 2004), 9.

122 Len Happ correspondence to Michael Claringbould 1986.

123 Len Happ correspondence to Michael Claringbould 1986.

124 The photo resolution was digitally enhanced by Michael Claringbould, from a Len Happ original.

125 Len Happ correspondence to Michael Claringbould 1986.

126 Ken Gastgeb, *The Transcript* newspaper of Norman, Oklahoma, April 1988. Ken Gastgeb was a member of the 345th Bomb Group. Contributions to the article were from Ed Hambleton of the 389th Bomb Squadron.

127 Len Happ correspondence to Michael Claringbould 1986.

128 Len Happ correspondence to Michael Claringbould 1986.

129 Ken Gastgeb, *The Transcript* newspaper of Norman, Oklahoma, April 1988.

130 Len Happ correspondence to Michael Claringbould 1986.

131 Ken Gastgeb, *The Transcript* newspaper of Norman, Oklahoma, April 1988.

132 Len Happ correspondence to Michael Claringbould, April 1987.

133 Russell L. Sturzebecker, *The Roarin' 20's, A History of the 312th Bombardment Group*, (Kennett Square, PA: KNA Press, 1976), 65.

134 Len Happ correspondence to Michael Claringbould, March 17, 1987.

135 Harry A. Gailey, *MacArthur's Victory: The War in New Guinea 1943-1944*, (New York, NY: Presidio Press, The Random House Publishing Group, 2004), 184.

136 Lawrence J. Hickey, et al., *Rampage of the Roarin' 20's*, (Boulder, CO: International Historical Research Associates, 2009), 116.

137 Detail, The New Guinea Area map, from the New Guinea Campaign Brochure, Edward J. Drea, University of Texas Libraries, Perry-Casteneda Library map collection.

138 Len Happ correspondence with Michael Claringbould, 14 April 1986.

139 Noemfoor, July 1944, from U.S. Air Force Museum, Dayton, OH, (2016). (The National Archives, Washington, DC).

140 Joseph W. Rutter, *Wreaking Havoc: A Year in an A-20*, (College Station, TX: Texas A & M University, 2004), 69.

141 Ibid., 74.

142 Lawrence J. Hickey, et al., *Rampage of the Roarin' 20's*, (Boulder, CO: International Historical Research Associates, 2009), 151.

143 Joseph W. Rutter, *Wreaking Havoc: A Year in an A-20*, (College Station, TX: Texas A & M University, 2004), 77, 78.

144 Ibid., 79.

145 Ibid., 79.

146 Ibid., 80.

147 Ibid., 93, 94.

148 Ibid., 94.

149 Harry A. Gailey, *MacArthur's Victory: The War in New Guinea 1943-1944*, (New York, NY: Presidio Press, The Random House Publishing Group, 2004), 250, 251.

150 Len Happ personal 201 files.

151 Joseph W. Rutter, *Wreaking Havoc: A Year in an A-20*, (College Station, TX: Texas A & M University, 2004), 107, 108.

152 Ibid., 108.

153 Len Happ correspondence to Michael Claringbould, April 1987 (undated, type-written). The letter continued, "*I have since seen Lt. Dyer at a convention reunion at Covington, Kentucky. We both re-hashed the flight and thanked God again for protecting us.*"

154 Joseph W. Rutter, *Wreaking Havoc: A Year in an A-20*, (College Station, TX: Texas A & M University, 2004), 108.

155 Ibid., 112, 113.

156 In 1585 as British Queen Elizabeth awaited an invasion by Spain, storms swept over the ocean and Spain's attacking fleet, referred to as the Armada, was sent to the bottom.

157 Joseph W. Rutter, *Wreaking Havoc: A Year in an A-20*, (College Station, TX: Texas A & M University, 2004), 113.

158 Ibid., 113.

159 Garrett Middlebrook, *Air Combat at 20 Feet: Selected Missions from a Strafer Pilot's Diary*, (Bloomington, IN: Author House, 2004), 605.

160 Lawrence J. Hickey, et al., *Rampage of the Roarin' 20's*, (Boulder, CO: International Historical Research Associates, 2009), 26.

161 Joseph W. Rutter, *Wreaking Havoc: A Year in an A-20* (College Station, TX: Texas A & M University, 2004), 116.

162 Len Happ Personal 201 file.

163 Joseph W. Rutter, *Wreaking Havoc: A Year in an A-20*, (College Station, TX: Texas A & M University, 2004), 115.

164 Ibid., 115.

165 Len Happ Correspondence.

166 Russell L. Sturzebecker, *The Roarin' 20's: A History of the 312th Bombardment Group*, (Kennett Square, PA: KNA Press, 1976), 32.

167 Garrett Middlebrook, *Air Combat at 20 Feet: Selected Missions from a Strafer Pilot's Diary*, (Bloomington, IN: Author House, 2004), 350, 351.

168 W. L. Craven and J. L. Cate, editors, *The Medical Service of the AAF*, 369, https://www.ibiblio.org/hyperwar/AAF/VII/AAF-VII-13.html.

169 Historical Studies Branch of the USAF, Aerospace Studies Institute at Maxwell Air Force Base Alabama regarding "*Combat Crew Rotation*", 1968.

170 Len Happ Personal 201 file.

171 Len Happ Personal 201 file.

172 Joseph W. Rutter, *Wreaking Havoc: A Year in an A-20*, (College Station, TX: Texas A & M University, 2004), 139.

173 Leo Hirrel, *Bismarck Archipelago: The U S Army Campaigns of WW II*, (Washington, DC: US Army Center of Military History, 2003), 25.

174 Linda D. Pendleton, *When Humans Fly High: What Pilots Should Know About High-Altitude Physiology, Hypoxia and Rapid Decompression*, (Aviation Publishing Group, Aviation News Magazine, AVWeb.com, November 7, 1999), http://www.avweb.com/news/aeromed/181893-1.html.

175 Ibid.

176 Ibid.

177 W. L. Craven and J. L. Cate, Editors, *The Army Air Forces in World War II*, (chapter 13 called *The Medical Service of the AAF*), (Washington, DC: Office of Air Force History, 1983), 392.

178 James S. Nanney, *Army Air Forces Medical Services in World War II* (Washington, D. C.: Air Force History and Museums Program, 1998), 3, http://www.afhso. af.mil/shared/media/document/AFD-100923-014.pdf.

179 Ibid., 33.

180 Russell L. Sturzebecker, *The Roarin' 20's, A History of the 312th Bombardment Group*, (Kennett Square, PA: KNA Press, 1976), 33.

181 Edward J. Drea, *New Guinea*, (Washington, D. C.: US Army Center for Military History, 2003), 10, http://www.history.army.mil/brochures/ new-guinea/ng.htm.

182 W. L Craven and J. L. Cate, Eds. *The Army Air Forces in World War II*, chapter 13 called "*The Medical Service of the AAF*". (Washington, DC: Office of Air Force History, 1983), https://www.ibiblio.org/hyperwar/AAF/VII/AAF-VII-13.html.

183 Ibid., 369.

184 Ibid., 369.

185 Ibid., 369.

186 Garrett Middlebrook, *Air Combat at 20 Feet: Selected Missions from a Strafer Pilot's Diary*, (Bloomington, IN: Author House, 2004), 605.

187 Mae Mills Link and Hubert A. Coleman, *Medical Support of the Army Air Forces in World War II*, (Washington, D. C.: Office of the Surgeon General, 1955), 848, http://www.afhso.af.mil/shared/media/document/AFD-101203-018.pdf.

188 Ibid., 849, 850.

189 Ibid., 839.

190 Ibid., 369.

191 Ibid., 834.

192 Ibid., 838.

193 Len Happ Personal 201 file.

194 Aerospace Studies Institute, *Combat Crew Rotation*, Maxwell Air Force Base, Alabama: The Historical Studies Branch of the USAF 1968, https://www.afhra. af.mil/Portals/16/documents/Timelines/USAF%20Rotation%20Policies/ AFD-080424-048.pdf?ver=2016-08-30-151431-133.

195 Len Happ Personal 201 file.

196 Joseph W. Rutter, *Wreaking Havoc: A Year in an A-20*, (College Station, TX: Texas A & M University, 2004), 204.

197 Ibid., 225.

198 Ibid., 237.

199 The Washington Hotel is now called "Washington Place", the home of the Indianapolis Symphony Orchestra, with offices occupying the upper floors. It was built in 1912 and is now listed on the National Register of Historic Places.

200 Phil Bradley, 2015, www.wanpela.com/holdouts/registry.html.

201 According to the Pacific War Online encyclopedia Phencyclidine.kgbudge.com.

202 Federal Aviation Administration, https://www.faa.gov/pilots/training/airman_education/aerospace_physiology/.

203 Garrett Middlebrook, *Air Combat at 20 Feet: Selected Missions from a Strafer Pilot's Diary*, (Bloomington, IN: Author House, 2004), Prologue page X.

204 Those aircraft were: A-20, A-24, AT-6, BC-1/A, BT-13, O-52, P-40, P-51, PT-19, B-25, and C-47, of the last two he was certified as both a pilot and as a copilot.